Stability and Change in Development

Stability and Change in Development

A Study of Methodological Reasoning

Edited by
Jens B. Asendorpf ■ Jaan Valsiner

SAGE PUBLICATIONS
The International Professional Publishers
Newbury Park   London   New Delhi

For information address:

SAGE Publications, Inc.
2455 Teller Road
Newbury Park, California 91320

SAGE Publications Ltd.
6 Bonhill Street
London EC2A 4PU
United Kingdom

SAGE Publications India Pvt. Ltd.
M-32 Market
Greater Kailash I
New Delhi 110 048 India

Printed in the United States of America

Library of Congress Cataloging-in-Publication Data

Main entry under title:

Stability and change in development: a study of methodological
   reasoning / edited by Jens B. Asendorpf, Jaan Valsiner.
      p.   cm.
   Proceedings of a conference held in the Benedictine Convent of
Bernried, F.R.G., in July 1989.
   Includes bibliographical references and index.
   ISBN 0-8039-3807-1 (cl).—ISBN 0-8039-3808-X (pb)
   1. Developmental psychology—Methodology—Congresses.
I. Asendorpf, Jens. B.   II. Valsiner, Jaan.
BF712.5.S73   1992   91-30890
155'.072—dc20   CIP

FIRST PRINTING, 1992

Sage Production Editor: Judith L. Hunter

Contents

Preface

This volume is an experiment in two respects. It is an experiment in scientific communication under conditions of diversity of perspectives. And it is an experiment in its readership's propensities to abandon the contemporary treatment of methodology as a mere collection of "right methods" in favor of an active research for new linkages between the theoretical and empirical sides of the science of developmental psychology. This search can be guided by a methodological viewpoint in the good old Continental-European sense. The aim of this volume is to make readers familiar with this methodological tradition rather than to provide cookbook recipes for fancy but unconnected methods.

The practical nature of our experiment took the form of a small conference in the Benedictine Convent of Bernried, F.R.G., in July, 1989. Somewhat as a surprise to a number of the invited participants, we replaced presentations of traditional papers with an intense roundtable discussion of different methodological orientations toward the study of development. All the participants were productive in constructing our discourse in ways that made it possible to understand one another's pet views. The present volume comes from the efforts of the participants to elaborate upon issues that were raised in Bernried.

We are first and foremost grateful to all the participants of the Bernried conference for their active participation in this joint effort and in its final product—the present volume. It is very rewarding for us as organizers of the conference and editors of this volume that many of the ideas that we discussed at Bernried have been followed up in greater depth in this volume, and that the cross commentaries in this volume preserve the attitude toward intellectual inquiry that we experienced within the friendly walls of the Benedictine Convent.

As it often happens, some of the original participants of the conference could not take part in this volume. We extend our gratitude to them for their participation. We thank Anthony Bryk, Bob Cairns, Avshalom Caspi, Annette Engfer, and Werner Wittmann for their intellectual stimulation and exchanges of views.

The whole project owes its success to the generous support that the Max-Planck-Gesellschaft and the Max-Planck-Institut für Psychologische Forschung provided at all stages of its preparation and execution. But, of course, the quiet and pleasant environment of the Bernried Benedictine Convent and the good care that it provided for our conference were the final guarantees for the success of the project. Finally, we thank Sage for its readiness to publish this volume.

JENS B. ASENDORPF
JAAN VALSINER

Editors' Introduction: Three Dimensions of Developmental Perspectives

JENS B. ASENDORPF

JAAN VALSINER

The landscape of research in developmental psychology is quite heterogeneous: Different researchers approach the same domain of development in different ways that reflect long-standing methodological traditions. The present volume aims at integrating this heterogeneity of approaches to development. Different contributors present their developmental perspectives from their distinctive points of view, and commentators respond to these contributions from their own perspectives. The concluding chapter aims at integrating this variety of views. In this way, we try both to demonstrate and to transcend the existing heterogeneity of developmental psychology.

Demonstrating and structuring different developmental perspectives is a methodological endeavor. This kind of methodological enterprise is quite different from what is also considered methodology in present-day psychology: describing and comparing particular research methods. Because the fundamental difference between methodological studies such as ours and the study of particular methods often is not recognized, we feel that it is necessary to start our introduction with a brief discussion of the difference between methodology and methods.

Methodology Versus Methods

It has always been striking to us that a traditional Continental European distinction is missing in present Anglo-American psychology: the distinction between *methodology* (German: *Methodologie;* French: *methodologie;* Italian: *metodologia;* Russian: *metodologia*) and *methods* (German: *Methodik;* French: *methods;* Italian: *metodica;* Russian: *metody*). The present use of the word *methodology* in Anglo-American psychology refers to distinctly different scientific enterprises such as (a) the study of particular methods of designing, conducting, and evaluating empirical studies (with a dominance of various kinds of statistical methods); (b) a comparative evaluation of these particular methods in terms of their appropriateness for particular psychological research questions; (c) an evaluation of the tacit assumptions underlying particular methods; and (d) an evaluation of the tacit assumptions underlying general approaches to psychological research.

In present Anglo-American developmental psychology, the vast majority of "methodological" endeavors consist of studies of particular methods and their comparative evaluation for particular developmental questions. Rarely are the tacit assumptions underlying particular methods or general approaches to development evaluated, although these are important, fundamental questions. The first, most frequent type of studies is concerned with methods, whereas the second, less frequent scientific enterprise is concerned with methodology proper.

To give a classic example outside of psychology, Einstein's relativity theory was not concerned with methods, it was a methodological contribution in the proper sense. In his critique of Newtonian mechanics, Einstein did not run an experiment, and he did not develop a new method. Instead, he reflected upon the tacit assumptions underlying the measurement of movement through time and space. He reinterpreted existing data (particularly the experiment by Michelson and Morley in 1881) within a new conceptual framework: the relativity of time. In order to model movement from his relativistic perspective, he had to use a new mathematical model instead of traditional differential calculus: tensor calculus. But this method already existed at his time. Thus Einstein's contribution to mechanics is a good example of a methodological contribution to science.

Of course, it does not always take an Einstein in order to make a decent methodological contribution to developmental psychology. We all could try it and profit from it if we now and then pause in business-as-usual and reflect upon the tacit assumptions of what we are doing in our daily work. The Bernried workshop, on which the present volume is based, was designed in order to stimulate a methodological reflection in the proper sense of developmental research.

The General Idea of the Bernried Workshop

Our general idea was to provide *empirical data* for a *methodological evaluation* by bringing together an extremely heterogeneous group of developmental researchers in terms of their theoretical orientation and the methods they use in their research, and to confront them with a single fictitious data base. This fictitious data base resembled a projective test. The data could be used from diverse developmental perspectives. We thereby hoped to achieve a high *variance of usage* that would reflect the great variety of existing approaches to human development. This variety of usage represented the empirical basis of the workshop, and it is also reflected in the contributions to this volume.

The mere existence of such a variety of approaches is not enough, of course. When we designed the Bernried workshop, we also hoped that we would be able to structure this variety by some rather simple dimensions of *inter-approach differences* that were, more concretely, reflected by interindividual differences among the participants of the workshop. We thought it might be better not to decide in advance what the particular dimensions would be; we left this to be worked out by the participants during the workshop. We regard the dimensional structure of the variety of contributions to the Bernried workshop to be the major outcome of this "experiment in science."

During the workshop and during our reflection on the workshop, it turned out that the great variety of developmental approaches to the same data set could be structured best by three dimensions of inter-approach differences that are not only specific to the Bernried participants but that also seem to underly present developmental-psychological research in general.

First, the *general* (universalistic) perspective focuses on developmental changes that are shared by most people, whereas the *differential* perspective assumes that these changes can differ greatly from individual to individual. Second, the analysis of *intermediate outcomes*

xii   *Stability and Change in Development*

in the course of development can be distinguished from the analysis of the *developmental mechanisms* that generate these outcomes. And third, existing developmental perspectives can be characterized by how they deal with the developing person-environment relationships. Many methodological traditions focus only or primarily on *changes of the person,* some others stress *changes of the environment,* and a few try to emphasize *changes in the link between person and environment* although there are only few research methods available for studying this link per se.

The General-Developmental Perspective

The general-developmental perspective is interested in *universal developmental changes,* that is, in intraindividual age-linked changes that are shared by most individuals of a population. Historically, the general-developmental perspective has been the primary research emphasis. Its roots in nineteenth century embryology and evolutionary thinking provided strong scientific backgrounds for the emergence of a number of particular versions of the general-developmental perspective in the present century. The research programs of Jean Piaget, Lev Vygotsky, Heinz Werner, Kurt Lewin, and many others were built around the notion of finding general (universal) laws by which development proceeds. Present information processing accounts of development also tend to emphasize general development.

Within the general-developmental view, interindividual differences in developmental change are most often simply regarded as error variance or are conceived of as spurts or delays of general development. The latter view was first explicitly taken by Binet and Simon (1905) who proposed to measure interindividual differences in intelligence by describing each individual's intelligence in terms of the mean intelligence of a particular age group (the individual's mental age). Thus within-age variations of intelligence were related to between-age variations of intelligence, assuming that all interindividual differences in a population can be explained in terms of spurts or delays in one developmental course common to all individuals.

It is not an historical accident that this view of interindividual differences was first made explicit in the cognitive domain of development. The same assumption has characterized most approaches to interindividual differences in the cognitive domain up to the present day (see, e.g., Sternberg & Powell, 1983; Wohlwill, 1973).

The Differential-Developmental Perspective

In his systematic and comprehensive treatment of differential psychology, William Stern (1911) distinguished three programs of differential psychology: the description and explanation of interindividual differences in traits and patterns of traits; the study of particular populations (e.g., the two genders, different age groups, different cultures); and single-case studies of particular individuals. These three programs were Stern's response to the neglect of interindividual differences and individuality in the general psychology of his time: The programs were designed in order to differentiate general psychology (Asendorpf, 1991).

This differentiation was achieved by two means that Stern did not always treat as separate, as they in fact are: contrasting different individuals or groups within a population, and studying specific subgroups of individuals up to the extreme case of studying one individual. Methodologically, there is a fundamental difference between studying a particular subgroup of a population (e.g., the psychology of women) and studying differences between individuals or groups (e.g., gender differences). Subgroups can be studied with the methodology of general psychology; the only difference is that the results achieved are limited to these subgroups. Comparing different individuals or groups within a population needs a new methodology because the units of analysis are not individuals but differences among individuals. Stern and many psychologists after him did not always keep this difference straight. For the sake of clarity, we will in the following exposition refer to the differential perspective only in terms of the study of *differences* among individuals or between groups of individuals.

If the differential perspective is applied to development, the units of analysis are not differences among individuals but *differential developmental changes,* that is, interindividual differences in developmental change (see Buss, 1979). Differential change can be due to differential spurts or delays of general-developmental change (see above), but this is only one possible mechanism for generating differential change. The differential-developmental perspective rather assumes that developmental processes can be qualitatively different between different individuals or groups.

At a descriptive level, two different orientations toward differential change can be distinguished: focusing on undirected stability, or focusing on directed change. Much of differential-developmental research is devoted to studying the *stability* of interindividual differences across different age groups in a particular sample. Most often, the *mean stability* between two points in time is evaluated by correlating an individual-difference variable between the two time points. If the mean stability equals $r = 1.0$, all individuals change in the same way, that is, there is no differential change. In this case, the differential-developmental approach is not needed because development can be completely captured by the general-developmental perspective.

The lower the mean stability is, the more differential change took place in the sample, that is, the more important is a differential-development perspective for explaining development. If a moderate mean stability is found, this can be the result of two quite different phenomena. First, most individuals of the population change to a moderate degree in their rank-order position. Thus most individuals are moderately unstable in their age-deviation scores. Second, most individuals are stable in their rank-order position but some individuals change very much in their rank, or, more generally, individuals vary greatly in the degree to which their age-deviation scores change over time. Interpretations of medium-sized correlations nearly always favor the first of the possible interpretations and neglect the second one (see Asendorpf, 1989; Valsiner, 1986). How this bias in interpretations can be avoided by studying interindividual differences in *individual stability scores* will be discussed in Chapter 5 of this volume.

In analyses of stability it does not matter whether a particular person shows an above-average increase or a below-average decrease over time; what does matter is the degree to which the person deviates from the average. This view of change is appropriate for analyses from a personality perspective where deviations from mean developmental change are considered as error. But from a developmental perspective, it makes a difference whether, for example, the IQ of a child increased or decreased between two points in time. The second orientation toward differential change takes different directions of change into account by focusing on *directed change*.

If two points in time are compared, this type of analysis compares individual change scores between individuals, or mean change scores between groups. If more than two points in time are compared, individual change can be described by *individual developmental functions* (see Wohlwill, 1973, for a systematic discussion). For example, step-functions describe when individuals jump from one developmental level to the next-higher level (see Chapters 1 and 2), or individual growth curves describe the quantitative increase of graded characteristics (see Chapter 4). Because development includes not only increase but also regression and decrease (see Uttal & Perlmutter, 1989), models that focus exclusively on increases can have limited value for describing particular developmental phenomena.

Outcomes Versus Mechanisms

Both the general-developmental and the differential-developmental perspective can focus on *intermediate outcomes* of development or on the *mechanisms* that may generate these outcomes. The first approach is a descriptive one, whereas the second view is concerned with explanation (see Chapter 7). The outcome-orientation is "diagnostic" in its focus: It tries to determine which functions have already come into being at particular age levels, and in what ontogenetic sequence these functions appear. This approach can also include the disappearance of ontogenetically earlier functions over age, and temporary regression, that is, the disappearance of an earlier established function for some period of time, and its later reappearance in ontogeny. What the outcome orientation cannot explain is how *novel* functions emerge. It can only register developmental changes *after* those have taken place, not before their emergence or during the process of emergence.

Developmentalists who are interested in the *mechanisms* of developmental change struggle with the gross difficulties of analyzing the emergence of novel functions within microgenetic studies. The basic problem that these microgenetic studies entail is: How are the observed changes in function related to ontogeny? A rather limited set of answers has been proposed throughout the history of psychology: equilibration through assimilation and accommodation (Spencer, Baldwin, Piaget), differentiation and integration (Werner), or the order-out-of-chaos metaphors of modern systems thinking (see Prigogine & Stengers, 1984; Thelen, 1989; Wolff, 1987).

All these views appear to be applicable at both microgenetic and ontogenetic levels (e.g., a child psychologist may use the same version of a "differentiation" model to explain the emergence of a new skill during a laboratory teaching experiment that lasts one hour, or the emergence of a new mental function over a time span of three years). But this fact is no proof for the direct (and full) transfer of emerging functions from the microgenetic to the ontogenetic sphere. Many of the everyday problems that developing children solve might have no long-term relevance for their ontogeny, but some may exert a great impact on their development. A deceptively easy solution to this problem is to consider each microgenetic life-experience contributing to ontogeny by way of some summative aggregation of similar events, similar to the belief of statistically minded psychologists in the strengthening of data by means of statistical aggregation. This idea is not acceptable, however, for many developmental psychologists.

Developmental mechanisms are most often studied from a general-developmental point of view. The differential-developmental view has less often been concerned with the mechanisms that are responsible for observed differential change. Examples are notions of genetic and environmental differential change as discussed in behavioral developmental genetics (see Plomin, 1986), and studies of the impact of critical life events on development (see, e.g., Hultsch & Plemons, 1979).

Focus on Persons, Environments, or Person-Environment Relations

All four perspectives on development discussed so far can focus on persons alone, environment alone, or on person-environment relationships. The first one has dominated developmental thinking since its beginning, and the second one (the study of the age-related change of environments) has rarely been taken (but, see Bronfenbrenner, 1989). Whether it is appropriate to reduce the person-environment relationship to one of its two components could—and should—be explicitly stated, but the practice of developmental psychology is far from that. Developmental research is traditionally biased toward a person-oriented view of development. How strong this bias is becomes obvious when the unit of development is clearly relational in nature but the analysis still tends to be person-oriented (e.g., studies of the development of attachment).

If a person-oriented perspective is taken, the developing person is most often reduced to a point on some continuum or to membership in some category system. Block (1971) and Magnusson (1988) have criticized this "variable orientation" of psychology, and have advocated a truly "person-oriented view" that treats individuals as complex organized systems. In Chapters 2, 4, and 5, readers will find approaches to differential development from such a person-oriented view.

The importance of studying person-environment relationships has been stressed time and again during the history of psychology, but only rarely has the *development* of person-environment been the primary focus (but, see Cairns, 1979; Sameroff, 1983; Valsiner, 1987; von Eye & Kreppner, 1989). During the last two decades, one line of arguments for focusing on person-environment relationships has been based on the assertion of thermodynamics and general systems theory that development can take place only in open rather than closed systems, that is, in systems that exchange matter, energy, or information with their environment (see Bertalanffy, 1968; Miller, 1978; Prigogine & Stengers, 1984; Sameroff, 1983; Valsiner, 1987).

Some developmentalists conclude from the openness of biological systems that it is "natural" to focus upon system-environment relationships in order to study development. This view has been questioned to some extent by Maturana and Varela (Maturana & Varela, 1980; Varela, 1979) who try to understand the functioning of biological systems, including their development, from a "self-referential" point of view. They stress the point that is often not sufficiently acknowledged by psychologists concerned with person-environment relationships, that biological systems function in a way that guarantees some degree of autonomy *despite* openness and changing environments. Maturana and Varela argue that concepts such as goal-directedness, adaptation, and development are introduced by observers in order to describe the system-environment relations from the observers' view although they are irrelevant from the *system's* point of view. From the developing system's point of view, development should be understood rather as the "history of the preservation of system identity" (Varela, 1979).

Although this is a one-sided view to some extent (Asendorpf, 1988, chap. v.8), the reasoning of Maturana and Varela reminds us that focusing on person-environment relations is not as natural or even "necessary" as some developmental psychologists assume. Understanding development means that we have to take into account that developing systems are partially open and partially autonomous, and that it depends on the particular research questions to be answered whether we ought to choose the system, the environment, or an out-side observer of both system and environment as the reference point for analysis.

The study of person-environment relations can focus on outcomes or on mechanisms. From an outcome point of view, an intermediate outcome of development is described in terms of the interaction of person and environmental influences. If the outcome view is paired with a general-developmental perspective, questions can be asked—such as how personal and environmental influences contribute to maintaining, facilitating, or inducing developmental outcomes (see Gottlieb, 1983, for a discussion). If the outcome view is paired with a differential-developmental perspective, intermediate developmental outcomes are treated most often within an analysis of variance frame-work that statistically separates the contributions of person variance, environmental variance, person-environment interaction, and person-environment covariance to the outcome variance (see Plomin, 1986, for a discussion).

Approaches that focus on developmental mechanisms are confronted with a severe problem: Presently, there are few methods available for studying the continuous transaction between persons and environments itself (not its outcomes). Persons act within a given environment, change it, and that change sets up conditions for further actions by the persons. Thus both persons and their environment develop, as well as the person-environment relationship (see Chapter 6).

It might be helpful for readers of this volume to have these three basic distinctions within developmental psychology in mind when they become immersed in the heterogeneity of developmental approaches as these emerged during the week-long discussions in Bernried, and as they also can be found in the following contributions. Each contribution is either a main chapter that tries to summarize a major methodological perspective within developmental psychology, or it is a commentary that tries to enlarge or to differentiate the picture that is presented by a main chapter.

Chapters 1 and 2 are concerned with qualitative change in development. Individual development is conceptualized in terms of discontinuous steps or stages that appear in a certain order or sequence during development. Schröder in Chapter 1 takes a general-developmental perspective by asking whether this sequence is the same for all individuals. Von Eye, Kreppner, and Wessels in Chapter 2 take the differential-developmental viewpoint by asking whether different subgroups of individuals in a population show systematic differences in their developmental sequences. Various statistical models are discussed and compared that allow analysis of these questions. The unit of analysis of all these models is the individual developmental function that refers to either a single developmental attribute or to a whole developing system (Chapter 2).

Thorngate in Chapter 3 assumes that the individual developmental function can be modeled at the ordinal level, that is, in terms of "greater-than, less-than" of a certain psychological quality. A simple statistical tool is proposed that allows researchers to compare actual ordinal individual sequences with theoretical predictions for development, both from a general- and from a differential-developmental point of view.

Chapter 4 by Alsaker is based on the stronger assumption that individual developmental functions can be measured at the level of an interval scale. They are modeled in terms of linear or nonlinear individual growth curves that are simultaneously analyzed for general- as well as differential-developmental change.

Whereas the first four chapters are concerned with directed developmental change, Chapter 5 by Asendorpf focuses on the stability of interindividual differences, that is, on undirected differential-developmental change. The analysis transcends traditional notions of trait stability in three respects. First, the continuity of a developmental continuum is distinguished from the stability of the individual differences in this continuum, and a method is proposed whereby continuity can be empirically studied independently of stability. Second, stability at the level of a sample is distinguished from stability at the individual level, and a method is described by which interindividual differences in the stability of traits can be analyzed and related to interindividual differences in the stability of the environment. Third, the stability of personality patterns is discussed from a person-oriented point of view; this discussion is further elaborated by the commentary by Bergman.

Kindermann and Skinner in Chapter 6 are concerned with developmental changes of persons' environment, and with the person-environment transaction during development. Various models are proposed for conceptualizing the interplay between environmental and individual developmental change. This chapter serves to balance against the focus of the preceding chapters on developing persons and the intermediate outcomes of their development.

Developing mechanisms are in full focus in the discussion of descriptions versus explanations of development in Chapter 7 by Lightfoot and Folds-Bennett who also stress once more the importance of studying individual developmental functions rather than changes at the sample level—a theme that runs through all contributions to this volume. In line with the present unsatisfactory conceptualization of developmental mechanisms, this chapter stresses the need for such explanatory models rather than offering new alternatives. In doing this, it points, according to our view, to the weakest point in today's developmental methodology.

Each of these seven chapters with their accompanying commentaries takes a different perspective on human development. The final integrative chapter is a methodological evaluation of the heterogeneity of these perspectives. It is organized around six biases in contemporary developmental psychology that are closely related to the three dimensions of developmental perspectives set out in this introductory chapter. Our hope is that spelling out these biases may stimulate some readers to transcend them in their own research.

As becomes evident from this short preview of the contributions, the methodological issues covered in this volume are clearly indicative of a variety of general methodological approaches. No contribution to the present book provides its readers with an easy solution to any of the problems that plague contemporary developmental psychology. Instead, the volume focuses on the ways of how we could construct new methods for our particular purposes on the basis of explicit methodological analysis. How the ideas that the reader will find in this book fit for different practical uses remains largely beyond the scope of our endeavor, the explicit goal of which was to avoid offering easy-looking "recipes" for very complex issues of developmental psychology.

References

Asendorpf, J. (1988). *Keiner wie der andere: Wie Persönlichkeitsunterschiede entstehen* [Like nobody else: How personality differences develop]. München: Piper.
Asendorpf, J. (1989). Individual, differential, and aggregate stability of social competence. In B. H. Schneider, G. Attili, J. Nadel, & R. Weissberg (Eds.), *Social competence in developmental perspective* (pp. 71-86). Dordrecht, Netherlands: Kluwer.

Asendorpf, J. (1991). *Die differentielle Sichtweise in der Psychologie* [The differential perspective within psychology]. Göttingen: Hogrefe.

Bertalanffy, L. v. (1968). *General system theory.* New York: Braziller.

Binet, A., & Simon, T. (1905). Méthodes nouvelles pour le diagnostique du niveau intellectuel des anormaux. *Année Psychologique, 11,* 191-244.

Block, J. (1971). *Lives through time.* Berkeley, CA: Bancroft Books.

Bronfenbrenner, U. (1989). Ecological systems theory. In R. Vasta (Ed.), *Annals of child development* (pp. 187-249). Greenwch, CT: JAI Press.

Buss, A. R. (1979). Toward a unified framework for psychometric concepts in the multivariate developmental situation: Intraindividual change and inter- and intraindividual differences. In J. R. Nesselroade & P. B. Baltes (Eds.), *Longitudinal research in the study of behavior and development* (pp. 41-59). New York: Academic Press.

Cairns, R. B. (1979). *Social development.* San Francisco: Freeman.

Gottlieb, G. (1983). The psychobiological approach to developmental issues. In P. H. Mussen (Ed.), *Handbook of child psychology* (Vol. 2, pp. 1-26). New York: John Wiley.

Hultsch, D. F., & Plemons, J. K. (1979). Life-events and life-span development. In P. B. Baltes & O. G. Brim, Jr. (Eds.), *Life-span development and behavior* (Vol. 2, pp. 1-36). New York: Academic Press.

Magnusson, D. (1988). *Individual development from an interactional perspective: A longitudinal study.* Hillsdale, NJ: Lawrence Erlbaum.

Maturana, H., & Varela, F. (1980). *Autopoiesis and cognition.* Dordrecht, Netherlands: D. Reidhel.

Miller, J. G. (1978). *Living systems.* New York: McGraw-Hill.

Plomin, R. (1986). *Development, genetics, and psychology.* Hillsdale, NJ: Lawrence Erlbaum.

Prigogine, I., & Stengers, I. (1984). *Order out of chaos.* New York: Bantam Books.

Sameroff, A. (1983). Developmental systems: Contexts and evolution. In P. H. Mussen (Ed.), *Handbook of child psychology: Vol. 1. History, theory, and methods* (pp. 237-294). New York: John Wiley.

Stern, W. (1911). *Die differentielle Psychologie in ihren methodischen Grundlagen* [Methodological foundations of differential psychology]. Leipzig: Barth.

Sternberg, R. J., & Powell, J. S. (1983). The development of intelligence. In J. Flavell & E. Markman (Eds.), *Handbook of child psychology* (4th ed.) (pp. 341-419). New York: John Wiley.

Thelen, E. (1989). Self-organization in developmental processes: Can systems approaches work? In M. R. Gunnar & E. Thelen (Eds.), *The Minnesota Symposia on Child Psychology: Vol. 22. Systems and development* (pp. 77-117). Hillsdale, NJ: Lawrence Erlbaum.

Uttal, D. H., & Perlmutter, M. (1989). Toward a broader conceptualization of development: The role of gains and losses across the life span. *Developmental Review, 9,* 101-132.

Valsiner, J. (1986). Between groups and individuals: Psychologists' and laypersons' interpretations of correlational findings. In J. Valsiner (Ed.), *The individual subject and scientific psychology* (pp. 113-151). New York: Plenum.

Valsiner, J. (1987). *Culture and the development of children's actions.* Chichester, UK: John Wiley.

Varela, F. J. (1979). *Principles of biological autonomy*. New York: North-Holland.

von Eye, A., & Kreppner, K. (1989). Family systems and family development: The selection of analytical units. In K. Kreppner & R. M. Lerner (Eds.), *Family systems and life-span development* (pp. 247-269). Hillsdale, NJ: Lawrence Erlbaum.

Wohlwill, J. F. (1973). *The study of behavioral development*. New York: Academic Press.

Wolff, P. H. (1987). *The development of behavioral states and the expression of emotions in early infancy*. Chicago: University of Chicago Press.

1

Modeling Qualitative Change in Individual Development

EBERHARD SCHRÖDER

In this chapter an order-theoretical approach to the analysis of qualitative change in individual development is presented. In the first part
of the chapter I discuss conceptual, methodological, and statistical
implications of the order-theoretical analysis of individual developmental trajectories; in the second part, in order to illustrate the order-
theoretical approach I present an empirical example from the domain
of cognitive development.

In contradistinction to such approaches to the analysis of qualitative
change in development that focus primarily on the aggregate level of
analysis, in the present contribution an individual-oriented approach
will be presented that focuses specifically on the intraindividual organization of behavior, that is, on differences between variables or
changes of developmental attributes over time *within the individual.*
In the individual-oriented approach hypotheses about the intraindividual organization of behavior are evaluated on the basis of developmental patterns or profiles of individuals (see also Editors'
Introduction, this volume). It has indeed been shown that statistical
parameters relating to the mean function of the whole group do not
necessarily show how each individual develops. Patterns of attributes
or temporal profiles adequately represent the intraindividual organization of behavior for each individual and therefore are taken to

1

represent the unit of analysis when qualitative change in individual development is being modeled. An order-theoretical approach to the analysis of qualitative change in development is proposed that models the order in the acquisition of distinct developmental steps under the assumption of uniformity and invariability in development. These developmental models may be applied to both synchronous relationships between developmental attributes and diachronous relationships across measurement occasions. Using this approach, order-theoretical models of development can be compared with the observed developmental trajectories of the individuals. Finally, the order-theoretical approach to the analysis of qualitative change in development will be discussed with respect to individual differences in development. A complementary approach to differential qualitative change in development is presented in Chapter 2.

The Analysis of Qualitative Change in Individual Development

Generally, empirical studies in developmental psychology are concerned with two major research topics: (a) the analysis of developmental change in behavior and (b) the analysis of individual differences in development. According to McCall (1977), change in development means that "a behavior can increase or decrease in frequency or amount across age, or one behavior can replace, supplement, or grow out of another with development." A growth curve of the amount or frequency of a given behavior across time for an individual or a group of individuals is called the *developmental function* (Kagan, 1980; Wohlwill, 1973). While continuous developmental functions derive from growth curves of quantitative attributes, discontinuous changes in development are found when qualitative attributes are analyzed. For example, the major focus of Piagetian research is on qualitative change in development because in this theory cognitive development is characterized by stepwise change involving qualitatively different but sequential stages.

The second perspective in analyzing development is on individual differences. "That is, does the relative rank ordering of individual subjects on a given attribute relate to the relative rank ordering of those individuals on the same or another attribute assessed at a subsequent age?" (McCall, 1977). The correlation between two attributes indicates the amount of consistency in the relation between two or more items, and the correlation of an attribute across two subsequent measurement occasions indicates the stability of individual differences.

These two perspectives on the analysis of individual development are independent because means or frequencies of a developmental curve can vary independently of the correlation between the attributes (see also Editors' Introduction, this volume).

The order-theoretical approach to the analysis of qualitative change in development takes into account both the analysis of developmental change and the analysis of individual differences. The approach focuses either on discontinuous growth curves or on individual differences in development. The order-theoretical analysis of discontinuous or qualitative change in development is designed to specify the order or sequence of the acquisition of distinct developmental steps or stages (Nagel, 1957) by comparing individual developmental trajectories in terms of their uniformity or diversification in development. Assuming a uniform developmental sequence means that it is true for all individuals that a specific developmental attribute is acquired earlier than some other attribute; thus the earlier attribute is a precursor of the later one. In contrast, multiple or divergent developmental sequences occur when different intraindividual developmental trajectories obtain in different groups of individuals, for example, if some individuals have acquired attribute A before B and others B before A (van den Daele, 1969, 1976).

Two kinds of developmental sequences can be distinguished: prerequisite and precursor sequences. While a prerequisite sequence means that a developmental stage is a necessary condition (antecedent) for the development of a subsequent stage, precursor sequences merely represent the empirical order in the acquisition of different tasks within one domain of development (Campbell & Richie, 1983). It is important to note—because sometimes neglected—that assuming an order-theoretical relationship between developmental attributes requires a task analysis of these relations. The assumed order-theoretical relationship must be validated by conceptual arguments because otherwise spurious relationships cannot be distinguished from theoretically meaningful ones. A meaningful empirical analysis of qualitative change in development thus requires theoretical and conceptual arguments that explain the postulated order of acquisition (Toulmin, 1981).

In the empirical literature three different procedures have been applied when analyzing qualitative change in development. First, differences in the means or frequencies of single or several developmental variables across different age-groups, or within the same sample across different measurement occasions, are taken as evidence for developmental change within individuals. The implicit assumption of this inference is that the developmental growth curve of each individual is congruent with the developmental function of the group. There is, however, no reliable inference from the mean curve to change within the subject as differences can occur between individual developmental trajectories that are not revealed in the global growth curve of the sample (Asendorpf, 1989; Bakan, 1967; Schröder, 1989). Therefore, the developmental trajectories of each individual cannot be approximated by the developmental function of the group.

Second, correlational statistics are applied in the analysis of qualitative change in development in order to examine the relationships between developmental variables. In this approach correlation coefficients are taken to indicate the amount of consistency between variables or the amount of stability of an attribute across different measurement occasions. However, correlation coefficients can be misleading when used to justify order-theoretical relationships between variables (for example, in the case of hypotheses about developmental sequences). In various studies it has been demonstrated that there were no significant correlations between developmental variables although sequential relationships between those variables existed (Edelstein, Keller, & Wahlen, 1984; Henning, 1981; Hudson, 1978; Rudinger, 1978; Schröder, 1989).

Third, Guttman-scaling has been used in order to analyze qualitative change in development. This procedure appears to be adequate for the purpose as it takes the individual patterns of attributes into account. Unfortunately, Guttman-scaling does not permit analysis of different developmental relationships as, for example, synchronous or precursor relationships in development. The procedure is restricted to prerequisite relationships only. Neither does the Guttman procedure permit longitudinal analysis of qualitative change in development since only intraindividual differences between variables, but not intraindividual changes over time, can be modeled by this method. Although these procedures have been used in the empirical literature they do not permit analysis of order-theoretical hypotheses about qualitative change in development. Therefore, empirical and methodological strategies have recently been developed that in part derive from the field of biostatistics, latent attribute scaling theory, or order theory. But before describing the statistical procedures for the analysis of qualitative change in development it is necessary to discuss the methodological implications of the analysis of qualitative change in development.

In order to clarify the analytical status of order-theoretical assumptions, specific hypotheses about qualitative change in development will be located in the data-box offered by Cattell (1952, 1988) and adapted for data-gathering strategies in developmental psychology by Buss (1979). Three analytical dimensions are relevant for the analysis of developmental change: individuals, variables, and measurement occasions. The following types of data-aggregation strategies can be adopted to analyze qualitative change in development under an order-theoretical perspective: (a) the analysis of interindividual differences in intraindividual differences, and (b) the analysis of interindividual differences in intraindividual change. Under the first strategy, individuals are compared (interindividual differences) in view of their differences in different variables at one measurement occasion (in terms of sampling across variables at one occasion—intraindividual differences). Under the second strategy, individuals are compared (interindividual differences) in view of change in a variable across different measurement occasions (in terms of sampling across occasions with regard to one variable—intraindividual change).

The two strategies correspond to the following perspectives in analyzing differential change in development: (a) The analysis of interindividual differences in intraindividual differences corresponds to a synchronous perspective, as order-theoretical hypotheses are tested on the basis of configurations of attributes within the individual for one measurement occasion (patterns of attributes or synchronous profiles); (b) The analysis of interindividual differences in intraindividual change corresponds to a diachronous perspective, as order-theoretical hypotheses are tested on the basis of constellations of attributes across different measurement occasions within the individual (patterns of change or diachronous profiles). In the case of synchronous analysis the order of developmental steps is inferred rather than observed, as repeated measures do not exist. On the contrary, the diachronous perspective necessitates repeated measurement of the variables, as the sequence of acquisition refers to observed changes in development across different measurement points.

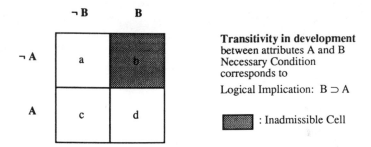

Figure 1.1. Transitivity in Development

In both synchronous and diachronous analysis different variables or measurement occasions are aggregated in the form of specific configurations of attributes or constellations of time occasions that represent courses of development within the individual. The patterns or profiles can be classified as admissible or inadmissible according to the order-theoretical model of development. The order-theoretical relationships between the attributes or the time occasions as postulated by a task analysis can be transformed into propositional statements (in terms of statement calculus). For example, if a developmental variable A is supposed to be a precursor of a developmental attribute B (i.e., if A is a necessary condition for the development of B), the co-occurence of $\neg A$ and B is inadmissible due to the assumed sequential relationship between $\neg A$ and B (see Figure 1.1). On the other hand, the combinations AB, $A \neg B$, and $\neg A \neg B$ are admissible according to the order-theoretical hypothesis. This relationship corresponds to an implicative relation between two developmental variables, A and B. The statement calculus of logical implication, however, only matches the ordered series of variables on a synchronous level; it adequately represents the relationships between variables at one time of measurement.

In contrast, the diachronous level of analysis focuses on the acquisition of concepts across times of measurement. Therefore an additional assumption has to be made on a diachronous level of analysis. This concerns the question of whether an acquired ability is retained during development. Assuming an implicative relationship between developmental variables (A is a necessary condition for the development of B) implies that these tasks emerge cumulatively during development; that is, once a task is acquired, it must be retained across

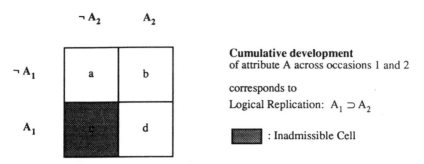

Figure 1.2. Cumulativity in Development

time. This diachronous relationship can be formulated as the propositional form of logical replication. Consider the case of two measurement occasions (t_1 and t_2). The propositional statement of logical replication then means that an attribute observed at the first time of measurement (A_1) must be present on the second measurement occasion (A_2). Therefore, the occurrence of attribute A at the first measurement occasion represents a sufficient condition for the occurrence of the same attribute at the second measurement point. Attribute A must be replicated at the second measurement occasion (see Figure 1.2).

Regarding the distinction between general analytical approaches in developmental psychology the order-theoretical approach to the analysis of qualitative change in development represents both the modeling of qualitative change in development and the modeling of individual differences in development. The analysis of qualitative change in development described in the present chapter combines two separate data-gathering strategies: (a) the analysis of interindividual differences in intraindividual differences, that is, individual differences in the order of acquisition of different tasks at one measurement occasion, and (b) the analysis of interindividual differences in intraindividual change, that is, individual differences in the order of acquisition of one task across two or multiple measurement occasions. Within this methodological framework ordered patterns of change in development can be analyzed (within the individual) in view of uniformity or diversification in development. While the analysis of patterns of change corresponds to the analysis of *qualitative changes* in development, the question of uniformity in development corresponds to the analysis of *individual differences*. Therefore, the methodological term *individual differences* is used differently in different models of qualitative change in development. Within an order-theoretical approach, analyzing individual differences in performance focuses on intrinsic processes in development. The developmental processes of hierarchical structuring, integration, and consolidation of cognitive operations, for example, represent intrinsic processes in development that are inherent to the regulation and organization of epistemic interactions and that derive from intrinsic constraints on development (Schröder & Edelstein, in press). In this case the focus of the analysis is on interindividual variability (or invariability) in intraindividual differences and change. A different focus for the analysis of individual differences is the explanation and prediction of differences between the developmental trajectories of individuals or groups. This approach focuses on external conditions of development such as opportunities or constraints located in the social life-worlds or ecologies that affect the development.

Having specified the methodological framework for the order-theoretical analysis of qualitative change in development, I will describe statistical procedures that are adequate for the testing of developmental hypotheses about intraindividual qualitative change and that have been applied in the context of order-theoretical analyses. (An overview of statistical procedures for the analysis of qualitative data is given in Henning & Rudinger, 1985; Rudinger, Chaselon, Zimmermann, & Henning, 1985.) Two different statistical procedures were selected for the special purpose of the present contribution. One procedure is a probabilistic validation procedure developed by Dayton and MacReady (1976). The other is the Unconditional Prediction Analysis (von Eye & Brandtstädter, 1988), a procedure based on the prediction analysis according to Hildebrand, Laing, and Rosenthal (1977). While both procedures permit the reconstruction of a postulated developmental model from developmental data they differ from each other in a variety of ways.

Dayton and MacReady's method proceeds as follows (see also Rudinger et al., 1985): In order to estimate the recruitment (conditional) probabilities the observed patterns must be classified according to the admissible patterns (true-score-patterns). Conditional probabilities (recruitment probabilities) are calculated for each configuration by means of the Maximum-Likelihood Method. Then the observed patterns are reclassified according to the postulated developmental model. Errors or misclassification that occur in this step of the procedure are expressed in terms of guessing and forgetting probabilities (positive error α_i and negative error β_i). After estimating the recruitment probabilities, the procedure computes the predicted frequencies for each pattern and the probability of each true-score pattern θ_i. In order to test the fit between the two distributions, the predicted and the observed frequencies of the patterns are compared by means of χ^2 statistics. If no difference is found between the two distributions, it can be assumed that the order-theoretical model of differential change in development adequately represents the distribution of the observed patterns.

Prediction Analysis (Hildebrand et al., 1977) evaluates statistically the prediction from certain states or categories of a predictor to specific states or categories of a criterion. A measure is computed for the proportional reduction in error (PRE), evaluating the difference between observed and predicted probabilities of those patterns or cells that are inadmissible according to the order-theoretical model postulated. In the Unconditional Prediction Analysis (von Eye & Brandtstädter, 1988) it is additionally assumed that all variables entering into the equation are statistically independent. For the statistical inference a binomial test is used that is relatively robust with regard to the distribution of the frequencies.

While the two statistical procedures were specifically designed for the analysis of sequential data, they differ with respect to basic assumptions. Comparing the two procedures, there are major differences concerning the statistical models for estimating the predicted frequencies and concerning the inferential procedures used. While in Dayton and MacReady's procedure frequencies were predicted on the basis of recruitment probabilities according to the sequential model postulated (conditional probabilities), in the Unconditional Prediction Analysis the distribution of inadmissible patterns is tested against a distribution model of total independence. Therefore, with respect to the specificity of the order-theoretical hypothesis, the Unconditional Prediction Analysis model is based on weaker statistical assumptions, because the PRE measure reflects the difference between observed inadmissible patterns and the predicted patterns under the assumption of total independence among all variables. Regarding the inferential test Dayton and MacReady's procedure and the Unconditional Prediction Analysis proceed in different ways. While in Dayton and MacReady's procedure the statistical fit between observed and predicted model is calculated by the means of χ^2 statistics, in Unconditional

Prediction Analysis a binomial test finds if there are significant differences between observed and predicted cells. Thus, Dayton and MacReady's procedure may be problematic because, on the one hand, the χ^2 statistic should be interpreted only when the expected frequency of each cell is not too low, and, on the other hand, no inadmissible pattern should obtain. The binomial test in von Eye and Brandtstädter's procedure does not lead to such problems.

An Empirical Example of the Analysis of Qualitative Change in Cognitive Development

The data of the present study derive from the project "Child Development and Social Structure," a longitudinal study conducted in urban and rural Iceland (Edelstein, Keller, & Schröder, 1990). The research was undertaken to analyze the interface between individual development and socialization in a society exposed to processes of rapid modernization since the end of the Second World War. Individual development was represented by the domains of cognitive and sociomoral development, personality and ego resources. Subjects of the present substudy were 121 urban children who were tested at ages 7, 8, 9, 12, 15, and 17 years. The stratification of the sample will not be described here because differential analyses of external conditions of development represented by various design variables (gender, social class, general ability) are not the focus of the present analyses. To measure the development of cognition, a variety of instruments were administered depending on the age and the developmental status of the subjects (see Schröder, 1989, for details). The order-theoretical analysis of the present study will be illustrated by the concept of conservation of continuous and discontinuous quantities at ages 7 and 8 years.

Conservation of continuous quantities was measured in the following manner (Goldschmid & Bentler, 1968): Subjects were presented two glasses of equal size filled with equal amounts of water. Subjects were asked if there was as much water in one of the glasses as there was in the other, or whether there was more water in one of the glasses. If the subject said that one of the glasses contained more water, the level of the water was adjusted until the subject said that both glasses contained equal amounts of water. When the subject assumed that there were equal amounts of water in both glasses, the water contained in one of the glasses was poured into five little glasses. The experimenter then asked the subject whether the large glass contained as much water as the five little glasses together, or whether the large glass or the five little glasses contained more water.

Conservation of discontinuous quantities was measured in the following manner (Goldschmid & Bentler, 1968): Subjects were presented two glasses of equal size filled with equal amounts of corn. Subjects were asked whether the two glasses contained the same amounts of corn, or whether there was more corn in one of the glasses. If the subject said that one of the glasses contained more corn, the corn in the glass was adjusted until the subject said that both glasses contained equal amounts of corn. If the subject said that both glasses contained some amounts of corn, the corn from one of the glasses was poured into a taller, but narrower glass. The subject was asked whether the large glass contained as much corn as the tall glass, or whether one of the glasses contained more corn.

Every response (judgment) was probed for the subjects' justification (explanation). Explanations that referred to arguments about equivalence (identity) or compensation between two dimensions were classified as adequate answers. Explanations referring to differences in the height of the level of water or corn when explaining differences in the amount of water or corn were scored as inadequate.

In the following section a developmental model of conservation of continuous and discontinuous quantities is presented.

TASK-ANALYSIS AND DEVELOPMENTAL HYPOTHESIS

Whereas in the task concerning the conservation of continuous quantities subjects have to compare quantities of the variable, that is, continuous amounts of water as a whole, the task of conservation of discontinuous quantities refers to an undefined amount of discontinuous elements (corn). It was hypothesized that the concept of conservation of discontinuous quantities is a prerequisite of the emergence of the concept of conservation of continuous quantities as the concept of continuous quantity (such as the concept of volume) is constructed by first quantifying invariable units of quantity (corn, in the present example). It is assumed that the difference between the reference systems of the tasks of conservation

Discontinuous quantities   →   Continuous quantities

→:   is precursor (necessary condition)

Figure 1.3. Synchronous Model: Conservation of Quantities

of quantities lead to décalages in the acquisition of the two tasks (see Piaget, 1941; Piaget, 1971).

FORMULATION OF THE DEVELOPMENTAL MODEL

According to the order-theoretical hypothesis that experience with discontinuous quantities is an antecedent condition for the development of continuous quantities, conservation of discontinuous quantities should be acquired earlier than the conservation of continuous quantities (hypothesis of transitivity in acquisition; see Figure 1.3).

Discontinuous quantities   →   Continuous quantities   Time 1

Discontinuous quantities   →   Continuous quantities   Time 2

→:   is precursor (necessary condition)

Figure 1.4. Synchronous Model for Two Measurement Occasions: Conservation of Quantities

The synchronous model of qualitative change is formulated as an implicative relation. This propositional relationship was postulated independent of the developmental status or age of the child. Therefore, at the second measurement occasion the same order-theoretical relationship between the conservation of discontinuous and continuous quantities was assumed (see Figure 1.4). Because in this study repeated measures of variables are available it was additionally assumed that the synchronous relationships are also valid in the diachronous perspective. Thus it was postulated that the concept of conservation of quantities develops cumulatively. This means that a task solved adequately at the first time of measurement will be retained at the next measurement occasion. This diachronous relationship can be formulated by statement calculus as a case of logical replication (see Figure 1.5).

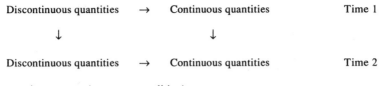

→: is precursor (necessary condition)
↓: cumulative development

Figure 1.5. Sequential Model for Two Measurement Occasions: Conservation of Quantities

STATISTICAL EXAMINATION AND RESULTS

In order to test statistically the postulated model of qualitative change in development the multiple relationships were transferred into a binary coded matrix (see Table 1.1). The developmental patterns differ with respect to the course and the rate of development: stagnation, progression, regression in development, and invariant developmental courses. There are 16 possible patterns of individual development, but only 6 of these represent admissible patterns (admissible patterns underlined).

In Table 1.2 the results of the statistical procedures are reported. While the results of the structural analysis (Dayton & MacReady, 1976) are listed in columns 3 through 5, the results of the Unconditional Prediction Analysis (von Eye & Brandtstädter, 1988) are shown in column 6. Column 1 contains all 16 possible patterns of development. Patterns that are admissible in the model are underlined. The observed frequencies are listed in the second column. The next parameter (column 3) represents the probability of true-score pattern k. In column 4 the frequencies predicted by Dayton and MacReady's procedure are tabulated. χ^2 tests of the difference between observed and predicted frequencies are tabulated in column 5. Measures for the α_i and β_i error as well as the summary χ^2 statistics are given at the bottom of Table 1.2. The last column in the table represents the predicted frequencies examined by Unconditional Prediction Analysis.

Differences between the frequencies predicted by Dayton and MacReady's procedure and the observed frequencies are relatively small. Seven out of 59 observed developmental trajectories are inadmissible. The statistical test of the fit between observed and predicted data still yields acceptable results. The hypothesis that the predicted

TABLE 1.1   Admissible Patterns in the Sequential Model: Conservation of Quantities

DIS7	CON7	DIS8	CON8	
0	0	0	0	Stagnation
1	0	0	0	Regression
0	1	0	0	Regression and invariant
1	1	0	0	Regression
0	0	1	0	Progression
1	0	1	0	Stagnation
0	1	1	0	Regresson and invariant
1	1	1	0	Regression
0	0	0	1	Invariant
1	0	0	1	Invariant
0	1	0	1	Invariant
1	1	0	1	Regression and invariant
0	0	1	1	Progression
1	0	1	1	Progression
0	1	1	1	Invariant
1	1	1	1	Stagnation

NOTE: 0: task not solved; 1: task solved. Admissible patterns are underlined. DIS7,8: Conservation of discontinuous quantities at age 7 (8) years. CON7,8: Conservation of continuous quantities at age 7 (8) years.

and the observed data derive from the same distribution (fit) was accepted statistically, as the observed χ^2 is about the same size as the critical value ($\chi^2 = 9.02$). About 9% of the developmental trajectories were classified as positive and 4% as negative errors (see α_i and β_i errors at the bottom of the table). The frequencies predicted by Unconditional Prediction Analysis (UPA) are listed in the last column. These frequencies were computed under the assumption that all variables are independent of each other. Differences between observed and expected frequencies are relatively large compared to those produced by Dayton and MacReady's procedure. As shown at the bottom of Table 1.2, the reconstruction of the postulated developmental model was statistically significant. According to the postulated order-theoretical model the proportional reduction in error achieved was nearly 60% (PRE = 0.58).

    Although both procedures yield comparable statistical results in testing the developmental model there are remarkable differences with respect to the prediction of frequencies and with respect to the inferential test. Predictions of frequencies in Dayton and MacReady's

TABLE 1.2 Results of Order-Theoretical Analyses—Developmental Model: Conservation of Quantities (N = 59)

Pattern	Obs. N	Theta	DM Pred. N	Chi^2	UPA Pred. N
0000	1	0.0448	1.8368	0.3812	0.0501
0001	2		1.0844	0.7731	1.4287
0010	0	0.0000	1.0844	1.0844	0.4428
0011	20	0.4439	20.1163	0.0007	12.6206
0100	1		0.1888	3.4852	0.0394
0101	0		0.1469	0.1469	1.1256
0110	0		0.1469	0.1469	0.3488
0111	2		2.8625	0.2599	9.9435
1000	0		0.2023	0.2023	0.0636
1001	1		0.4476	0.6717	1.8134
1010	0	0.0000	0.4477	0.4477	0.5620
1011	9	0.1434	9.5668	0.0336	16.0185
1100	0		0.0571	0.0571	0.0501
1101	1		0.8582	0.0234	1.4287
1110	0		0.8583	0.8583	0.4428
1111	22	0.3676	19.0950	0.4419	12.6206
Σ	59			9.0243	

NOTE: $chi^2(8)$ = 9.0243
PRE = 0.580
α_i = 0.0925
z = 2.800
β_i = 0.0429
$p(z)$ = 0.003
Pattern: Configuration of items DIS7, CON7, DIS8, and CON8 (see legend in Table 1.1)
Theta: Probability of pattern
Obs. N: Observed frequency
Pred. N: Predicted frequency
α_i: Positive error (guessing probability)
β_i: Negative error (forgetting probability)
DM: Dayton and MacReady's procedure
UPA: Unconditional Prediction Analysis

procedure are very accurate since they represent conditional probabilities according to the postulated model. But predictions of frequencies in the UPA procedures appear to be less accurate. These predictions were computed under the assumption of total independence between all variables. Concerning the inferential test, the χ^2 statistics in Dayton and MacReady's procedure can lead to problems of over-fit when the expected frequency of each cell is less than 1. In the present model more than half of the cells show expected frequencies that are lower than 1. Therefore, the results of the statistical inference in the model tested by Dayton and MacReady's procedure may be problematic.

Conclusions

This chapter presents an order-theoretical approach to the analysis of intraindividual qualitative change in development. According to the distinction between the two major analytical strategies in developmental psychology, the order-theoretical approach represents both the modeling of qualitative change in development and the modeling of individual differences in development. Two different data-gathering strategies are combined in this approach: (a) individual differences in the order of acquisition of different tasks at one measurement occasion, and (b) individual differences in the order of acquisition of one task across two or multiple measurement occasions. Empirically, questions concerning intraindividual change in development can be adequately assessed only on the basis of the individual developmental patterns, because aggregate developmental curves for groups of individuals do not necessarily show how the individual develops over time. Therefore, questions about the invariability or diversification in developmental trajectories were analyzed within the individual on the basis of ordered patterns of change. These patterns of change represent both the synchronous configurations of attributes and the diachronous constellations of an attribute over time. Within the order-theoretical approach individual differences were analyzed in view of intrinsic processes in development to determine whether change in development (within the individual) forms an invariable developmental sequence and whether uniformity or diversification is obtained in the developmental trajectories of the individuals. Thus within the methodological framework of Buss (1979) the order-theoretical approach is concerned with the interindividual invariability in intraindividual differences and change.

Within this framework, hypotheses about qualitative changes in development can be formulated in terms of statement calculus. With regard to the synchronous perspective the assumed prerequisite order in the acquisition of developmental attributes was formulated as an implicative relationship (transitivity in development). With regard to the diachronous perspective the postulated cumulative development was formulated as a replicative relationship (cumulativity in development). After specifying the order-theoretical model, admissible and inadmissible patterns of development were distinguished.

The two statistical procedures that were selected for the special purpose of the present investigation were specifically designed for the analysis of qualitative change in development. However, they differ with regard to the basic statistical models. While in Dayton and MacReady's procedure frequencies are predicted on the basis of re-cruitment probabilities (conditional probabilities according to the spe-cific model) and the inferential test refers to the differences between observed and predicted frequencies of both admissible and inadmissi-ble patterns, in the Unconditional Prediction Analysis only the fre-quencies of the inadmissible patterns are tested against a model of total independence.

In the empirical example chosen for the demonstration of the order-theoretical approach, both statistical procedures reconstructed the postulated order-theoretical model of the development of the conser-vation of quantities quite satisfactorily. The assumption was con-firmed that the concept of conservation of discontinuous quantities is a prerequisite (or necessary condition) for the development of conser-vation of continuous quantities. Both the synchronous hypothesis con-cerning transitivity in development and the diachronous hypothesis concerning cumulativity in development were accepted using each of the two statistical procedures. Individual differences in the sense of variable or multiple developmental trajectories (differential change) were not found in the order of acquisition. Thus individuals acquired the concept of conservation of quantities in the same order. Neverthe-less, large differences between individual levels of development (de-velopmental status) were observed.

Compared to the prediction by Unconditional Prediction Analysis, Dayton and MacReady's procedure predicted the frequencies rather accurately and without sizeable misclassifications. These differences in the predictive accuracy, however, are not surprising when the basic assumptions of the two statistical models are taken into account. While Dayton and MacReady's procedure focuses on the statistical fit between observed and predicted model, the binomial test of Uncondi-tional Prediction Analysis tests whether there are differences between observed and predicted frequencies. But besides these differences be-tween the statistical models of the two procedures, Dayton and MacReady's procedure refers more directly to the specification of the postulated model. With regard to this specificity in modeling qualitative change and with regard to the methodological purpose of this chapter, the analysis of specific order-theoretical hypotheses about qualitative change in development, Dayton and MacReady's procedure appears to be more adequate than the model underlying the von Eye and Brandtstädter procedure. With respect to the inferential test, however, Dayton and MacReady's procedure was less robust since summary χ^2 statistics are based on cells with predicted frequencies less than 1.

In the present study the focus was on an order-theoretical approach. A further step in the analysis would be to trace observed interindividual differences back to external conditions of development such as opportunities or constraints in the social life-worlds or developmental ecologies of children. One assumption about individual differences due to external conditions of development might be that, while children from deprived socioecological origins show diversification in the acquisition of specific cognitive domains, children originating from enriched social ecologies show uniform developmental sequences in their acquisition profiles leading to consolidated and mature cognitive structures. One way of analyzing this kind of question within an order-theoretical approach is to formulate, and compare, two separate models of development, one for each particular group of children (for example children from enriched and from deprived social backgrounds). Another way would be to combine the separate models of development for each group into an integrated model of development for the whole sample. In the case of a differential model of development an indicator must be introduced that represents the social origin of the individual. Research questions about differential change in development, however, transcend the conceptual framework of the present chapter and will be discussed in Chapter 2.

References

Asendorpf, J. B. (1989). Individual, differential, and aggregate stability of social competence. In B. H. Schneider, G. Attili, J. Nadel, & R. Weissberg (Eds.), *Social competence in developmental perspective* (pp. 71-86). Dordrecht, Netherlands: Kluwer.

Bakan, D. (1967). *On method: Toward a reconstruction of psychological investigation.* San Francisco: Jossey-Bass.

Buss, A. R. (1979). Toward a unified framework for psychometric concepts in multivariate developmental situations: Intraindividual change and inter- and intraindividual differences. In J. R. Nesselroade & P. B. Baltes (Eds.), *Longitudinal* research in the study of behavior and development: Design and analysis (pp. 41-59). New York: Academic Press.

Campbell, R. L., & Richie, D. M. (1983). Problems in the theory of developmental sequences. *Human Development, 26,* 156-172.

Cattell, R. B. (1952). The three basic factor analytic research designs—their interrelations and derivates. *Psychological Bulletin, 49,* 499-520.

Cattell, R. B. (1988). The data box: Its ordering of total resources in terms of possible relational systems. In J. R. Nesselroade & R. B. Cattell (Eds.), *Handbook of multivariate experimental psychology* (pp. 69-130). New York: Plenum.

Dayton, C. M., & MacReady, G. B. (1976). A probabilistic model for validation of behavioral hierarchies. *Psychometrika, 41,* 189-204.

Edelstein, W., Keller, M., & Wahlen, K. (1984). Structure and content in social cognition: Conceptual and empirical analyses. *Child Development, 55,* 1514-1526.

Edelstein, W., Keller, M., & Schröder, E. (1990). Child development and social structure: Individual differences in development. In P. B. Baltes, D. L. Featherman, & R. M. Lerner (Eds.), *Life-span development and behavior* (Vol. 10). Hillsdale, NJ: Lawrence Erlbaum.

Goldschmid, M. L., & Bentler, P. M. (1968). *Manual: Concept assessment kit—conservation.* San Diego, CA: Educational & Industrial Testing Service.

Henning, H. J. (1981). Suche und Validierung kognitiver Strukturen, Entwicklungssequenzen und Lern-/Verhaltenshierarchien mit Hilfe probabilistischer Modelle [Search for and validation of cognitive structures, developmental sequences and learning or behavioral hierarchies by the means of probabilistic models]. *Zeitschrift für Psychologie, 189,* 437-461.

Henning, H. J., & Rudinger, G. (1985). Analysis of qualitative data in developmental psychology. In J. R. Nesselroade & A. von Eye (Eds.), *Individual development and social change: Explanatory analysis* (pp. 295-341). New York: Academic Press.

Hildebrand, D. K., Laing, J. D., & Rosenthal, M. (1977). *Prediction analysis of cross-classifications.* New York: John Wiley.

Hudson, L. M. (1978). On the coherence of role-taking abilities: An alternative to correlational analysis. *Child Development, 49,* 223-227.

Kagan, J. (1980). Perspectives on continuity. In O. G. Brim, Jr., & J. Kagan (Eds.), *Constancy and change in human development* (pp. 26-74). Cambridge, MA: Harvard University Press.

McCall, R. B. (1977). Challenges to a science of developmental psychology. *Child Development, 48,* 333-344.

Nagel, E. (1957). Determinism and development. In D. B. Harris (Ed.), *The concept of development* (pp. 15-34). Minneapolis: University of Minnesota Press.

Piaget, J. (1941). Le mécanisme du développement mental [The mechanism in the development of the mind]. *Archives de Psychologie, 17,* 215-285.

Piaget, J. (1971). The theory of stages in child development. In D. R. Green, M. P. Ford, & G. B. Flamer (Eds.), *Measurement and Piaget* (pp. 1-11). New York: McGraw-Hill.

Rudinger, G. (1978). Erfassung von Entwicklungsveränderungen im Lebenslauf [Assessment of developmental change across the life-span]. In H. Rauh (Ed.), *Jahrbuch für Entwicklungspsychologie* [Annual report of developmental psychology] (pp. 157-214). Stuttgart: Klett-Cotta.

Rudinger, G., Chaselon, F., Zimmermann, E. & Henning, H. J. (1985). *Qualitative Daten: Neue Wege sozialwissenschaftlicher Methodik* [Qualitative data: New approaches in the methodology of social sciences]. *München: Urban & Schwarzenberg.*

Schröder, E. (1989). *Vom konkreten zum formalen Denken: Individuelle Entwicklungsverläufe von der Kindheit bis zum Jugendalter* [From concrete to formal thought: Individual developmental trajectories from childhood to adolescence]. Bern: Huber.

Schröder, E., & Edelstein, W. (in press). Intrinsic and external constraints on the development of cognitive competencies. In M. Chandler & M. Chapman (Eds.), *Criteria for competence: Controversy in the assessment of children's abilities.* Hillsdale, NJ: Lawrence Erlbaum.

Toulmin, S. (1981). Epistemology and developmental psychology. In E. S. Gollin (Ed.), *Developmental plasticity* (pp. 253-267). New York: Academic Press.

van den Daele, L. D. (1969). Qualitative models of development. *Developmental Psychology, 1,* 303-310.

van den Daele, L. D. (1976). Formal models of development: A. Organization and transformation. In K. F. Riegel & J. A. Meacham (Eds.), *The developing individual in a changing world* (pp. 69-78). The Hague: Mouton.

von Eye, A., & Brandtstädter, J. (1988). Evaluating developmental hypotheses using statement calculus and non-parametric statistics. In P. B. Baltes, D. L. Featherman & R. M. Lerner (Eds.), *Life-span development and behavior* (Vol. 8, pp. 61-97). Hillsdale, NJ: Lawrence Erlbaum.

Wohlwill, J. F. (1973). *The study of behavioral development.* New York: Academic Press.

2

Differential Change in Systems of Categorical Variables

ALEXANDER VON EYE

KURT KREPPNER

HOLGER WESSELS

This chapter deals with the statistical analysis of differential change in categorical, nominal-level variables. Change is a term that describes variations in behavior relative to some anchor. A widely used anchor is the absence of change (e.g., Asendorpf, 1989). Possible other anchors include change patterns of other individuals, expected change, optimal change, maximal change, and speed of change. In any instance, change can be considered a relational term that describes the behavior of variables relative to other variables or constants (cf. Maier, 1983). In the developmental behavioral sciences researchers consider the following four types of change:

(1) *Individual change.* Here, one individual changes his or her behavior in one or more variables. Possible anchors include earlier

AUTHORS' NOTE: The authors are indebted to Eberhard Schröder, Jens Asendorpf, Jaan Valsiner, and the conference participants for constructive comments on earlier versions of this chapter.

behaviors of the same individual or ipsative change. Directed change involves approximation of a priori specified goals.

(2) *Universal change.* All or almost all individuals change in the same way. Again, possible anchors include earlier behaviors and goals. Examples include societies moving from one political system to another.

(3) *Aggregate change.* Change averaged across all members of a population. Aggregate change may be an artifact because outliers or large variances may be ignored.

(4) *Differential change.* Change in smaller units of the population that differs from change in other units. The units contain one or more individuals, all of which belong to the same population. The anchor is most often provided by other units of the population or by measures of aggregate change.

This chapter focuses on differential change. In addition, we confine ourselves to discussing change in nominal-level variables. There are many statistical methods suitable for analysis of ordinal, interval, or ratio scale level variables. Examples include regression methods for repeated observations (cf. Lorch & Myers, 1990), least squares estimations of trends (cf. Games, 1990; Metzler & Nickel, 1986), and structural equation modeling (McArdle & Aber, 1990). There is, however, only a very small arsenal of methods to analyze change in qualitative or nominal-level data (see Clogg, Eliason, & Grego, 1990; Rindskopf, 1987, 1990; von Eye, 1990; von Eye, Kreppner, & Wessels, in prep.; von Eye & Nesselroade, in press).

EXAMPLE OF DIFFERENTIAL CHANGE: CRIMINAL BEHAVIOR

In the Cambridge Study in Delinquent Development (Farrington, 1989), 411 males, mostly born in 1953, are observed in crime- and delinquency-related behaviors. The participants were interviewed at ages 8, 10, 14, 16, 18, 21, and 32. In addition, information is available from and about parents, peers, and teachers, and from psychometric tests.

At age 32, about 95% of the still alive members of the sample could be interviewed. Of those, only 240 were still unconvicted.

Viewed cross-sectionally, at age 32, convicted men differed from unconvicted ones in most variables investigated, or, as Farrington (1989, p. 241) put it, "in most aspects of life." The convicted men have more unsatisfactory accommodation, more divorce or separation from wives, children separated from them, more unemployment, and lower earnings. In addition, they spend more evenings out of their homes, are involved in more fights, do more heavy smoking, more drunk driving, more heavy drinking, more drug taking, more theft from work, more tax evasion, and more other offenses than unconvicted men.

From a developmental perspective, three groups can be distinguished that follow differential pathways. The first is the group of *latecomers*. These are the 22 individuals first convicted after their 21st birthday. The men in this group do not differ greatly from unconvicted men. They were, however, more likely to be heavy drinkers and divorced or separated. Also, they report the lowest earnings in the sample, went out most frequently in the evening, were involved in fights, were heavy smokers, admitted many offenses, and displayed the highest psychiatric disorder scores.

The second group contains the so-called *desisters*. These are 55 individuals last convicted before their 21st birthday. These men also did not differ greatly from unconvicted men, showing a profile somewhat similar to the one displayed by the latecomers. They were the worst drunk drivers and drug-takers, however, and admitted frequent theft from work.

The *persisters* are the most extreme group. These are the 61 individuals who continued to commit offenses after their 21st birthday. They were the worst in most categories.

In general, results of the Cambridge Study show that both offenders and nonoffenders turn less deviant between ages 18 and 32. Nevertheless, the differences between the two groups are still statistically significant at age 32. In addition, factors observed at ages 8-10 predicted factors observed at age 32 well. Furthermore, results suggest that at this age differences between convicted and unconvicted men replicate in many ways differences between their parents. Specifically, this applies to the categories low family income, poor housing, erratic job record, marital disharmony, and separation from children.

The three groups of latecomers, desisters, and persisters exemplify the concept of differential change in the following way: Each group follows a distinct change pattern. This pattern is unique and allows the researcher to define a disjunct classification. In this particular example, the anchor used to describe the changes is provided by measures of aggregate change. Despite the differences in change patterns, all individuals belong to the same well-defined population of working-class males within a London school district. All of them were born in 1953.

Analyzing Differential Development in
Nominal-Level Variables

The following sections introduce methods for analysis of the two types of change in nominal-level variables' *symmetry* and *transition patterns*. For each type of change we present tests of log-linear models and data examples. *Differential development* is assumed to be present when groups of individuals differ in change patterns (and hence in parameters of log-linear models).

Contingency tables result from crossing categorical variables. For instance, crossing the two categorical variables *A* and *B* yields a table that combines each level of *A* with each level of *B* and vice versa. *A* and *B* can be different variables like gender and type of car owned. In developmental applications, however, researchers often cross the same variable observed at different occasions. The cells in contingency tables or cross-classifications contain the numbers of instances in which each combination of variable states was observed.

For the following example suppose 100 voters answered the question which party they favor before and after the last tax rise. The result of this poll appears in Table 2.1, which shows that 25 individuals consistently voted for the Democrats (cell DD). Fifteen voted for the Republicans after, but for the Democrats before, the tax rise (cell DR), and so on. Overall, we see that before the tax rise the Republicans were preferred by 60 individuals. After the tax rise, this number dropped to 55. Also, we see that the Democrats attracted more voters (RD = 20) than did the Republicans (DR = 15).

SYMMETRY IN NOMINAL-LEVEL VARIABLES

There are four concepts of symmetry in square contingency tables (cf. Lienert, 1978): (1) diagonal, or axial symmetry, (2) marginal symmetry, or marginal homogeneity, (3) point symmetry, and (4) point-axial symmetry. Diagonal symmetry is by far the most frequently discussed concept. In many instances, authors just say

TABLE 2.1 Stability of Voters' Decisions

		after		
		D	*R*	*Total*
	D	25	15	40
before	R	20	40	60
	Total	45	55	100

D = votes for Democrats
R = votes for Republicans

"symmetry" when they mean diagonal symmetry (e.g., Bishop, Fienberg, & Holland, 1975; Wickens, 1989).

Testing Diagonal Symmetry

Diagonal symmetry proposes that the number of individuals in each of any given pair of cells mirrored at the diagonal of a square matrix is the same. In other words, by symmetry in a two-dimensional square table we mean that

$$y_{ij} = y_{ji} \qquad \text{for all } i \neq j \qquad [2.1]$$

Table 2.1 above displays such a two-dimensional table. We see from (2.1) that the diagonal cell frequencies are not part of the definition of diagonal symmetry. Thus we may neglect them.

From a development perspective, symmetry can be a useful concept if patterns of change in nominal-level variables are of interest. Suppose a researcher assumes that in the ontogenetic development of schizophrenia, speech anomalies (S) and paranoid ideas (P) follow each other with equal probability. Then, the researcher may test the null hypothesis

$$y_{PS} = y_{SP}$$

Accordingly, suppose an investigator of family development assumes that emotional rejection (E), affective warmth (D), and neutral family climate (N) follow each other with equal probability. Then, the null hypothesis of symmetry involves

$$y_{ED} = y_{DE} \qquad y_{EN} = y_{NE} \qquad y_{DN} = y_{ND}$$

Statistically, there are several ways to test the hypothesis of axial symmetry. For 2×2 tables there is, for instance, the well-known McNemar χ^2 test of fourfold symmetry

$$\chi^2 = \frac{(b - c)^2}{b + c}, \quad df = 1. \qquad [2.2]$$

Please notice that both the above formulations and this test assume the researcher focuses on symmetry with respect to the main diagonal. If one wishes to test symmetry relative to the other diagonal, one uses

$$\chi^2 = \frac{(a - d)^2}{a + d}, \quad df = 1. \qquad [2.3]$$

rather than Equation 2.2. In both Equations 2.2 and 2.3, a through d denote the cell frequencies in a fourfold table, clockwise beginning with the upper left cell. In the remainder of this chapter we confine the discussion to symmetry relative to the main diagonal. Formulations that use the other diagonal are straightforward.

Bowker (1948) proposed a generalization of the fourfold test suitable for $k \times m$ tables. The test statistic for $i \neq j$ is

$$\chi^2 = \sum_{ij} \frac{(y_{ij} - y_{ji})^2}{y_{ij} + y_{ji}}, \quad df = (m^2 - m)/2 \qquad [2.4]$$

Log-Linear Model Representations of Diagonal Symmetry

In this section we give two log-linear model representations of *diagonal or axial symmetry*. The first is called "regular log-linear model representation" (Bishop et al., 1975). The second is a design matrix representation.

Following Bishop et al. (1975, pp. 282-283), the log-linear model for this assumption is, in a two-dimensional table,

$$\log(y_{ij}) = u_0 + u_{A(i)} + u_{A(j)} = u_{AB(ij)} \qquad [2.5]$$

with side constraints

$$u_{AB(ij)} = u_{AB(ji)} \qquad\qquad [2.6a]$$

and

$$\sum_i u_{A(i)} = \sum_i u_{AB(ij)} = 0 \qquad\qquad [2.6b]$$

(Notice that the third term on the right-hand side of Equation 2.5 is $u_{A(j)}$ rather than $u_{B(j)}$.) Assuming multinomial sampling, maximizing the equation

$$\sum_{ij} y_{ij} \log(\hat{y}_{ij}) = Nu_0 + \sum_i (y_{i\cdot} + y_{\cdot i}) u_{A(i)} + \sum_{ij} 1/2 (y_{ij} + y_{ji}) u_{AB(ij)} \quad [2.7]$$

yields the expected cell frequencies for the off-diagonal cells

$$\hat{y}_{ij} = (y_{ij} + y_{ji})/2 \qquad \text{for all } i \neq j. \qquad\qquad [2.8]$$

The case $i = j$, that is, the main diagonal, need not be considered because the hypothesis concerns only the off-diagonal cells so that

$$\hat{y}_{ij} = y_{ij} \qquad \text{for all } i = j$$

Standard programs for log-linear modeling cannot easily handle models of diagonal symmetry. It is, however, possible to express the assumption of diagonal symmetry using dummy coding in a design matrix. The design matrix contains one vector for each *ij*-pair. This vector contains a 1 for each of the two cells mirrored at the diagonal, and a 0 for all other cells.

The following example, taken from Lienert and von Eye (cf. Funke & Hussy, 1979; von Eye & Nesselroade, in press), investigates the time needed to solve tasks in the "master mind" game. A sample of $n = 118$ adolescents played master mind with a personal computer. Each subject was allowed 8 trials. Table 2.2 contains the data of the $N = 106$ subjects who needed 6 and 7 guesses to solve the puzzle. Problem solving time was categorized into the three categories: 1 = less than 11 sec, 2 = between 11 and 20 sec, and 3 = more than 20 sec. Table 2.2 also contains the frequencies expected under the assumption of

TABLE 2.2   Log-Linear Analysis of Assumption of Axial Symmetry of
Problem Solving Times

Trials		Frequencies		Design Matrix				
6	7[a]	Obs.	Exp.	u_{12}	u_{13}	u_{23}	u_{11}	u_{22}
1	1	27	27.0	0	0	0	1	0
1	2	10	9.0	1	0	0	0	0
1	3	2	3.0	0	1	0	0	0
2	1	8	9.0	1	0	0	0	0
2	2	13	13.0	0	0	0	0	1
2	3	12	8.5	0	0	1	0	0
3	1	4	3.0	0	1	0	0	0
3	2	5	8.5	0	0	1	0	0
3	3	25	25.0	0	0	0	0	0

a. 6 = problem solving time in trial 6
7 = problem solving time in trial 7

symmetrical shifts between categories. The design matrix appears in
the right-hand panel of the table.

This design matrix contains vectors that specify the assumption of
diagonal symmetry and vectors needed to obtain the correct degrees
of freedom and parameter estimates. The first vector in the matrix
specifies the assumption that cells 12 and 21 contain the same frequencies. The second vector specifies this assumption for cells 13 and
31, and the third vector for cells 23 and 32.

Two vectors are needed to make sure the χ^2 for the diagonal symmetry model is not inflated by components that are not part of the assumptions. For the present example this means that we do not want
the χ^2 to increase because estimated expected frequencies differ from
the observed frequencies in the main diagonal. To guarantee that for
cells 11, 22, and 33 there is no such discrepancy, we add two vectors.
The first contains a 1 only for cell 11, and elsewhere zeros. The second vector contains a 1 only for cell 22, otherwise also only zeros.
For cell 33 there is no need for a vector of this type, because it is the
only cell not included in any of the vectors of the design matrix.
Therefore, the estimated expected frequency for this cell is equal to
the observed one. (Notice that any pair of such vectors would have
done for the present example. The resulting L^2 and χ^2 values will always be the same. The parameter estimates, however, may differ.)

The degrees of freedom for two-dimensional axial symmetry models equal the number of cell pairs. The present example analyzes three

TABLE 2.3 Log-Linear Analysis of Two Models of Problem Solving Times

Trials 6	7	Obs.	Frequencies Exp. 1	Exp. 2			Design Matrix for Second Model			
1	1	22	22.00	22.00	0	0	0	0	1	0
1	2	14	9.50	12.60	1	0	0	0	0	0
1	3	9	6.00	10.38	0	1	0	0	0	0
2	1	5	9.50	3.60	−1	0	0	0	0	0
2	2	18	18.00	18.00	0	0	0	0	0	1
2	3	15	9.00	15.02	0	0	1	0	0	0
3	1	3	6.00	5.38	0	−1	0	0	0	0
3	2	3	9.00	3.02	0	0	−1	0	0	0
3	3	20	20.00	20.00	0	0	0	1	0	0

cell pairs. The L^2 for the model is 3.872, which, for df = 3, has p = 0.2756. We may therefore conclude that the shifts between levels of problem solving time are equally likely.

Differential change patterns discriminate two or more groups of individuals from each other. Suppose a second group of high school students, cognitively more advanced than the first, participated in the same experiment as the first group. The same experimental procedures applied, and problem solving times were categorized as before. Table 2.3 summarizes results from two model tests. The first model proposes axial symmetry as in Table 2.2. The second model makes the following assumption: Students who need more than six trials to solve a master mind problem tend to invest more time before they make a decision. As a consequence, we expect above average frequencies in cells that contain cases with longer problem solving times following shorter times.

Table 2.3 shows that the cognitively more advanced students' frequency distribution is not axial symmetrically distributed. The likelihood ratio χ^2 = 16.31 (df = 3) suggests that this model must be rejected (p = 0.001). It is worth noting that three of the five parameters of this model suggest that significant portions of variability in this table have been explained. Since the overall model does not fit, however, the parameters cannot be interpreted.

The second model proposing that $y_{ij} > y_{ji}$ provides a clearly better explanation of the observed frequency distribution. We calculate a likelihood ratio χ^2 = 1.31 (df = 2) for which p = 0.5192. This is a very impressive fit. Five of the six model parameters are statistically significant. Only the second one falls short of statistical significance. Dropping this vector leads to a model fit of χ^2 = 3.894 (df = 3) for which p = 0.2731. Thus the more parsimonious model provides a very good fit and is not statistically inferior to the less parsimonious model.

From these results we conclude that:

(1) Same age students who reached different levels of cognitive performance display different patterns of problem solving times. While the more advanced students tend to invest more time when not successful, the less advanced students show a more erratic pattern: they switch as often from shorter to longer problem solving times as from longer times to shorter ones.

(2) While diagonal symmetry can appropriately be tested using design matrices with only dummy coding vectors (see Table 2.1), the alternative model can be as easily specified using effect coding vectors. Notice that the models in Tables 2.2 and 2.3 address the same cells. The matrices differ in that (1) they use effect versus dummy coding and (2) the effect coding model requires one more vector.

In addition to the practical uses of axial symmetry illustrated above (cf. Lienert, 1978), there are implications for further analysis. Many methods of clustering and scaling presuppose the matrix of pairwise distances of similarities is symmetric. If the model of axial symmetry cannot be rejected the cell frequencies in the off-diagonals can be interpreted as reflecting intercategory similarities. The larger the cell frequencies, the more likely the two categories co-occur. Methods of cluster or scaling analysis can provide an adequate spatial representation of the categories. If the model of axial symmetry must be rejected scaling and clustering solutions may be incomplete.

Marginal Homogeneity and Quasi-Symmetry

The concept of marginal symmetry proposes the marginal distribution of a variable is the same across two occasions (cf. Bishop et al., 1975; Green, 1989). Marginal symmetry is often called marginal homogeneity. If the expected cell frequencies follow the model of marginal homogeneity we have

$$\hat{y}_{i\cdot} = \hat{y}_{\cdot i} \qquad\qquad [2.9]$$

for $i = 1, \ldots I$. For fourfold tables, the model of marginal homogeneity implies that

$$\hat{y}_{12} = \hat{y}_{21} \qquad [2.10]$$

Please notice that Equation 2.10 is also satisfied if the model of axial symmetry applies.

The model of marginal symmetry given in Equation 2.9 cannot be transformed into a simple parametric log-linear model for estimating expected values (cf. Bishop et al., 1975, p. 282). It can, however, be inferred from comparing the models of axial symmetry and quasi-symmetry. This model can be explained as follows. Suppose category c_i is preferred to category c_j $(i \neq j)$. If this relationship applies one can expect

$$\hat{y}_{ij} > \hat{y}_{ji} \qquad [2.11]$$

The model of quasi-symmetry is the model of choice if certain categories are selected more often than others. Such a preference makes axial symmetry very unlikely. However, once preference patterns of this type are taken into account, confusion among alternative categories may be symmetric. In other words, the model of quasi-symmetry removes the hypothesis of equal margins (see Equation 2.9) but assumes the odds ratios are still symmetric. Using the notation from the Appendix we obtain for the complete model of quasi-symmetry

$$\log(y_{ij}) = u_0 + u_{A(i)} + u_{B(j)} + u_{AB(ij)} \qquad [2.12]$$

with

$$u_{AB(ij)} = u_{AB(ji)}$$

To evaluate the assumptions of marginal homogeneity we consider the following. The model of diagonal symmetry implies marginal homogeneity. The model of quasi-symmetry only implies symmetry of association parameters. Thus we have a hierarchical relationship that can be used for a test: The difference between the likelihood chi-square values for the two models is the likelihood chi-square estimate for the model of marginal homogeneity. (For a complete example, see Wickens, 1989, pp. 259-265.)

Point Symmetry

The concept of point symmetry proposes that cells on both sides of the center cell of a square table have equal frequencies. Consider a 3×3 table. The model of point symmetry for this table implies that, $\hat{y}_{11} = \hat{y}_{33}$, $\hat{y}_{12} = \hat{y}_{21}$, $\hat{y}_{13} = \hat{y}_{31}$, and $\hat{y}_{23} = \hat{y}_{32}$. Point symmetry implies that the marginal distributions are point symmetrical also, but not necessarily the same.

The above example of point symmetry in a 3×3 table can lead to the assumption that a table must have an odd number of rows and columns in order that models of point symmetry can be tested. This is not the case. The point of symmetry can be imaginary. Consider a 2×2 table. Here, the model of point symmetry implies that $\hat{y}_{11} = \hat{y}_{22}$ and $\hat{y}_{12} = \hat{y}_{21}$.

The model of point symmetry is easily translated into design matrices using dummy coding. For each pair of cells one specifies one coding vector that postulates equivalence. If the table has an odd number of rows and columns, the point of symmetry is not part of the hypothesis. Main effects need not be considered.

As for other models of symmetry, point symmetry is easily applied to three and higher dimensional tables. Consider a $2 \times 2 \times 2$ table. For this table, the model of point symmetry implies that $\hat{y}_{111} = \hat{y}_{222}$, $\hat{y}_{112} = \hat{y}_{221}$, $\hat{y}_{121} = \hat{y}_{212}$, and $\hat{y}_{122} = \hat{y}_{211}$.

Developmental applications of point symmetry typically test distributional assumptions for behavior patterns. Suppose a sample of $n = 50$ families is observed on three occasions. The observers count the presence (1) versus absence (2) of conflict in decision-making situations. The observed joint frequencies of these counts appear in Table 2.4. The table also contains the expected frequency distribution estimated under the model of three-dimensional point symmetry, and the design matrix.

Please notice that the design matrix has only three vectors rather than four as one might conclude from the above model implications. This can be explained by the characteristics of the coding vectors. Reading columnwise, the vectors specify which cell frequencies are expected to be equivalent. However, reading row- or cellwise we realize that cells 122 and 211 were not included in any specification. The coding vectors show only zeros for these cells. As a consequence, the program assumes the average of these cells as expectancy. Therefore, the specification of an additional coding vector would be redundant. Please notice that a test of this part of the point symmetry model is possible by substituting this vector for any of the other three.

TABLE 2.4 Analysis of Conflicts Under the Model of Three-Dimensional Point Symmetry

Conflicts on 3 Occasions	*Frequencies* Obs.	Exp.	*Design Matrix*		
111	1	2	1	0	0
112	6	8	0	1	0
121	5	3	0	0	1
122	15	12	0	0	0
211	9	12	0	0	0
212	1	3	0	0	1
221	10	8	0	1	0
222	3	2	1	0	0

The goodness of fit for the point symmetry model in Table 2.4 is satisfactory. We calculate a likelihood ratio $\chi^2 = 6.167$ (df = 4) for which $p > 0.187$. Thus we may conclude that the occurrence of conflicts is point symmetrically distributed in these families. This conclusion has the following implications:

(1) Presence and absence of conflict is equally likely at all three occasions. This follows from marginal symmetry. Examples of application of marginal symmetry include the analysis of test items or psychiatric symptoms. Here, one can apply models of point symmetry only if the items have difficulty indices of about 0.5. (For transformations that generate such difficulty indices without affecting the association pattern see Lienert, von Eye, & Rovine, 1988.) To illustrate this point, we calculate the observed univariate marginal conflict frequencies for each occasion. We obtain $y_{1..} = 27$, $y_{2..} = 23$, $y_{.1.} = 17$, $y_{.2.} = 33$, $y_{..1} = 25$, $y_{..2} = 25$. Obviously, the assumption of marginal symmetry applies to the second occasion only to a lesser extent.

(2) The autocorrelations of the conflict variable across the three occasions are not constrained. In other words, we do not expect the autocorrelations to be equal. Indeed, we calculate the correlations $\varphi_{12} = -0.185$, $\varphi_{13} = -0.602$, and $\varphi_{23} = 0.127$, where the subscripts denote the occasions.

Point-Axial Symmetry

The combination of point symmetry and diagonal or axial symmetry is called point-axial symmetry. Consider a 3×3 table. For this table, the model of point-axial symmetry implies that $y_{11} = y_{33}$, $y_{21} = y_{12} = y_{23} = y_{32}$, and $y_{31} = y_{13}$. It follows from this combination of characteristics that matrices that display a point-axial frequency distribution have identical, symmetrically distributed marginals. (For an example of a statistical analysis of point-axial symmetry see Lienert, 1978.)

Differential Patterns of Change:
Status and Developmental Trajectory

The following paragraphs analyze patterns of change in nominal-level variables. Suppose a developmental theory assumes that qualitatively different states develop in an a priori specified sequence. To test this assumption, the researcher can specify those patterns that confirm this theory, or are admissible, in contrast to those patterns that contradict the theory, or are inadmissible (for an example see Chapter 1). In the present context, the terms *admissible* and *inadmissible* do not imply deterministic models. Although, in theory, inadmissible patterns should occur with zero probability, measurement error or less than perfect psychometric instruments lead us to classify individuals in cells where they do not belong. Thus statistical testing seems more appropriate than rejecting a theory because of a small number of contradicting instances.

Examples of sequences of qualitatively different states can be found in many developmental theories. Piagetian theory, for example, assumes that the cognitive stages of concrete and formal operations represent the changing ability of individuals to perform qualitatively different operations (cf. Schröder, 1989; Chapter 1 this volume). In addition, researchers assume that later stages can develop only after the development of earlier stages is complete. Thus a sequence of admissible stages is predetermined.

Developmental theories covering other domains also assume a sequence of stages. There is, however, not always an inherent logic that predetermines what state can follow what other state. Rather, the theory may propose that certain sequences are more likely than others. In either case, we have a finite set of states that individuals can be in or not. If one forms cross-classifications from the stages, cells will contain individuals who display admissible patterns, and other cells will contain individuals who display unlikely patterns.

Many methods for analysis of sequence patterns have been discussed. Examples include prediction analysis of cross-classifications (Hildebrand, Laing, & Rosenthal, 1977; von Eye & Brandtstädter, 1981; Schröder, 1989, this volume) and scaling methods (Dayton & MacReady, 1976; Schröder, 1989, this volume). The following paragraphs apply nonstandard log-linear models.

(1) *The analysis of life trees.* In life event analysis researchers focus on sequences of life events. Examples of life events include marriage, job history, and military service. Life events change the state an individual is in. A marriage, for instance, changes the state from single, divorced, or widowed to married. At each point in time life events do or do not occur and the states following these events last or do not last. The cross-classification of a series of life events is termed *life tree* (Müller, 1980; von Eye & Brandtstädter, 1981). Thus, life-tree research is a special case of life event research.

Each branch of a life tree specifies a particular *life path* through a sequence of events. As stated above, developmental theories propose that some of the paths are admissible while others are inadmissible. In weaker terms, some of the paths are more likely and others are less likely to be observed.

Using standard log-linear modeling we can analyze life trees to identify patterns of associations between life events. Logistic regression can be used to define path analysis of life events. In the following paragraphs, we analyze life trees using the design matrix approach. The hypotheses we analyze concern variable relationships and differential development in particular groups of individuals. Hypotheses of both kinds can be analyzed simultaneously. Thus we are able to analyze differential development within a system of variables.

Suppose life events, *A, B, C,* and *D* are observed one after the other. These variables can be crossed to form an $I * J * K * L$ contingency table. Each cell of this table defines a life path. For example, cell 1221 contains the individuals who experienced state 1 of variable *A,* state 2 of variables *B* and *C,* and state 1 of variable *D.* The table as a whole defines a complete life tree.

For the following example suppose we investigate a life tree of married couples that involves the following events and states: counselor visit (*V*; 1 = yes, 2 = no), employment status (*J*; 1 = employed, 2 = unemployed), number of children (*C*; 1 = no children, 2 = children), and experienced marital happiness (*H*; 1 = happy, 2 = unhappy). The working hypothesis is that seeing a counselor increases chances for a happy marriage. In other words, we expect all cells with the index 1 for counselor visit and 1 for subjective marital happiness to display above, and cells with indexes 12 below average frequencies. This hypothesis is proposed to hold regardless of the states assumed by the variables J and C, that is, across all states of J and C. We expect the following result: cells 1112, 1122, 1212, and 1222 show below, and cells 1111, 1121, 1211, and 1221 show above average frequencies. (The order of variables is as listed above.)

This example shows that the number of cells confirming or disconfirming a hypothesis does not depend on the order of variables. This can be explained as follows. In the example, the variables J and C assume categories 11, 12, 21, and 22. This is the case regardless of whether they are observed before or after the variables V and H. Thus the present approach does not allow the researcher to discriminate between designs in which variables are observed in different order (cf. von Eye & Brandtstädter's, 1981, critique of other methods in this respect). The reason is the confound between time and observed life event.

The following data example analyzes retrospective data presented by von Eye and Brandtstädter (1981). A sample of $n = 207$ undergraduates in psychology answered a questionnaire that contained the following variables: gender (G; 1 = male, 2 = female), internal locus of control (IPC; Krampen, 1981; 1 = below average, 2 = above), subjective amount of time needed to make a decision on an academic major (T; 1 = short, 2 = long), and subjective satisfaction with present life (S; 1 = happy, 2 = unhappy). We analyzed these data under the following hypotheses:

(1) male psychology students are more likely to display below than above average internal control scores,

(2) male psychology undergraduates scoring below average in internal locus of control are more likely to be happy if they needed only little time to decide for a major in psychology than when they needed more time.

In addition to these hypotheses we consider the main effects for the variables gender and life satisfaction. The first main effect takes into account that more female ($n = 130$) than male students ($n = 77$) participated in the study. The second main effect accounts for variations

TABLE 2.5 Analysis of Life Tree of the Variables Gender (G), Internal Locus of Control (L), Decision-Making Time (D), and Happiness (H)

Variables GLDH	Frequencies Obs.	Exp.	Design Matrix			
1111	5	2.36	−1	1	−1	−1
1112	11	15.64	−1	1	1	0
1121	14	11.36	−1	1	−1	1
1122	15	15.64	−1	1	1	0
1211	2	3.98	−1	−1	−1	0
1212	17	12.02	−1	−1	1	0
1221	2	3.98	−1	−1	−1	0
1222	11	12.02	−1	−1	1	0
2111	7	8.08	1	0	−1	0
2112	27	24.42	1	0	1	0
2121	7	8.08	1	0	−1	0
2122	24	24.42	1	0	1	0
2211	5	8.08	1	0	−1	0
2212	28	24.42	1	0	1	0
2221	12	8.08	1	0	−1	0
2222	20	24.42	1	0	1	0

due to the higher frequency of "happy" answers. Table 2.5 contains the observed and estimated expected frequencies, and the effect coding vectors of the design matrix.

The results for the data in Table 2.5 show that the model cannot be rejected (likelihood ratio $\chi^2 = 13.633$, df = 11, $p < 0.254$). None of the differences between the estimated expected and the observed frequencies is significant. Three of the four estimated parameters are significant. The only one falling short is the one contrasting the above and below average internally controlled males ($z = 1.103$, $p < 0.135$). To make the model more parsimonious we omitted this parameter in a recalculation. The model test revealed a likelihood ratio $\chi^2 = 14.855$ (df = 12). This value also suggests a very good fit ($p = 0.2495$). All of the parameter estimates are significant. Thus we may adopt the more parsimonious model. It is statistically not inferior to the more elaborate one.

(2) *The analysis of developmental trajectories. An example from family development.* Recent literature on log-linear modeling has focused on the analysis of linear relationships in ordinal categorical data (see Agresti, 1984; Green, 1988; Haberman, 1978, 1979). In longitudinal research, however, linearity appears to be unlikely in many cases,

especially when the time variable is included in the analysis as an ordinal variable with discrete states. Using a more general approach, von Eye, Kreppner and Wessels (in prep.) and Wessels (1990) have shown that orthogonal polynomial coding of design-matrix vectors is a method suitable for analysis of time trends of observational behavioral data. The following section illustrates this method for analysis of differential change using an example of family development.

The data for this example are taken from a longitudinal study that explored changes in socialization patterns inside the family. The arrival of a second child was taken as the starting point for a series of observations in the families' homes to study the process of this child's integration in its natural environment. Sixteen families were observed during seven time periods, when the second child was 6/8 weeks, 4/5 months, 8/9 months, 12/13 months, 16/17 months, 20/21 months, and 23/24 months old. Seven hours of videotaped material from each family covering the entire two years were subdivided into interaction episodes lasting between 20 and 40 seconds each, yielding about 1,100 episodes for each family. All episodes were scored according to initiative/target combination and socialization activities. For this example, two dyadic initiative/target combinations and two socialization activities were selected to demonstrate the differential analysis of change.

The first example studies the activity "situation control" in the mother-2nd child dyad over time, that is, the intentional intervention in an ongoing interaction in order to continue or to change an activity according to the initiator's interest. The second example deals with the activity "transmission of rules" in the father-child1 dyad over time, that is, the conveyance of norms and regulations for proper conduct in the family. For studying differences across families, a cluster analysis was conducted by entering scores describing differences between mothers and fathers in controlling socialization activities. Two groups could be isolated, one group (cluster 1) with high difference scores, that is, a low degree of parental cooperation during this period of time, and a second group (cluster 2) with moderate to small difference scores or a higher degree of parental cooperation.

The study's aim was to find adequate models for the two groups' specific trajectories in the mother-child2 "situation control" or father-child1 "transmission of rules" socialization activities over time. Therefore, a two-dimensional table was introduced for the analysis with the variables "time period" (T) and "family group" (cluster 1 and cluster 2).

Consider for example a variable "time period" (T) of family development data having 7 states within the first two years after the birth of the second child. In nominal log-linear modeling, one model to be tested for this variable is the assumption that each cell has the same probability. The log-linear model for this assumption is

$$\log(y_i) = u_0 \qquad [2.13]$$

where $u_0 = \log (N/I)$ if I defines the number of states of the variable (see Haberman, 1978). Since we are analyzing change over time, however, a uniform frequency distribution is not very likely. The next possible model in nominal log-linear analysis would be the main effect model but this model is already saturated (since we are analyzing only one variable).

At this point, ordinal log-linear models become important. A simple assumption about the frequencies in the different states of T would be to assume a linear rise or decline of the frequencies. A log-linear model reflecting this assumption would be

$$\log(y_i) = u_0 + \beta(v_i - v_m) \qquad [2.14]$$

where u_0 denotes the arithmetic mean of the natural logarithms of the cell frequencies y_i, β denotes a parameter estimate, v_i usually denotes an integer score with $v_i < v_{i+1}$ (for all $i = 1, 2 \ldots I$), and v_m denotes the mean of the scores v_i. In this log-linear time-trend model (Haberman, 1978) the deviation from the uniform distribution model of each $\log(y_i)$ is a linear function with slope $\beta(v_i - v_m)$ (Agresti, 1984).

In nominal log-linear modeling the inclusion of the main effect of T requires $7 - 1 = 6$ design matrix vectors. Each design matrix vector binds 1 degree of freedom for the significance test. However, the log-linear time-trend model estimates only one additional parameter when compared to the uniform distribution model. Therefore, only one more degree of freedom is invested. The use of coefficients of orthogonal polynomials for the scores v_i provides several advantages when the Newton-Raphson algorithm is applied for parameter estimation[1] (see von Eye, Kreppner, & Wessels, in prep.): First, trend analysis using polynomial scoring is well-known from trend analysis in analysis of variance. Second, the coefficients of orthogonal polynomials meet the criteria for effect coding of design matrices (see Appendix for details). Therefore, they can simply be inserted in the design matrix. Moreover, since the mean of these vectors is 0, Equation 2.14

reduces to $\beta(v_i)$. This results in simplified calculations. Third, the coefficients of orthogonal polynomials may be taken simply from standard statistical tables.

Using these results, an extension of the procedure to more complex functions is at hand. Recall that polynomials have the general form

$$y = \sum_i a_i x_{ii} \qquad [2.16]$$

For $i = 0$ one obtains $y = a_0 x_{00} = a$ and for $i = 0, 1$ one obtains

$$y = a_0 x_{00} + a_1 x_{11}$$

which is the linear regression equation (see von Eye, Kreppner, & Wessels, in prep.). Since variable T has 7 states, we may introduce up to $7 - 1 = 6$ polynomial vectors in the design matrix. The maximum order of the polynomial is 6. The saturated ordinal log-linear model is, therefore

$$\log(y_i) = u + \beta_i (v_{i\,1}) + \beta_2 (v_{i\,2}) + \beta_3 (v_{i\,3}) + \beta_4 (v_{i\,4}) + \beta_5 (v_{i\,5}) + \beta_6 (v_{i\,6})$$
$$[2.17]$$

where the v_{in} are the coefficients of an orthogonal polynomial of order n (Wessels, 1990).

With these results we may turn to differential analysis of time-trends. There can be two types of differences in developmental trajectories: First, the groups' trajectories may be equivalent in the slopes, but the trajectories differ in their elevation. Second, there may be divergent trajectories for different groups. In the following sections we give examples of both cases.

To illustrate the case, where two groups follow the same trajectories, we use frequencies of the variable "situation control" of the mother in regard to the second child in two groups of families. The cross-tabulation of these frequencies with the variable "time period" appears in the three left-hand columns of Table 2.6.

A nominal log-linear main effect model yields $L^2 = 6.101$ and $\chi^2 = 5.651$ with 6 degrees of freedom. Thus we may conclude the two groups display the same trends. However, this model provides no information about the character of the development of the groups and we decide to use an ordinal log-linear model to assess the type of the developmental trajectory in the different groups.

TABLE 2.6 Log-Linear Analysis Using Orthogonal Polynomials for Situation Control of Mother to the Second Child in Two Groups of Families Over 7 Points of Observation

| | | Frequencies | | | Design–Matrix | | | |
| | | Obs. | Exp. | | | | | |
C	T	Obs.	Exp.	$u_{C(i)}$	β_1	β_2	β_3	β_4
1	1	7	3.99	1	−3	5	0	0
1	2	6	9.56	1	−2	0	0	0
1	3	15	18.70	1	−1	−3	0	0
1	4	33	29.83	1	0	−4	0	0
1	5	42	38.84	1	1	−3	0	0
1	6	40	41.28	1	2	0	0	0
1	7	35	35.80	1	3	5	0	0
2	1	5	2.15	−1	0	0	−3	5
2	2	3	5.98	−1	0	0	−2	0
2	3	10	12.38	−1	0	0	−1	−3
2	4	19	19.01	−1	0	0	0	−4
2	5	23	21.67	−1	0	0	1	−3
2	6	23	18.32	−1	0	0	2	0
2	7	8	11.49	−1	0	0	3	5

Since the cross-tabulation involves two variables and the number of frequencies for the two clusters is not fixed, we include the main effect variable C in the model. To fit the developmental trajectories independently for both groups of families we add four vectors to the design matrix specifying a linear and a quadratic trend for each group. The complete design matrix is displayed on the right-hand side of Table 2.6.

Fitting this model to the observed frequencies yields $L^2 = 12.24$ and $\chi^2 = 13.06$ with 8 degrees of freedom indicating a good model fit.[2] Thus we conclude that the frequency of mother's "situation control" to the second child shows a general increase over the two-year time period. It peaks around the 3rd/4th time period, however, and declines later in both groups. The parameter estimates for the quadratic components are nearly identical for both groups. The negative sign of these parameters suggests that the quadratic slopes are not shaped like a valley as was postulated by the design matrix vector. Rather, the opposite is true. The slopes are shaped like a hill (see Table 2.7).

This example illustrates that the families in both groups show the same developmental trajectory within the two-year time period. The trend components differ across family groups, however: The mothers

TABLE 2.7 Parameter Estimates for Table 2.6

	τ	$s(\tau)$	$\tau/s(\tau)$
$u_{C(i)}$	.320	.084	3.812**
β_1	.366	.057	6.385**
β_2	−.102	.027	−3.731**
β_3	.280	.077	3.636**
β_4	−.149	.039	−3.812**

** $\alpha < .05$

of group 1 show much more controlling behavior than the mothers of group 2.

For the second of the two cases stated above, when the trajectories are different for both groups, consider the frequencies of "transmission of rules" of the father to the first child displayed in Table 2.8.

Fitting the same model to these data provides no satisfactory fit (L^2 = 24.72, χ^2 = 22.74, df = 8, $\alpha < .05$). Adding two more components to the model, a cubic and a quartic one (for both groups) yields L^2 = 7.42, χ^2 = 7.25 with df = 4, which is insignificant at $\alpha = .05$. Now, parameter estimates for the different trends per family group (Table

TABLE 2.8 Log-Linear Analysis Using Orthogonal Polynomial Scoring for Situation Control of Father to the First Child in Two Family Clusters Over 2 Years

		Frequencies			Design–Matrix							
C	T	Obs.	Exp.	$u_{C(i)}$	β_1	β_2	β_3	β_4	β_5	β_6	β_7	β_8
1	1	10	10.42	1	−3	5	−1	3	0	0	0	0
1	2	17	14.86	1	−2	0	1	−7	0	0	0	0
1	3	17	21.37	1	−1	−3	1	1	0	0	0	0
1	4	21	16.47	1	0	−4	0	6	0	0	0	0
1	5	5	7.43	1	1	−3	−1	1	0	0	0	0
1	6	5	4.42	1	2	0	−1	−7	0	0	0	0
1	7	16	16.03	1	3	5	1	3	0	0	0	0
2	1	27	26.51	−1	0	0	0	0	−3	5	−1	3
2	2	26	28.53	−1	0	0	0	0	−2	0	1	−7
2	3	27	21.74	−1	0	0	0	0	−1	−3	1	1
2	4	12	17.60	−1	0	0	0	0	0	−4	0	6
2	5	20	16.87	−1	0	0	0	0	1	−3	−1	1
2	6	15	15.83	−1	0	0	0	0	2	0	−1	−7
2	7	9	8.93	−1	0	0	0	0	3	5	1	3

TABLE 2.9 Parameter Estimates for Table 2.8

	τ	$s(\tau)$	$\tau/s(\tau)$
$u_{C(i)}$	−.227	.075	−3.035**
β_1	−.078	.058	−1.339
β_2	−.010	.030	−0.324
β_3	.450	.129	3.480**
β_4	−.052	.026	2.010**
β_5	−.168	.048	−3.464**
β_6	−.022	.028	−0.782
β_7	−.041	.099	−0.412
β_8	−.021	.018	−1.157

** $\alpha < .05$

2.9) exhibit salient differences for the two family groups' developmental trajectories: While for group 2 only the linear decreasing trend is significant ($\alpha = -.168$, $z = -3.464$), the linear component is insignificant for the families in group 1. For this group, however, the cubic and the quartic components are significant while they are insignificant for the families in group 2.

These results suggest that the family groups show different patterns of transmission of rules from father to first child. While in group 1 frequencies seem to oscillate in a somewhat erratic manner with an increase toward the end of the two-year period, frequencies in group 2 follow a linear decrease over time.

These examples illustrate how ordinal log-linear modeling can be used as a tool for differential analysis of change with categorical data sets. Notice, however, that orthogonal polynomial fitting of developmental trajectories is only one possibility among several. Other functions include trigonometric, exponential, and step functions. While orthogonal polynomials offer several advantages, as already discussed in this chapter, there is one major disadvantage: Cyclical processes cannot be parsimoniously fitted.

Conclusion

This chapter discusses the analysis of differential development from the perspective of a researcher that

(1) collects nominal level data in repeated measurement designs
(2) adopts a multivariate perspective
(3) compares groups of individuals, and
(4) performs explanatory rather than exploratory research.

The chapter discusses nonstandard log-linear modeling as a suitable methodology that enables one to test developmental hypotheses in a custom tailored fashion. The focus is on two model types, symmetry and developmental trajectory models. Symmetry models, often discussed only from a methodological perspective (Green, 1989; Wickens, 1989), have major developmental implications.

The model of *marginal symmetry* implies two equivalent marginal distributions. This implies that if a variable is observed on two occasions it has the same marginal distribution at both occasions. This can be a very important characteristic. Suppose a researcher administers a personality questionnaire on two occasions. Then, marginal symmetry implies that items have the same difficulty on both occasions. Thus if less than perfect autocorrelation is measured, but the model of marginal symmetry cannot be rejected, we can assume developmental change that is not necessarily confounded with changes in item characteristics. Similarly, one can assume differential development if there are distinct groups of individuals displaying differential autocorrelation patterns.

The model of *axial or diagonal symmetry* implies equally likely transitions between categories. If the model of axial symmetry cannot be rejected, we may conclude that there are no systematic developmental transition patterns. If, however, there is reason to reject the model, we have strong and clear indicators of systematic shifts. In most instances, it is not just one cell that shows a significant deviation from expectancy. Rather, as we know from configural research (Krauth & Lienert, 1973; von Eye, 1990), cells with unexpectedly high frequencies typically go hand in hand with cells containing fewer cases than expected from the model. Whenever this is the case, we have identified differential patterns of development. This can be of great importance in differential diagnostics of psychopathological development.

It is worth noting that the anchor used to identify differentially developing groups of individuals is twofold. First, groups of individuals are compared with other groups showing different developmental patterns. Second, each group is compared with the model of symmetry.

In a similar fashion, one can discuss the other concepts of symmetry, quasi-symmetry, point symmetry, and point-axial symmetry. For the present context, it is most important that each concept of symmetry can be coupled to a developmental hypothesis. This hypothesis can become differential in two ways. First, model rejections can often be explained by the presence of groups of individuals who deviate from model assumptions while other groups confirm the expectations. Methods of residual analysis or Configural Frequency Analysis (Krauth & Lienert, 1973; von Eye, 1990) allow one to identify these groups. The configural approach is mostly used in exploratory research. In contrast, in explanatory research a priori specified groups are expected to develop differently. For these groups, conditional models or separate models can be estimated (see Tables 2.2 and 2.3).

The second group of methods discussed in this chapter includes life-tree models. The main characteristic of these models is that observation points and life events are confounded. Thus the methods for cross-classification of time with variables or repeatedly observed variables (von Eye & Nesselroade, in press) cannot be applied. The only option is to cross-classify the variables that identify the life events and states that follow these events. Each cell in the resulting cross-classification represents a life path. Comparing life paths implies testing hypotheses on differential development.

Most important in the analysis of life trees or life events with log-linear models is that hypotheses on differential development can be tested within a system of variable main effects and interactions. For instance, in Table 2.5 we test the assumption that psychological well-being in male students depends on the amount of trouble they had earlier while deciding on their major. This test is done simultaneously with two tests on main effects. Other examples can be conceived with variables showing more complex interaction patterns.

Developmental implications of the present approach to the analysis of developmental trajectories are straightforward. The researcher has the following options.

(1) *Modeling slopes of developmental functions*: Here, there is a plethora of options. The researcher can smooth orthogonal polynomials, trigonometric functions, step-functions, exponential functions, and so on. In each case the present methods can be used to determine the degree to which data follow a particular type of function.

(2) *Outlier analysis*: The researcher can analyze residuals; that is, some form of the discrepancies between observed and estimated (expected) frequencies (for an example see Wessels, 1990). Outliers are either local deviations that suggest model modifications or they are interpreted as local associations present beyond a particular model. This is done in Configural Frequency Analysis (Krauth & Lienert, 1973; von Eye, 1990).

(3) *Specification of group differences*: Both outlier analysis and modeling slopes can be done in ways that contrast two or more groups. Results are expressed in terms of, for instance, group differences in developmental patterns (see Table 2.6) or outliers that define distinct groups.

From a data analysis perspective it should be noted that the methods of log-linear modeling present one among many other approaches of analyzing qualitative developmental data. Other methods include Configural Frequency Analysis (CFA) (von Eye, 1990), latent class or variable analysis (LCA) (Hagenaars, 1990), and scaling methods (Wood, 1990).

APPENDIX

Log-Linear Models for Analysis of Differential Change

Standard log-linear modeling allows the researcher to decompose the variability in a contingency table into main effects and interaction terms. Consider a contingency table made up by the four variables A, B, C, and D. Then, the following model provides a complete description of the variability in this table:

$$\log(y_{ijkl}) = u_0 + u_{A(i)} + \ldots + u_{D(j)} \qquad \text{[A1]}$$

$$+ u_{AB(ij)} + \ldots + u_{CD(kl)}$$

$$+ u_{ABC(ijk)} + \ldots + u_{BCD(jkl)}$$

$$+ u_{ABCD(ijkl)}$$

where $\log(y_{ijkl})$ is the observed frequency in cell $ijkl$. The model described in Equation A1 is well-known as the *saturated model*. It contains all possible main effects and interactions. In Equation A1, main effect terms contain only one-variable subscripts. Interactions contain two- or more variable subscripts.

To make the values of the u-parameters unique, one typically places side-constraints, also known as identifying restrictions. The most common convention used is that the sum of all parameters with the same subscript be zero. Thus we have for instance:

$$\sum_i u_{A(i)} = \sum_j u_{B(j)} = \sum_{ij} u_{AB(ij)} = \sum_{ik} u_{AC(ik)} = \sum_{ikl} u_{ACD(ikl)} = 0$$

Other constraints include fixing parameters and setting parameters equal to zero (Plackett, 1974).

Unlike in standard analysis of variance where the researcher estimates parameters for all main effects and interactions, the researcher attempts to find a model more parsimonious than the saturated one. Parsimonious log-linear models have the following three characteristics:

(1) They reflect the researcher's substantive assumptions.

(2) They contain fewer main effect and interaction terms than the saturated model, and the interaction terms are of the lowest possible order; that is, they involve the smallest possible number of variables.

(3) No more complex model reproduces the observed frequency distribution significantly better.

In hierarchical log-linear models terms for higher order effects subsume the terms for lower order effects. For instance, the interaction term $u_{ABC(ijk)}$ subsumes all pairwise interactions, $u_{AB(ij)}$, $u_{AC(ik)}$, and $u_{BC(jk)}$, and all main effects, $u_{A(i)}$, $u_{B(j)}$, and $u_{C(k)}$. In nonstandard models this type of hierarchy can also be generated. In addition, however, it is possible to perform comparisons analogous to contrasts in analysis of variance. This chapter focuses on the application of nonstandard models.

The estimation of log-linear parameters is typically performed using either of the following three methods. The first starts from an equation that expresses the model under study. The form of the model is exemplified in Equation A1. Unlike in the model specification for which one needs only one equation, however, one formulates one equation for each cell under consideration. Additional equations can be formulated to specify the side constraints. The equations are solved one after the other. A straightforward way to solve them is by working up, starting from low-order terms. A complete example is given in Wickens (1989, pp. 112-115). Many programs for log-linear modeling apply this strategy (e.g., SYSTAT, BMDP).

Another method, less popular in software packages, is the well-known weighted least square technique. In ordinary least squares one calculates the parameter vector from

$$\mathbf{b} = (\mathbf{X}'\mathbf{X})^{-1}\mathbf{X}'\mathbf{y} \qquad [A2]$$

(see Neter, Wasserman, & Kutner, 1985; von Eye, 1988), where $\mathbf{X}$ denotes the design matrix that specifies the model under study. The chapter explains in more detail how to use a design matrix to analyze specific developmental hypotheses.

The ordinary least squares solution for the parameter vector minimizes the squared differences between the observed frequencies in vector $\mathbf{y}$ and the expected frequencies in vector $\mathbf{Xb}$. This solution is not satisfactory in the analysis of frequency data for several reasons. One very important one is that each cell frequency is given the same weight. As is well-known, however, the cell frequencies may very well have greatly differing variances. As a result, the errors attached to them are not the same. To meet with the desideratum that frequencies with smaller errors have more weight than frequencies with bigger errors one can weight the error in $\mathbf{y} = \mathbf{Xb} + \mathbf{e}$ by the variances of cell frequencies. As a result, one obtains a weighted least squares estimator for the parameter vector via

$$\mathbf{b} = (\mathbf{X}' \mathbf{S}_y^{-1} \mathbf{X})^{-1} \mathbf{X}' \mathbf{S}_y^{-1} \mathbf{y} \qquad [A3]$$

where $\mathbf{S}_y$ is the estimated covariance matrix (cf. Bishop et al., 1975). One major advantage of this approach is that one can minimize the residuals in **e** using the same algorithm as for linear models with normally distributed errors. Another advantage is that there is far more flexibility than in the first estimation approach. One specifies in the design matrix what effect one is interested in. Some of the models discussed by von Eye, Kreppner, and Wessels (in prep.) cannot be estimated using standard log-linear modeling as programmed in some of the major program packages.

However, the weighted least squares approach has a number of drawbacks. Numerically, there can be problems when several cell frequencies are zero. As a cure, researchers often add a constant, the so-called delta, to each cell frequency. The effects of this procedure are still not fully explored.

A third approach gaining in popularity (cf. Rindskopf, 1987, 1990; von Eye, Kreppner, & Wessels, in prep.) uses also design matrices. In this case, the expected cell frequencies and parameters are estimated using a Newton-Raphson method, a method for maximizing functions. To apply this method one treats the likelihood equations as a function of a single parameter so that it has the form $f(b) = 0$. Using the Newton-Raphson method one estimates in the next steps of the iteration the next approximation for the maximum likelihood estimate of b as follows:

$$b_{i+1} = b_i - \frac{f(b_i)}{f'(b_i)} \qquad [A4]$$

where $f'(b_i)$ is the first derivative of $f(b_i)$. Geometrically, the resulting point estimate can be interpreted as the abscissa value of the tangent that $f(b)$ has at the point $b = b_i$ (cf. Reinhard & Soeder, 1978). The univariate Newton-Raphson method for estimation of parameters in log-linear modeling was introduced by Goodman (1979). The method has the following characteristics:

(1) If the starting point b_0 is close enough to the true solution it will always converge.

(2) If there is convergence it is quadratic or better (which, compared to other algorithms, can still be slow).

(3) The calculations are simple compared to those in the multidimensional Newton-Raphson method because no matrix inversion is necessary.

(4) The covariance matrix for the b-estimates is not a by-product of the calculations. Rather, it must be calculated separately.

For the calculations for the examples in this chapter we apply Rindskopf's (1987) program that estimates parameters using the unidimensional Newton-

Raphson method. The program expects (or generates) model specifications in form of a design matrix.

Design matrices. The design matrix **X** in Equations A2 and A3 contains vectors that specify what effects are assumed to enable the researcher to reconstruct the observed frequency distribution. One specifies the values in these vectors following the rules of either dummy or effect coding.

Dummy coding generates a number of vectors such that, in any given vector, a variable category is assigned a 1 while all other categories of the same variable are assigned a 0. Dummy coding can also be used to amalgamate categories or, in extreme cases, to categorize variables. For a variable with c categories there can be no more than $c - 1$ nonredundant dummy coding vectors. In more technical terms, we have, as in Equations A2 or A3, the $n \times 1$ column vector y_i of cell entries y of the observed frequency table, arranged in lexicographic order, and the $n \times (r + 1)$ design matrix **X**. The matrix **X** is of rank $r + 1 \le n$. One constraint that must be placed on **X** in order to obtain a unique solution for Equations A2 or A3 is that the columns, or vectors, of **X** be linearly independent. (For a more detailed discussion see, e.g., Gokhale & Kullback, 1978, who also give extensive examples of design matrices set up using dummy coding [e.g., pp. 140 and 141].)

Effect coding in analysis of variance reflects the effects of treatments. The standard code values are 1, 0, and −1. Accordingly, contingency table analysis effect coding vectors express assumptions about deviations from average. Most frequently, researchers put the constraint on effect coding vectors that, for any given vector, the sum of its values is 0. In some examples, for example in orthogonal polynomial coding, the product sum of any two vectors is 0 also.

In *standard application of log-linear modeling,* computer programs generate the design matrix or estimate parameters using the first method described above. The user can only specify the main effects and interactions he or she wants to be part of the model. In most instances the models are hierarchical.

In nonstandard log-linear modeling the user has the option to specify the likelihood functions or vectors of the design matrix, thus focusing on the effects he or she is interested in. The above sections give examples of design matrices for analysis of repeatedly observed nominal-level variables. The examples include the analysis of models for symmetry and shifts in categories. For data analysis we use Rindskopf's (1987) program. Other programs that allow one to handle nonstandard log-linear modeling include the SPSSX LOGLINEAR module.

Notes

1. Note that there are versions of the well-known IPF algorithm for the calculation of ordinal log-linear models (Agresti, 1984; Fienberg, 1980). These versions, however, do not apply with orthogonal polynomial scoring for the v_i.

2. The reader should notice that addition of a cubic component improves the fit of the model significantly. However, the parameter estimate is significant only for the first cluster.

References

Agresti, A. (1984). *Analysis of ordinal categorical data*. New York: John Wiley.

Asendorpf, J. (1989). Individual, differential, and aggregate stability of social competence. In B. H. Schneider, G. Attili, J. Nadel, R. Weissberg (Eds.), *Social competence in developmental perspective* (pp. 71-86). Dordrecht, Netherlands: Kluwer.

Bishop, Y.M.M., Fienberg, S. E., & Holland, P. W. (1975). *Discrete multivariate analysis: Theory and practice*. Cambridge: MIT Press.

Bowker, A. H. (1948). A test for symmetry in contingency tables. *Journal of the American Statistical Association, 43,* 572-574.

Brockwell, P. J., & Davis, R. A. (1987). *Time series: Theory and methods*. New York: Springer.

Clogg, C. C., Eliason, S. R., & Grego, J. (1990). Models for the analysis of change in discrete variables. In A. von Eye (Ed.), *Statistical methods for longitudinal research, Vol. 2*. New York: Academic Press.

Dayton, C. M., & MacReady, G. B. (1976). A probabilistic model for validation of behavioral hierarchies. *Psychometrika, 41,* 189-204.

Farrington, D. P. (1989). Later adult life outcomes of offenders and nonoffenders. In M. Brambring, F. Lösel, & H. Skowronek (Eds.), *Children at risk: Assessment, longitudinal research, and intervention* (pp. 220-244). Berlin: deGruyter.

Fienberg, S. E. (1980). *The analysis of cross-classified categorical data* (2nd ed.). Cambridge: MIT Press.

Funke, J., & Hussy, W. (1979). Informationsverarbeitende Strukturen und Prozesse: Analysemöglichkeiten durch Problemlöseparadigmen [Structures and processes of information processing: Analysis via paradigms of problem solving]. *Trierer Psychologische Berichte, 6.*

Games, P. (1990). Alternative analyses of repeated measures designs by ANOVA and MANOVA. In A. von Eye (Ed.), *Statistical methods in longitudinal research, Vol. 1*. New York: Academic Press.

Gokhale, D. V., & Kullback, S. (1978). *The information in contingency tables*. New York: Marcel Dekker.

Goodman, L. A. (1979). Simple models for the analysis of association in cross-classifications having ordered categories. *Journal of the American Statistical Association, 74,* 537-552.

Green, J. (1988). Log-linear analysis of cross-classified ordinal data: Applications in developmental research. *Child Development, 59,* 1-25.

Green, J. (1989, July). *Log-linear models for evaluating developmental data*. Paper presented at the meetings of the ISSBD, Jyväskylä, Finland.

Haberman, S. J. (1979). *Analysis of qualitative data* (Vol. 1). New York: Academic Press.

Haberman, S. J. (1979). *Analysis of qualitative data* (Vol. 2). New York: Academic Press.

Hagenaars, J. A. (1990). *Categorical longitudinal data.* Newbury Park, CA: Sage.

Hildebrand, D. K., Laing, J. D., & Rosenthal, H. (1977). *Prediction analysis of cross-classifications.* New York: John Wiley.

Krampen, G. (1981). *IPC-Fragebogen zu Kontrollüberzeugungen* [IPC questionnaire for locus of control]. Göttingen: Hogrefe.

Krauth, K., & Lienert, G. A. (1973). *KFA. Die Konfigurationsfrequenzanalyse und ihre Anwendung in Psychologie und Medizin* [KFA. Configuration Frequency Analysis and its application to psychology and medicine]. Freiburg: Alber.

Lienert, G. A. (1978). *Verteilungsfreie Methoden in der Biostatistik* [Nonparametric methods in biostatistics], Vol. 2. Meisenheim am Glan: Hain.

Lienert, G. A., von Eye, A., & Rovine, M. J. (1988). Factor analysis: Difficulty adjustment of item-intercorrelations using symmetry transformations. *EDP in Medicine and Biology, 18,* 118-124.

Lorch, R. F., & Myers, J. L. (1990). Regression analyses of repeated measures data in cognitive research. *Journal of Experimental Psychology: Learning, Memory, and Cognition, 16,* 149-157.

Maier, D. (1983). *The theory of relational data bases.* Rockville, MA: Computer Science Press.

McArdle, J. J., & Aber, M. S. (1990). Patterns of change within latent variable structural equation models. In A. von Eye (Ed.), *Statistical methods in longitudinal research, Vol. 1* (pp. 151-224). New York: Academic Press.

Metzler, P., & Nickel, B. (1986). *Zeitreihen- und Verlaufsanalysen* [The analysis of time series and repeated observations]. Leipzig: Hirzel.

Müller, N. (1980). Functions on life-trees for explaining social phenomena, with special reference to political socialization. *International Journal of Policy Analysis and Information Systems, 4,* 317-330.

Neter, J., Wasserman, W., & Kutner, M. H. (1985). *Applied linear statistical models* (2nd ed.). Homewood, IL: Irwin.

Plackett, R. L. (1974). *The analysis of categorical data.* London: Griffin.

Reinhard, F., & Soeder, H. (1978). *dtv Atlas zur Mathematik* [dtv handbook of mathematics], Vol. 2 (2nd ed.). München: dtv.

Rindskopf, D. (1987). A compact BASIC program for log-linear models. In R. M. Heiberger (Ed.), *Computer science and statistics* (pp. 381-386). Alexandria, VA: American Statistical Association.

Rindskopf, D. (1990). Testing developmental models using latent class analysis. In A. von Eye (Ed.), *Statistical methods in longitudinal research* (Vol. 2, pp. 443-469). New York: Academic Press.

Schröder, E. (1989). *Vom konkreten zum formalen Denken: Individuelle Entwicklungsverläufe von der Kindheit bis zum Jugendalter* [From concrete to formal thinking: Patterns of individual development from childhood to adolescence]. Bern: Huber.

von Eye, A. (1988). The general linear model as a framework for models in Configural Frequency Analysis. *Biometrical Journal, 30,* 59-67.

von Eye, A. (1990). *Introduction to Configural Frequency Analysis: The search for types and antitypes in cross-classifications.* Cambridge, UK: Cambridge University Press.

von Eye, A., & Brandtstädter, J. (1981). Lebensbäume als entwicklungspsychologische Modelle: Ansätze zur Analyse von Lebensereignissequenzen [Life trees as developmental models: Approaches to the analysis of sequences of life events]. *Trierer Psychologische Berichte, 8.*

von Eye, A., Kreppner, K., & Wessels, H. (in prep.). *Log-linear modeling of categorical data in developmental research.*

von Eye, A., & Nesselroade, J. R. (in press). Types of change: Application of configural frequency analysis in repeated measurement designs. *Experimental Aging Research.*

Wessels, H. (1990). *Zur multivariaten Analyse diskreter Daten: Über einige Erweiterungen und spezielle Parametrisierungen des allgemeinen log-linearen Modells* [The multivariate analysis of categorical data: Some extensions and particular parameterizations of the general log-linear model]. Doctoral dissertation, The Technical University of Berlin.

Wickens, T. D. (1989). *Multiway contingency tables analysis for the social sciences.* Hillsdale, NJ: Lawrence Erlbaum.

Wood, P. K. (1990). Applications of scaling to developmental research. In A. von Eye (Ed.), *Statistical methods in longitudinal research* (Vol. 1, pp. 225-256). New York: Academic Press.

COMMENTARY ON CHAPTERS 1 AND 2:

Modeling Qualitative Data

JEANETTE A. LAWRENCE

AGNES E. DODDS

Schröder in Chapter 1, and von Eye, Kreppner, and Wessels in Chapter 2 provide developmentalists with the means of examining change when the data are categorical. They present sophisticated techniques for analyzing change within individuals, and change in some individuals in relation to others, in ways that take account of more than one variable at a time. These chapters will be welcome to researchers who do not wish to force their subjects' qualitative responses into false ordinal or interval form.

A colleague in the late seventies once flatly refused to discuss nonparametrical analyses of categorical data. That type of data could not be analyzed. In our dust-bowl empiricist university, ANOVA reigned. Chi-squares were frowned on as the choice of the ignorant. Researchers who used nonparametric statistics, did so in shame and peril. Qualitative analyses that involved words and propositions, rather than scores and means, simply did not exist in that form of "scientific psychology." Many researchers have moved from that position in the eighties, and these two chapters are evidence of new encounters between statistical modelers and data-collectors, or better, Valsiner's (in press) "data constructors" who use methods to act upon the phenomena to make the data.

Let us assume the devil's advocate role and ask some questions about the models and their relation to theory and data, and make some suggestions about what developmentalists need from the types of

54

statistical models Schröder and von Eye et al. describe. Of course, in the spirit of the chapters, we cannot aggregate over developmentalists, so our stance is that of simple researchers with theoretical assumptions about development that require qualitative data for examining how individuals change, and how they change differently from each other.

There are at least two things that developmental researchers with qualitative data are likely to want from statistical modelers: statistical procedures that fit their theoretical assumptions and predictions; and assurance that the models will not do violence to their data. It is possible for methodological tools to distort the intentions and expectations of the theory, for example, by trivializing significant psychological processes with nonsensical operational definitions. It is also possible to distort qualitative phenomena by reducing them to more readily quantifiable forms that lose their richness, or by neglecting their essentially interactive organization (Kindermann & Valsiner, 1989).

A statistical model should allow theoretical assumptions and statements to be expressed in suitable empirical form, for potential falsification. Then, statistical transformations of the phenomena should be true to the theory so that trends in the analyzed data can feed back into theory building in a cyclical relationship (Glaser & Strauss, 1967). From this perspective, as Feyerabend (1975) argues, counterexamples that disagree with theory may be the most informative empirical data, because they can lead to novel and revolutionary theory development. There is a three-way linkage between theory, method, and data (Lawrence, 1981; Valsiner 1989) that means each component of the researcher's activity informs the others. Distortion of one component reduces the usefulness of the whole enterprise. As Valsiner (in press) argues, if we view the researcher's task as the construction of knowledge, relationships between theories and methods will be guided by theoretical assumptions at one end of the connection with the phenomena being studied at the other.

Both the Schröder and the von Eye et al. approaches adhere to principles of using theory-appropriate statistical models to test theoretical predictions about developmental change, and support the view that some data of change and constancy are most appropriately presented in categorical form. Each chapter is aimed at demonstrating how qualitative data can be analyzed to reveal developmental sequences, and to test hypotheses about multivariate relationships between nominally categorized variables. The authors disagree with statisticians who demand that the researcher produce aggregated data to document all developmental trends and differences.

Concerning the course of development, Schröder focuses more on intraindividual change, examining synchrony in the individual's acquisition of different developmental abilities at a given time, and diachronous patterns of changes over time. Von Eye and his associates are mainly oriented toward testing patterns of differential change where temporally related changes are compared for identifiable subject groups.

Schröder makes two predictions about changes in children's cognitive development that are derived from his order-theoretical assumptions about development. First, he claims that some abilities are prerequisites of others. In his special case, conservation of discontinuous quantities is proposed as an antecedent (necessary) prerequisite of conservation of continuous quantities. Next, he claims that acquired attributes are cumulative, in the sense that once acquired, they are retained. Once a researcher has observed that a child can conserve discontinuous quantities, then he or she will expect to see a similar performance at later times of measurement. These are very strong claims about the course of development, and we will return to their status vis-à-vis the patterns in Edelstein, Keller, and Schröder's (1990) data.

In contrast, von Eye et al.'s main focus is on demonstrating the mathematical properties of their design matrix representation of a nonstandard log-linear model, and then on putting the model through its paces with illustrative cases that explain differential change. Their claims about the fit of statistical model to theory are more modest, with a disclaimer that using their procedure does not imply that deterministic relations exist in the data. Thus, unlike Schröder's case, their approach is not oriented to psychological theory as much as to the statistical procedures that model and test its assumptions, although the statistical model is proposed as a technique to be used for explanation rather than simply exploration.

In terms of fitting statistical procedures to theory, Schröder is rather gentle on the two different statistical approaches that he uses to test his hypotheses of invariant developmental sequences to children's qualitative changes in conservation performances. Both procedures allow him to test his assumption that development of conservation of discontinuous quantities is a necessary condition for development of conservation of continuous quantities. He concludes that Dayton and MacReady's (1976) probabilistic validation model is superior to von Eye and Brandtstädter's (1988) Unconditional Prediction Analysis in generating more accurate expected frequencies in individual cells, more directly confronting the theory-model fit, and not requiring the assumption that variables are independent. However, Dayton and MacReady's inferential test is less robust because of the relatively large number of very small expected cells, leading to violations of chi-square assumptions. Given that Schröder has a large stake in testing the hypotheses of his strong theoretical position, we could reasonably expect a stronger conclusion about the choice of statistical models, vis-à-vis the relative costs of an over-fitting model and statistical assumptions of independence.

Von Eye and Brandtstädter (1988) admit the problems incurred by the independence assumption of the model and the repeated structure of the observations. In his current account, von Eye is fulfilling the von Eye and Brandtstädter (1988) promise by using a nonstandard log-linear modeling procedure that allows the researcher to specify the relationships of interest, and to combine systems of main effect and interacting variables.

Their longitudinal study of interactive socialization patterns in families addresses the statistical model-data fit, without ignoring the theoretical implications. In this example, models are "custom tailored" to fit the phenomena by revealing and analyzing differential time trends in complex arrays of factors. Cluster analyses are combined with a nonstandard log-linear model to take into account the significant feature of levels of parental cooperation in socializing their children. Having a global measure of the quality of family interactions is important for understanding the developmental trajectories of mothers' controlling behaviors and fathers' transmissions of rules with the same children over seven well-separated video-taped episodes of family interactions.

Von Eye et al. had made a definite effort to preserve something of the complexity of natural co-occurrences of mother/child and father/child interactions and to incorporate repeated measures in the analysis so that differential trends could be examined. Cluster analyses uncovered two groups of families with low versus high incidents of parental cooperation. They provided a global identification of the interactive nature of the parents' activities, and the conditions these set up for examining trends in mothers' and fathers' socialization activities. The analyses reveal how the controlling actions of mothers from families with low and high levels of parental cooperation follow the same trajectory for increases in control over the two-year period, but with the difference that mothers are more controlling in families where parent cooperation is low. Nevertheless, the trajectories for fathers' transmissions of rules differed for the two groups of families.

This example gives us an elegant demonstration of a sensitive response to the nature of the phenomena. Had the interaction of parental styles been neglected, and had the modeling process been unable to handle the complex sets of observations, then hypothesized differences in family development would have been untested.

To illustrate the full theory-statistical model-data connection, let us take Schröder's strong, potentially falsifiable hypotheses drawn from what appears to be a "simple stage model" of universal, invariant development (Flavell, 1977). Schröder's explicit predictions admittedly are derived from broad theoretical presuppositions, and a task analysis, and they are stated in testable form. But it is questionable how well either of the chosen statistical procedures could fit the assumptions, even in the best of experimental circumstances. The problem is not with the statistical models as much as with the expression of the A, B connections. Schröder claimed that A (conservation of discontinuous quantities) is a prerequisite, antecedent (or necessary) condition of B (conservation of continuous quantities). Necessity is not a relationship to be found in the empirical world. Necessary relations belong to the domain of logic, and to claim that something (B) must necessarily follow something else (A) in observed data is to ignore the emergent properties of the empirical order. Yet, Schröder equates necessity with prerequisite and antecedent conditions at several places in his argument and in his Figure 1.5. Even a weaker formulation of the A, B linkages means that counterinstances in the data need to be explained in relation to theoretical assumptions and not just in terms of methodological imperfections. For instance, von Eye et al. admit contrary-to-theory observations in some cells, by designating statistically tolerable error levels.

Reading Schröder's Table 1.2, we see that 7 out of 59 (11.9%) of the observations are directly contrary to theory, but he does little to explain how these may have occurred, and what they mean for the theory. How strongly must the researcher hold to the antecedent condition clause, and is it good enough according to the order-theoretical assumptions to accept that the meaning of antecedent in the theory agrees with its interpretation under the analytic technique? Can probabilistic statistical models really say what is acceptable? Yet, it is difficult in the face of an acceptable level of statistical significance to say one wants more, that is, a better theory-data fit. A qualitative orientation behooves the theorist to confront the data directly (Cairns, 1986), at least with exploratory analyses of the outliers, and preferably to report his or her explanations in more qualitative ways than simply categorizing or naming chunks of information.

Admittedly, Schröder makes suggestions about the direction of follow-up investigations, for example, into the external conditions behind the performances that do not fit the theoretical predictions. Of course we do not expect those analyses to appear in the chapter. Given the overall emphasis on individual change, however, we would expect that ad hoc hypotheses should focus on qualitative facets of the data that have been subsumed in the naming categories. It is reasonable to ask for explanations, or suggestions for appropriate exploratory follow-ups. What was happening in the data sessions in the counterexamples? Schröder's suggestions of places to look for evidence to shore up the holes in the theory left by the counterexamples do not inspire confidence that he is prepared to reexamine his hypotheses in the light of the data. By not first paying attention to the immediate theory-model-data connection, one neglects the possibility that finer, and therefore more inherently qualitative, analyses may lead to further problems for the theory.

Designation of nominal-level categories may of itself cause distortion of the phenomena, for example, when the episode of events includes more that one active agent, and the researcher names and records the activities of only one. For example, researcher-child interactions may be significant in understanding Schröder's findings. Von Eye et al.'s ability to handle multivariate relations in the family data is impressive. The coded video segments are not reduced to single target observations, as is so often the case. Nevertheless, the simple developmentalist is likely to be greedy for more information than the categorized data provide, and this is a place where exploratory uses of the model probably would be fruitful. With so many coded episodes and a total period of 2 years, and with the analysis of differences in developmental trajectories, we would like to know how those families interacted with each other on the significant occasions where the trajectories had fluctuations, for example, the similar valleys and hills in the development of mothers' controlling actions, and the fluctuations in fathers' rule transmission actions. Indeed, it would seem to be important to know how the mothers transmitted rules and the fathers transmitted controlling behaviors, and the changing cross-overs.

The story is not over once we have established the pattern of differential change across people. Finding patterns of change whets the developmentalist's appetite. More questions are raised: "How did these differential changes come about?" "What do they mean at the level of individualized analyses?" It may seem unfair to ask such questions in the context of von Eye's innovative statistical modeling, but they contain further issues about qualitative data.

We have hinted at the naming issue, in which the researcher makes segregating choices out of the array of observational material and then names the variables to be submitted to qualitative analysis, with coding instructions for making sure that anomalies are smoothed out in coding schemes (see Cairns's, 1986, exposé of the coding culture). Even while accounting for parental cooperation, von Eye et al. miss the responsiveness of the child and its effect on either or both parents' activities. It would seem that their current model or a later version could cope with more variables. But we want to know from both examples what was happening in the outlier cases. Later in this volume, Lawrence (see Commentary to Chapter 7) argues for fine-grained analysis of temporally antecedent processes leading to developmental outcomes, and Lightfoot and Fold-Bennett (Chapter 7) make a strong plea for examining target behaviors wholistically within the episodes where they occur. Von Eye et al.'s modeling would give good leads about what to reexamine in the data to discern how the significant factors interact, and how their linkages influence each other and developmental outcomes. Similarly, Schröder's theoretically inadmissible observations should make us curious about those individual children.

Therefore it is pertinent to ask, "What is qualitative data?" The question here is not as simplistic as it may seem, for there is a growing coterie of psychologists who have joined other social scientists in affirming the place of qualitative analyses in psychology. A range of methodologies have evolved, including at one extremity, closer to traditional quantitative methods, the type of analysis of nominal numerical data exemplified in the two chapters; and modeling of patterns in data in words at the other end, closer to ethnography. Examples of rigorously documented verbal modeling of patterns in data are presented by

Miles and Huberman (1984). Another theory-driven technique of qualitative analysis is our method of preserving in tabulated form the patterns of inferential linkages found in subjects' verbal protocols (e.g., Lawrence, 1988; Volet & Lawrence, 1990). This approach involves using words as analogues of numbers and presenting tables that show relationships and linkages between theoretically interesting statements of subjects.

In Lawrence (1988), a theory of judicial decision making and information processing first directed the investigation of a sample of magistrates' selection of different pieces of information from case details about offenders. The technique of choice was on-line verbal protocol analysis that would reveal the information a magistrate chose as significant. Next, we wanted to see how that selected information was used, in terms of the interpretive inferences that were made, and the decisions that followed those interpretations. The qualitative analysis involved constructing a notational scheme analogous to laying out the premises and derivations of logical syllogisms. Concepts are described in tables that show the linkages of subjects' reasoning processes. These data are not easily transformed into statistically manipulable categories without losing the flow of the reasoning.

In other verbal and behavioral episodes, qualitative analyses require the ability to link sequences of events to each other within and across occasions—for example, the type of exchange that takes place between parent and child when management of a task is being learned. We may want to preserve the order of who leads on Occasion1, and then on Occasion2 six months later, either parent (p), or child (c). Thus the [pcpcppc] structure of the sequenced leads on Occasion1 may change to a [pccpccc] structure on Occasion2, as the child gains in proficiency and confidence. We can imagine how von Eye's modeling procedures may be able to analyze the trajectories of sequences of processes involved in episodes reflecting the child's changing abilities. The categories and hypothesized linkages would be different in modeling these microanalytic interactions. Instead of looking at behaviors in different episodes, the models could be applied to the processes that together form small segments of single episodes, for example, strings of words or sequences of interlocking activities with the [pcp] structure. Microanalytic data could become grouping variables or repeated measures in larger segments. Once the value of this type of model is seen as valuable for revealing the theory-model-data connections, then a developmental researcher and a statistical modeler together may profitably tackle some new issues involved in analyzing qualitative change. These are exciting prospects. The secret is to preserve theory-model-data connections.

References

Cairns, R. B. (1986). Phenomena lost: Issues in the study of development. In J. Valsiner (Ed.), *The individual subject and scientific psychology* (pp. 97-111). New York: Plenum.

Dayton, C., & MacReady, G. B. (1976). A probabilistic model for validation of behavioral hierarchies. *Psychometrika, 41,* 189-204.

Edelstein, W., Keller, N., & Schröder, E. (1990). Child development and social structure: Individual differences in development. In P. B. Baltes, D. L. Featherman, & R. M. Lerner (Eds.), *Life-span development and behavior* (Vol. 10). Hillsdale, NJ: Lawrence Erlbaum.

Feyerabend, P. (1975). *Against method: Outline of an anarchistic theory of knowledge.* London: Verso.

Flavell, J. H. (1977). *Cognitive development.* Englewood Cliffs, NJ: Prentice-Hall.

Glaser, B. G., & Strauss, A. L. (1967). *The discovery of grounded theory: Strategies for qualitative research.* Chicago: Aldine.

Kindermann, T., & Valsiner, J. (1989). Research strategies in culture-inclusive developmental psychology. In J. Valsiner (Ed.), *Child development in cultural context* (pp. 13-50). Toronto: Hogrefe & Huber.

Lawrence, J. A. (1981). A case for the usefulness and plausibility of thinking-aloud data. In M. Lawson (Ed.), *Inquiry and action in education: Proceedings of the annual conference of the Australian Association for Research in Education* (Vol. 1). Adelaide: AARE, 95-103.

Lawrence, J. A. (1988). Expertise on the bench. In M.T.H. Chi, R. Glaser, & M. Farr, (Eds.), *The nature of expertise* (pp. 229-259). Hillsdale, NJ: Lawrence Erlbaum.

Miles, M. B., & Huberman, A. M. (1984). *Qualitative data analysis: A sourcebook of new methods.* Beverly Hills, CA: Sage.

Valsiner, J. (in press). Theories and methods in the service of data construction in developmental psychology. In P. van Geert & L. P. Moss (Eds.), *Annals of theoretical psychology: Vol. 7. Developmental psychology.* New York: Plenum.

Volet, S. E., & Lawrence, J. A. (1990). Adaptive learning in university students. In H. Mandl, E. de Corte, N. Bennett, & H. F. Freidrich (Eds.), *Learning and instruction: European research in an international context* (pp. 497-515). Oxford, UK: Pergamon.

von Eye, A., & Brandtstädter, J. (1988). Evaluating developmental hypotheses using statement calculus and non-parametric statistics. In P. B. Baltes, D. L. Featherman, & R. M. Lerner (Eds.), *Life-span development and behavior* (Vol. 8, pp. 61-97). Hillsdale, NJ: Lawrence Erlbaum.

3

Evidential Statistics and the Analysis of Developmental Patterns

WARREN THORNGATE

I am not a developmental psychologist, so I was pleasantly surprised to be invited to the wonderful conference at which this book was conceived. My task there was to present Ordinal Pattern Analysis (OPA) (see Thorngate, 1986a; Thorngate & Carroll, 1986), a simple technique for comparing "greater-than, less-than" predictions to similar observations obtained from single individuals over time. I began to develop OPA about 15 years ago hoping to solve a specific problem in my own research on human decision making. Like the musical notation that inspired it (Parsons, 1975), OPA soon became a hobby, then an obsession. I began to see uses for OPA almost everywhere. I was thus excited by the possibility of introducing the technique to those who might find it useful for understanding developmental processes.

I was also apprehensive. The great philosophical debates about probability and statistics (cf. Edwards, 1972; Nagel, 1939; Savage, 1962) teach us that the dominant statistical techniques in psychology (variance partitioning, null hypothesis testing, etc.) are often inappropriate for answering many of our most important questions. OPA seems to be a useful method for addressing many of the leftovers. But OPA is based on a statistical philosophy rather different from the one psychologists have for so long learned to embrace. It is hard to teach old colleagues new tricks, and new colleagues are reluctant to use a statistical procedure not recognized by the editorial establishment. Would developmental psychologists use OPA? At Bernried I was surrounded by some of the best statistical minds in psychology anxious to explore the recondite issues of human development with new and sophisticated variations on established statistical methods. There I was with my little technique, ready to instruct the participants how to understand their data by counting on their fingers. Perhaps the developmental psychologists would be amused by my contribution, but they would surely patronize the competition. I began to wonder why I came; indeed, I began to suspect that others wondered the same.

As I listened to the conference discussion, however, I discovered what most developmental psychologists have apparently long known. There are at least two fundamentally different approaches to the study of human development. One, which I shall call the *formalist* approach, emphasizes quantitative research methods, rigorous statistical controls, laboratory settings, sophisticated designs, large numbers of subjects, short observation periods, and omnivariate statistical analyses. The other, which I shall call the *naturalist* approach, emphasizes intensive observation, qualitative description, nonlaboratory settings, long observation periods, small numbers of subjects, and simple data analyses. A similar distinction can be found between experimentalists and naturalists in botany and zoology. There are numerous variants of both approaches, but their themes appeared to account for much of the variation of opinion in conference debates. Curiously, almost all the formalists in the conference were men; most of the naturalists were women. I am not sure why the sex difference would be so large. Yet it did sustain what I observed as a very creative tension between two complementary epistemologies.

Noting my epistemological affinity with the naturalists, I quickly concluded that OPA might have a future in their camp. My conclusion was half correct. The philosophical foundations of OPA seem appropriate to addressing many of the questions that naturalists ask. However, OPA deals with the goodness of fit between ordinal predictions and the ordinal properties of observations. A large proportion of naturalistic research generates categorical or nominal data, and thus requires methods for assessing categorical or nominal fit. At the end of the conference, Jaan Valsiner challenged me to extend some OPA ideas in order to develop these methods. Here is the result.

SOME CONCEPTUAL PRELIMINARIES

Naturalists who wish to analyze categorized observations currently have at their disposal two popular statistical techniques: Markov modeling and log-linear analysis. Though these techniques are occasionally useful, they suffer from two major limitations. First, the techniques require data in quantities or under circumstances that are often difficult or impossible for naturalists to obtain. Log-linear tests for category dependencies, for example, require independent observations in numbers that at least double each time a category variable is added.[1] Markov models require large numbers of observations under stationary conditions to estimate transition probabilities. Second, the techniques address properties of data that are often irrelevant to testing important developmental ideas. Log-linear partitionings address only the epicyclic manifestations or "residuals" of data structures and generative processes; Markov models address only crude forms of "state-space" processes assumed to be identical across individuals. Many naturalists feel obliged to adapt their research to these Procrustean limitations. Some collect observations that meet the requirements of the techniques; others ask only those questions the techniques can answer. Neither adaptation is likely to produce the kind of understanding that characterizes good science.

It thus seems advisable to reverse the adaptive process, to develop statistical procedures that meet the conditions of naturalistic research and that address the important questions this research can answer. It is unlikely that traditional statistical procedures can be extended toward these ends. Most, if not all, rich and potentially informative naturalistic observations are gathered from only a few subjects observed at many different times under many different conditions. As a result, the data obtained rarely meet the assumptions on which traditional statistical procedures are based. Fortunately, the problem is by no means intractable. To solve it we need only embrace a statistical perspective better suited to the goals and conditions of naturalistic enquiry.

What is this perspective? Perhaps it is best developed by first considering what naturalists are trying to do. Judging from their great traditions in natural science and natural history, most naturalists observe nature in order to derive, test, or modify ideas. As a result, the goal of most naturalistic enquiry is to assess how well and how often sets of predictions drawn from theoretical ideas match samples of data drawn from natural observations. Their goal is *not* to assess the chances that aggregated properties of these samples will generalize to some vaguely defined population. We need only recall the great works of Linnaeus, Lyell, Darwin, Brahe, Hubble, and others to remind ourselves that not all scientific achievements require manipulated variables, random samples, or a thorough knowledge of SPSS. Many require instead only a wide variety of observations, a wide variety of ideas, and a mind sufficiently tempered to cull ideas unfit for the observations until only the fittest survives.

Accordingly, the statistical methods most useful for naturalistic enquiry are methods that tell us the extent to which our theories generalize to or are consistent with our observations. We sample our observations according to the conditions of our theories, not according to the limitations of our statistical methods; any sample sufficient to test a theory is acceptable. We compare two or more theories by finding and observing circumstances in which at least one theory makes different predictions than the others; good naturalists must be good finders as well as keen observers. If different theories best account for different sets of observations, we are challenged to determine what distinguishes these sets; good naturalists must also be good theoreticians.

Naturalists do not need more inferential statistics to accomplish these tasks. Instead, they need more *evidential statistics,* numbers that help them to determine when, where, how well, and how often their predictions match their observations, and that help them to choose what to explain or observe next. Evidential statistics lie somewhere between or beyond the popular descriptive and inferential groupings. Though they do not describe the relations among observations, they do describe the relations between predictions and observations. Though they cannot be used as aids to empirical inference, they can be used as aids to conceptual preference. Evidential statistics are designed to be simple, informal, and exploratory. They are meant to be understood, and to be helpful in finding the patterns of data that are most in need of understanding. Together they form what we may call the evidential perspective.

Ordinal Pattern Analysis and the Evidential Perspective

Before meeting Jaan Valsiner's challenge to create what we may call evidential statistics for nominal data, I should like to illustrate the evidential perspective by considering an Ordinal Pattern Analysis of a small archival study. There are two reasons for this ordinal interlude. First, OPA is the example of the evidential perspective I know best, and it can serve to develop a feel for the perspective. Second, naturalists often do have data with ordinal properties, and do wish to test some ordinal predictions with them. The following exposition should serve as a working introduction to OPA (see also Thorngate, 1986a; Thorngate & Carroll, 1986).

Suppose we wish to evaluate two theories of social development concerned with sociability. Both theories predict that the number of social interactions will increase with age. In addition, theory X predicts that at any given age until puberty females will engage in more social interactions than will males. Theory Y predicts that males will engage in more social interactions than will females until age 12, then the difference will reverse.

When comparing any two theories using OPA we are interested in the accuracy of three sets of predictions: those made by both theories (e.g., social interactions will increase with age); those made by one theory but not the other (e.g., only theory Y makes predictions past puberty); and those contested by the theories (e.g., X and Y make opposite predictions for males and females who have not reached puberty until after 12). Though the most dramatic theoretical comparisons come from the contested set, common and unique predictions are also important components of theoretical evidence. Both theories may be worthless if their common predictions are numerous and wrong. One theory that makes slightly fewer contested predictions may still be preferred if it correctly predicts numerous unique events. Some methods of assessing such tradeoffs are presented in Thorngate and Carroll (1986).

By happy coincidence we find five people who have kept daily diaries for most of their childhood years. From these we count the number of social interactions mentioned in each diary for each year, and decide that these numbers are acceptable indicants. The numbers are shown in Table 3.1. Not surprisingly, the data are extremely difficult to analyze using traditional statistical methods, but quite simple to analyze using OPA.

WITHIN-SUBJECT PREDICTIONS

Consider first the common prediction: Interactions will increase with age. If the prediction were correct, then we should expect each

TABLE 3.1 Number of Social Interactions Mentioned in Five Diaries

Person	\ 7	\ 8	Age of person (* indicates year of puberty) 9	10	11	12	13	14	15
A (female)			93	81	102	157	*189	180	203
B (female)	31	44		69	97	*118	101	60	62
C (female)		60	58	92	*116	90	227		239
D (male)	28	12	46			*94	78	83	189
E (male)			38	74	90	113	*121	80	

person to have more interactions for any year of age than for every previous year of age. Person A, for example, should have more interactions at age 10 than at age 9, more at age 11 than at ages 10 and 9, and so on. Indeed, for all 7 years that person A kept a diary, we can make an ordinal prediction about each pair: (A9 < A10), (A9 < A11), . . . (A14 < A15). There are 21 such ordered pairs for person A. How many of them are matched by the observations? Clearly A10 (= 81) is less than A9 (= 93): no match. A11 (= 102) is greater than both A10 and A9: two matches. We tally the number of matches (hits) and mismatches (misses) for all 21 pairs, and insert the numbers into the OPA formula for an *Index of Observed Fit* (IOF):

$$\text{Hits} = 19; \text{Misses} = 2;$$

$$\text{IOF(A)} = (\text{Hits} - \text{Misses})/(\text{Hits} + \text{Misses})$$
$$= (19 - 2)/(19 + 2) = 17/21 = +0.81.$$

The IOF index ranges from +1.00 (all hits) to −1.00 (all misses). By chance we might expect half of the ordered predictions to be matched by the observations; if so, then Hits = Misses and IOF = 0. The IOF(A) indicates that the prediction of theories X and Y improved our hit rate over guessing by 81%.

Eight years of data for person B give us $(8 \times 7)/2 = 28$ pairs of years for which theories X and Y make ordinal predictions: (B7 < B8), (B7 < B10), . . . , (B14 < B15). We tally how many of these 28 predictions hit and miss the observed ordinal relations:

$$\text{Hits} = 19; \text{Misses} = 9;$$

$$IOF(B) = (Hits - Misses)/(Hits + Misses)$$
$$= (19 - 9)/(19 + 9) = 10/28 = +0.36.$$

In similar manner we calculate the IOF for persons C, D, and E:

$$IOF(C) = (18 - 3)/(18 + 3) = +0.71;$$

$$IOF(D) = (19 - 2)/(19 + 2) = +0.81;$$

$$IOF(E) = (12 - 3)/(12 + 3) = +0.60.$$

In aggregate, the prediction is matched by $(19 + 19 + 18 + 19 + 12)$ $= 87$ of the $(21 + 28 + 21 + 21 + 15) = 106$ ordered data pairs. It is thus correct $(87/106) = 82\%$ of the time, a 64% improvement over random guessing $(IOF(total) = (87 - 19)/106 = +0.64)$. In different words, the prediction "generalizes to" 82% of our observed sample, a 64% increase over chance. The prediction improves our guesswork for all five subjects.

We may note that each subject shows one consistent predictive error: a drop in social interaction the year following puberty. We could thus eliminate five of our errors by predicting that social interactions will increase in every year but the one following puberty. However, this conditional prediction does not greatly increase our predictive accuracy $[(86 + 5)/106 = 86\%$; $IOF = +0.72]$, and we yet have no theory to account for postpuberty drop. We might therefore not yet wish to reject theories X and Y that generate the unconditional prediction, for in Popperian terms they have not yet been falsified.

When I lecture about OPA, it is usually at this point that someone asks, "Yes, but are those IOFs statistically significant?" It is possible to develop randomization tests for IOFs that may pacify those nursed on the null hypothesis (see Thorngate, 1986a). From the evidential perspective, however, the question is spurious. Neither theory X nor theory Y can be eliminated by an insignificant difference, nor can either be accepted by a significant one. We might wish to reject the theories if all IOFs were high and negative, and doubt them if the IOFs were low and negative. Yet no number can tell us the difference between acceptance, rejection, and doubt. The IOFs we have calculated tell us something important about the fit of a prediction to a population of five diaries. The prediction may also fit other populations, but we will not know until we examine them. Alas, the beautiful assumptions of

sampling theory that inspire so many inferential statistics can almost
never be met in psychological research simply because we can so rarely
specify the populations of people, tasks, times, memories, motives,
skills, and so on from which our samples came (Thorngate, 1986b). We
have allowed statistical significance to become a powerful rhetorical device, but it remains an ineffective cogitative instrument.

Note how we have examined the theory-data fits of five individuals
before aggregating across these fits. This reverses the usual practice
of first aggregating across individuals with "summary statistics" then
examining the fit of a theory to the aggregate. Often the two methods
do not produce the same results, and thus may lead us to different theoretical conclusions. In general, the first method should be preferred
(see Thorngate, 1986b). It is sometimes useful, however, to determine
how well an aggregate exemplifies its constituents. The most useful
aggregate for OPA is usually not the "average individual." Instead it
is "the prototypical individual" constructed from the more popular
order in each pair of intraindividual data.

I hasten to illustrate. Consider all of the 36 pairs of ages (columns)
in Table 3.1. For example, two persons keep a diary at ages 7 and 8;
one (B) increases social interactions with age, and one (D) decreases
them. Thus neither trend is more popular so there is no typical order
in the 7,8 pair. The one person (D) keeping a diary at ages 7 and 9 increases social interactions, so the typical 7,9 pair increases . . . All
four of the 9,12 pairs increase, so the typical 9,12 pair increases . . . Three of the four 11,12 pairs increase, so the typical
11,12 pair increases . . . Finally, all three of the 14,15 pairs increases,
so the typical 14,15 pair increases. String these 36 typical pairs together and by "majority rule" we obtain the prototypical subjects, that
is, the ordinal configuration that maximizes the number of hits aggregated across all subjects. Like a least-squares solution, any theory
that fits the prototype will give the best aggregated fit to its constitu-
ent individuals. And if the prototype does not give a good fit to its
constituents (i.e., if the IOFs between the prototype and the individuals are low), then we should probably not spend too much time trying
to account for the prototypical finding.

Prototypes need not be constructed lock-step with age. We are
quite free, for example, to examine a pre-post puberty prototype by
sliding each subject's data back or forth across ages until all their puberty years align down one column. The columns could then be labeled Puberty, One Year Before, One Year After, and so on. If the

resulting puberty prototype showed a much better ordinal fit to the data of its five constituents than did the chronological age prototype (above), then we might disregard or drop age and invoke puberty as an explanatory concept.

Like all ordinal tests, OPA must have rules for dealing with such thing as missing data or ties. Missing data are handled by default; the number of observations available to test predictions obviously decreases, but OPA "takes what it can get." No special adjustments are necessary for calculating OPA indices when data are missing; the researcher must only become more cautious in drawing conclusions from the data that remain. OPA is thus more useful than traditional repeated measure analyses in dealing with the common problem of missing data in longitudinal designs.

Ties are a bit more contentious. Though admittedly arbitrary, when strong ordinal predictions are made (greater than, less than), OPA handles ties as missing data; they are not used in IOF and related equations, and thus can neither support nor refute a prediction. Some theories, of course, make weak predictions (equal to or greater than, equal to or less than), and it is then tempting to use ties as support for them. Those who cannot resist the temptation should calculate the OPA results in two ways: with ties and without. If most predictive support comes from ties, consider what it implies for the survival of the weakest.

In addition to orders of numbers, we often have occasion to predict orders of relations between numbers. Most common are predictions about orders of differences. We may wish, for example, to predict that increases in social interaction will be greater following puberty than before it. One translation of this prediction for the data in Table 3.1 might be that the differences between adjacent years after puberty will be greater than differences in adjacent years before puberty. In the case of Person B this would reduce to the following set of differences in age pairs:

$$(8 - 7) < (12 - 13), (10 - 11) < (12 - 13), (11 - 12) < (12 - 13),$$

$$(8 - 7) < (13 - 14), (10 - 11) < (13 - 14), (11 - 12) < (13 - 14),$$

$$(8 - 7) < (14 - 15), (10 - 11) < (14 - 15), (11 - 12) < (14 - 15).$$

Other translations of the prediction are possible; many predictions are ambiguous, and about all we can do with them is to find what seems a reasonable translation and give it a go. (Incidentally, none of the nine predictions above are matched by Person B's data, so the IOF = −1.00.)

As I hope you have gathered by now, OPA is not intended to be a collection of recipes for cooking up helpings of truth. Instead, it attempts to accomplish some of the tasks of evidential statistics previously noted. Science is the craft of detecting and the art of explaining patterns (Thorngate, 1986b). OPA, like all statistical techniques, is part of the craft. The art lies beyond numbers.

BETWEEN-SUBJECT PREDICTIONS

Consider now the second prediction of theory X: At any given age females will engage in more social interactions than will males until puberty. Because the prediction places no restrictions on the males or females, we are free to test it using the data in Table 3.1 for every female/male pair at a given age below puberty. At age 7, for example, female B has more interactions than male D (31 > 28), confirming the prediction. It is confirmed twice more at age 8: Females B and C have more interactions than male D (44, 60 > 12). All four tests at age 9 are hits: (A > D), (A > E), (C > D), (C > E). At age 10, one of the three tests is a miss: (B < E). Female C reaches puberty at age 11 and no longer meets the condition of the prediction, but the remaining two valid tests are hits: (A > E), (B > E). Finally, at age 12 only one test remains, and it is a hit: (A > E). In sum, the second prediction of theory X can be tested 13 times using the data from Table 3.1. Of these, we have tallied 12 hits and a single miss. Thus

$$\text{IOF}(X) = (12 − 1)/(12 + 1) = +0.85.$$

Is this a good fit? It is certainly not a bad one, but the question can better be answered when we have some bases of comparison. The second prediction of theory Y gives us one such basis. Note that theory Y predicts the opposite of theory X regarding sex differences up to age 12: Theory Y predicts more social interaction for males. We can thus hold a little predictive contest between the two theories using most of the 13 pairs selected above. All but one of the 10 relevant pairs at ages 7, 8, 9, and 10 support the prediction of theory X. The two pairs that test both theories at age 11 also support theory X. Thus when contested on the playing field of Table 3.1, theory X wins over theory Y by a score of 11 to 1.

There is one remaining pair that further tests Y at age 11, but does not support it (E < C). So far, therefore, the "until 12" condition of theory Y has been tested 13 times, and missed on 12 of them, giving an

$$\text{IOF(Y for "until 12")} = (1 - 12)/(1 + 12) = -0.85.$$

Theory Y, however, further predicts that females will have more social interactions than will males from age 12 on. In fact, theory Y makes a prediction about all of the 32 female/male pairs across all the ages in Table 3.1. As noted above, theory X addresses only 13 of these pairs. In OPA parlance this gives Y more *scope* than X. Scope is often important in assessing the fit of theories, especially when a theory of small scope gives a better fit than a theory of large scope. The details and equations useful for analyzing scope are provided in the two original OPA references.

How does theory Y fare in its "12-plus" predictions? The theory makes 4 hits and 2 misses at age 12, 5 hits and 1 miss at age 13, 2 hits and 2 misses at age 14, and 2 hits and 1 miss at age 15. Thus,

$$\text{IOF(Y for "12-plus")} = (13 - 6)/(13 + 6) = +0.37,$$

so across all ages,

$$\text{IOF(Y)} = (14 - 18)/(14 + 18) = -0.12.$$

To summarize, though theory Y has more scope than theory X, and has a moderately good fit (IOF = +0.37) in its own 12-plus domain, in the aggregate it is better to guess (IOF = 0.00) than to use theory Y (IOF = −0.12) in predicting social interaction differences between the three females and two males in Table 3.1.

In view of the aggregated predictive failure of theory Y, we may wish to reject it. This does not mean, however, that we must accept our one alternative. Other alternatives may exist; indeed, in view of the results we may now wish to create one. Because theory X gives a good fit until age 12 and theory Y gives a fair fit beyond, it is tempting to combine them. We can easily do so by dropping the puberty condition of theory X. A theory Z predicting that females will have more social interactions than boys at any age will address all 13 + 19 = 32 female/male pairs in Table 3.1, and correctly predict 12 + 13 = 25 of them; thus, it is

$$IOF(Z) = (25 - 7)/(25 + 7) = +0.56.$$

It is tempting to invent a theory that makes this prediction, but how do we do it? For all of our putative sophistication in testing theories, most psychologists are astonishingly naive about their nature, variety, and development. As a result, many psychologists continue to keep box scores of significant differences, offer generalizations as explanations, provide "how" answers to "why" questions. Unsullied by theoretical acumen, they blithely retest the first assumption of empiricism ad nauseam in the name of science. Sure enough, with a little skillful pilot testing, similar conditions once again produce similar observations. Empiricism is reconfirmed. Yet understanding is not advanced.

This is not the place to discuss theory building, although I can recommend Stinchcombe (1968), Akerlof (1984), and Powers (1989) for examples of how it is done. Here common sense should tell us that it is probably foolish to rush into a post hoc explanatory frenzy at the sight of a few numbers in five diaries. It seems more sagacious to collect data from other times and other places that are further addressed by theories X and Y, and to keep tabs of the hits and misses in their common and separate predictive domains. It is also sagacious to keep our eyes and minds open. If there are consistent patterns of development beyond the lab and behind the questionnaire, then receptive naturalists are likely to find them. And those who have by then learned the art of theory will likely beat the others to a good explanation.

Fuzzy Categories and Nominal Pattern Analysis

Having done our ordinal warm ups, it is now time to consider how we might determine the fit between categorical predictions and nominal data. At least two useful approaches now exist for doing some of it. The first is called *prediction analysis* (Hildebrand, Laing, & Rosenthal, 1977), and is very well suited for testing such cross-classified, categorical predictions as "Children will vote for the same political party as their parents." A second approach is concerned with *sequence comparisons* (cf. Sankoff & Kruskal, 1983). It is useful for examining such propositions as "The sequence of developmental stages will be more similar for children in the same culture than for children in different cultures." Both are excellent examples of nominal statistical analyses from the evidential perspective. What passes for Nominal Pattern Analysis below is an attempt to supplement these two fine works.

At the risk of exposing my shameful ignorance of developmental psychology, permit me to abstract from the naturalists' discussions at Bernried. Many naturalists watch individual children in their own habitats, and keep written, filmed, or taped records of what they see. If the records are good, they provide a text of each child's activities and the contexts in which these activities occur. Eventually, the resulting words, sounds, or pictures must be encoded in a set of categories. Sometimes the categories are derived from a theory or conceptual framework, but as often as not they are borrowed from other research or inferred from a careful reading of the text. The categories become repositories of tick marks. The tick marks are totaled. The totals are taken to a statistician for cross-tabulatory advice. This progression is usually undertaken on the assumption that categorizing and analyzing are quite separate processes. Naturalists are often frustrated to learn that their categorizing schemes must conform to the requirements of extant statistical procedures. Statisticians are rarely embarrassed to learn that extant statistical procedures do not conform to categorizing schemes. Neither group pays much attention to the possibility that their tasks are inseparable. So it may do us some good to examine briefly the intimate connections between categorizing, analyzing, and theorizing.

I think most naturalists and statisticians would agree that an ideal categorizing scheme provides a set of precisely defined, exclusive, and exhaustive categories. Most would also agree that this ideal is virtually never attained—and for good reason. A category is simply a synopsis of two or more texts that somehow captures their common meaning. But when the meaning of a text depends on its context, then as contexts proliferate, so too do categories. Category proliferation creates big problems for statistics and science alike. If we must create a new category for almost every sentence of recorded observation, then virtually nothing will happen "in general" or even "often." As a result, there will be no common patterns to explain. Any theory based on our categories will in effect become a theory of our sentences, and will say more about our descriptive proclivities than about the consistencies of human development.

What to do? We seem to have only three options to limit category proliferation. First, we can study only phenomena that are context free. Second, we can limit the domain of our observations to a handful of contexts. Third, we can introduce ambiguity into our categories.

I understand that it is extremely exciting to find phenomena that occur regardless of cultural, historical, personal, or other contexts and that can be easily classified in, say, 3-6 categories. Such, I suspect, is the stuff of naturalist dreams. Alas, these phenomena do not seem to be common (Thorngate, 1976), nor do they stand up and shake our hands. They hide. We seek. We can often spend a lifetime seeking. Yet we have no reason to assume that these phenomena, if they do exist and if we do find them, will be in any way important for understanding human development. Indeed, they may not even be interesting. My father, for example, claims to have discovered a universal law of eating behavior: Every time the elbow bends, the mouth flies open (Mitchell Thorngate's Law). I think his claim is justified. But it may be some time before his law becomes the foundation of a universal theory of consumption.

If we must live with context and the proliferation of categories it brings, then we can limit the categories by limiting the contexts we observe. Rather than observing children's learning activities, for example, we can limit ourselves to children's learning activities in the classroom context, or further limit ourselves to the questions that English-speaking children aged 9 ask in French immersion class. With such reductions of our observational domain, we might expect reasonable summaries of our observations with 10-20 categories. The categories might also suffice for the study of French-speaking children, children aged 7, English classes, and so on. It is less likely, however, that the categories will suffice for teenage Iranian females taking ice skating lessons, or for Micmac Indian males learning animal tracking from their elders. Many of the original categories may be meaningful, but we should expect that additional categories would be needed. If category additions are needed, it is highly likely that theoretical additions would be needed as well. We should not dismiss the possibility that some day a Mendelian Table of categorical elements will be constructed and used to account for all texts in all contexts. But until then we might make do with the ambiguous option.

Most scientists are interested in explaining common features of diverse phenomena, and in seeking these features they often resort to either of two feature detection strategies. The first is *overview*, rising above details to see the forest in the trees. The second is *oversight*, ignoring details to see what features remain. Scientific overviews are usually attained by creating higher levels of abstraction, and scientific oversights are usually attained by resorting to statistical synopses. The latter, of course, is aided in no small way by the theory of the random variable—a theory that has led most psychologists to view human behavior as signal plus noise.

Overview and oversight are not the only strategies for determining common features in diverse phenomena. A third is *perspective,* viewing the diversity from different angles or attitudes to see what does and does not change. As any good artist knows, perspective is aided in no small way by ambiguity simply because ambiguity, by definition, provokes us to examine phenomena in different ways. Ambiguity is thus crucial for creating the variety of ideas that compete in our scientific experiments, and presumably from which only the best-fitting survive.

Ironically, ambiguity has a bad reputation in science, and conventional scientific wisdom prescribes that it should be minimized whenever possible. Most psychologists accept this wisdom, and attempt to reduce the ambiguity of their concepts and measurements in conventional ways. For example, measurement ambiguity is conventionally equated with intrajudge and interjudge reliability. As a result, even developmental naturalists conventionally ask two or more judges to categorize samples of text in context two or more times. If judges consistently place a text in the same category, then the category is retained; if they are not consistent, then the judges are retrained or the categories are altered or discarded. The net effect of this procedure is to reduce the variety of perspectives from which judges view the texts. Ultimately, the texts are viewed from only one perspective, the "signals" from this perspective are separated from the "noise" by statistical synopsis, and variations of the signals are examined from various levels of abstraction that include ANOVA or log-linear equivalents of main effects, low-order interactions, and higher order interactions.

Perhaps by now it should not be surprising that the evidential perspective suggests an alternative to conventional wisdom. The alternative embraces judgmental variety, and attempts to make good use of ambiguity in assessing theory-data fit. It begins with the assumption that the data in category judgments do not come from individuals but from groups—specifically, dyads composed of a judge and a person

being judged. Each person provides samples of text that we assume
is related to the person's perspective on their contexts. Each judge
provides a categorical translation of the texts that we assume is related to the judge's perspective on their contexts. The primary task
of the Nominal Pattern Analysis adumbrated here is to determine
how well predictions from theoretical perspectives match texts
generated from both perspectives. To do so we must disambiguate
the perspectives of persons from the perspectives of judges. Alas,
the task is practically impossible. About the best we can do is to
ask persons to serve as their own judges in hopes that they retain
the same perspective as actor and observer (see Harré & Secord,
1973). Our second best option requires at least two judges to categorize the texts of at least two persons. Then, after reciting the
magical incantation "Ceteris paribus!" we can look across persons
and examine the fit of theoretical perspectives to judges' perspectives, then look across judges and examine the fit of theoretical
perspectives to persons' perspectives.

The magical task becomes more manageable by requiring judges
to categorize in a manner adapted from notions of fuzzy set theory
(cf. Kaufmann, 1975; Smithson, 1987). Each judge is asked to
evaluate text samples of two or more persons for their *degree of
membership* in two or more categories. Each evaluation is expressed by distributing 100 membership points across the categories, including a "wastebasket" or "et cetera" category, according
to the perceived degree of category membership.[2] For example, a
judge evaluating text sample T1 with respect to categories A, B, C,
and Other may assign 85 membership points to category A, 5 to
category B, 0 to C, and 10 to Other. The same judge may evaluate
text sample T2 by assigning 25 points to each of the four categories. Note that the concentration versus dispersion of membership
points across categories provides an elegant indicant of ambiguity:
As the concentration of points in a single category decreases, ambiguity increases. Note as well that when a judge assigns all membership points to only one category, then the fuzzy classification
scheme reduces to a conventional, single-membership categorizing
task. Assigning membership points can be more time consuming
than making single-category placements, but it does alleviate much
of the agony that judges often experience when trying to place
texts in two or more categories.

AN EXAMPLE

Let us now consider how the idea of perspective comparison and the method of membership assignment can be used in the Nominal Pattern Analysis of another hypothetical example. Suppose we are interested in exploring the development of social motives in children (e.g., see McClintock, 1978). We accept from previous research the idea that individuals can exhibit any of five basic motives in varying degrees:

(1) individualism (maximizing own gain);
(2) competition (maximizing the difference between own gain and other's gain);
(3) vindictiveness (minimizing others' gain);
(4) cooperation (maximizing the total of own gain and other's gain);
(5) altruism (maximizing others' gain).

Yet we also have some hunches about the trajectory of motive development. In particular, we believe that children are motivated primarily by consideration of their own outcomes, but the direction and extent of their consideration of others' outcomes varies with age and cultural context. As children age, their behavior will be increasingly influenced by its effects on others. Children raised in a cooperative environment will increase activities beneficial to others. Children raised in a competitive environment will increase activities deleterious to others. As a result, children from cooperative families should increase their cooperation and altruism, and reduce their competition and vindictiveness. Children from competitive families should do the reverse.

In order to test our hunches, suppose we obtain one-hour videotapes of two children in classroom group-activity situations every two years from ages 5 to 15. The first child is from a communal Haida Indian family on the Queen Charlotte Islands off the northwest coast of British Columbia. The second child is from an upwardly mobile, professional family in Vancouver on the southwest coast of British Columbia. Two judges (A and B) watch the tapes and distribute membership points across the five motive categories and the Other category according to their overall impressions. Their distributions are shown in Table 3.2. Judge A, for example, allocated 75 of 100 membership points to the Individualism category after watching the tape of the Haida child at age 5; Judge B allocated 45 points to the same.

TABLE 3.2 Motive Category Membership Ratings (A.B) of Judges A and B

	Age					
	5	*7*	*9*	*11*	*13*	*15*
Haida child						
Individualism	75.45	70.60	65.50	50.45	60.40	40.40
Competition	05.20	00.20	10.15	10.20	05.10	00.10
Vindictiveness	00.00	00.00	05.00	00.05	00.05	05.05
Cooperation	10.15	05.15	10.20	20.10	25.10	40.15
Altruism	10.05	10.00	05.05	10.10	10.20	10.25
Other/Unknown	00.15	15.05	05.10	10.10	00.15	05.05
Professional child						
Individualism	35.35	40.35	50.45	70.60	65.60	60.65
Competition	10.15	20.15	20.15	25.25	20.20	30.25
Vindictiveness	05.00	10.00	05.10	00.05	05.05	00.05
Cooperation	15.10	10.05	15.00	00.05	05.00	00.00
Altruism	05.15	00.10	05.10	00.00	00.00	00.00
Other/Unknown	30.25	20.35	05.20	05.05	05.15	10.05

How well do our hunches fit these membership distributions? Taking our cue from Ordinal Pattern Analysis, we answer this question by examining the ordinal patterns of the membership allocations. For example, each child provides six tests of the proposition that Individualism predominates, one test at each of the six ages. According to the membership allocations of Judge A, the Haida child shows more individualism than any other motive at all ages except one; at 15, Individualism and Cooperation are tied for dominance at 40 points each. Thus our "predominant Individualism" prediction hits the "Judge A and Haida child" data five times and misses once for an IOF of $(5 - 1)/(5 + 1) = +0.67$.

As a second example, our hunch that competition increases with age in the Professional child can be tested 11 times with the "Judge B and Professional child" data because 11 of the 15 pairs of membership points show a clear ordinal relation (i.e., the points are not tied). One of these 11 tests comes from age pair 5 and 11 (Competition membership points = 15 and 25); another test comes from age pair 5 and 13 (Competition membership points = 15 and 20). Of the 11 pairs, 10 match our hunch; only the pair of ages 11 and 13 misses (Competition points = 25 and 20). As a result, the "competition increases" IOF for "Judge B and Professional child" data is $(11 - 1)/(11 + 1) = +0.82$.

TABLE 3.3 IOFs for Various Hunch/Data Combinations

	Judge A			Judge B			Total		
	tests	hits	IOF	tests	hits	IOF	tests	hits	IOF
Haida child									
Individualism predominates	6	5	+0.67	6	6	+1.00	12	11	+0.83
Competition declines	12	7	+0.17	10	8	+0.60	22	15	+0.36
Vindictiveness declines	8	2	−0.50	9	0	−1.00	17	2	−0.88
Cooperation increases	14	13	+0.86	11	4	−0.27	25	17	+0.36
Altruism increases	5	3	+0.20	14	13	+0.86	19	16	+0.68
subtotal	45	30	+0.33	50	31	+0.24	95	61	+0.28
Professional child									
Individualism predominates	6	6	+1.00	6	5	+0.67	12	11	+0.83
Competition increases	12	11	+0.83	11	10	+0.82	23	21	+0.83
Vindictiveness increases	11	2	−0.64	11	8	+0.45	22	10	−0.09
Cooperation declines	13	11	+0.69	11	10	+0.82	24	22	+0.83
Altruism declines	8	7	+0.75	11	11	+1.00	19	18	+0.89
subtotal	50	37	+0.48	50	44	+0.76	100	81	+0.62

We have five hunches to test about the Haida child, and five more to test about the Professional child. We can test each hunch with the membership distributions of Judge A and of Judge B. The results of all these 20 tests are shown in Table 3.3.

There are many noteworthy features of Table 3.3, but only a few will be noted here. Judging from the positive IOFs in the subtotals, our hunches generally improve over chance our abilities to predict the ordinal relations of category membership allocations. In general, our hunches do better at predicting judgments of the Professional child (IOF = +0.62) than predicting judgments of the Haida child (IOF = +0.28). In general, our hunches about the Haida child agree with Judge A (IOF = +0.33) slightly more than Judge B (IOF = +0.24). In contrast, our hunches about the Professional child agree very well with Judge B (IOF = +0.76) and only moderately well with Judge A (IOF = +0.48). Across judges and children our hunches about the predominance of Individualism, and about the rise and fall of Altruism, fit quite well. Our hunches about the fall and rise of Vindictiveness, however, are more often wrong than right.

What can be said about our hunches in summary? They seem to generalize to two judges' evaluations of two children moderately well. The indicants of fitness in Table 3.3 suggest that we would improve the overall fit by reversing our hunch about the development of

Vindictiveness, but it makes no theoretical sense. Before abandoning our original hunches, therefore, we may be well advised to test them with additional data. Our hunches are obviously far from a fully developed theory, and we obviously must remind ourselves that their respectable fit does not give us license to conclude that social environment determines social motives. Nevertheless, I am confident in suggesting that the Nominal Pattern Analysis represented in Table 3.3 does give us a valuable method to examine empirical evidence for and against our hunches. Indeed, I think we learn far more about our hunches by this evidential exercise than by attempting to pour the same data through a more traditional statistical filter.

Conclusion

The Nominal Pattern Analysis generated above is only one of many that may be constructed to test the fit of our theories to our observations. The technique it exemplifies may not be the best or most useful one. To be frank, I literally made it up as I went along, and should not be surprised if it falls short of the requirements of most naturalist research in developmental psychology. I hope, however, that the technique will provide a prototype for those wishing to extend the evidential perspective on categorical data. I encourage developmental naturalists to develop variations best suited for their particular research. And I look forward to a time when evidential statistics become as natural as inferential statistics in our attempts to understand why people develop as they do.

Notes

1. Thus, for example, a $2 \times 2 \times 2$ analysis of three dichotomous variables will generally require double the number of observations of a 2×2 analysis of two such variables.

2. We may also allow each judge to rate the category memberships on separate scales (e.g., 1-100 for individualism, 1-100 for competition), and perhaps then choose to standardize their ratings by dividing each by their totals. There is no fixed procedure for eliciting fuzzy membership estimates (cf. Smithson, 1987).

References

Akerlof, G. (1984). *An economic theorist's book of tales.* Cambridge, UK: Cambridge University Press.

Edwards, A.W.F. (1972). *Likelihood.* Cambridge, UK: Cambridge University Press.

Harré, R., & Secord, P. (1973). *The explanation of social behavior.* Totowa, NJ: Littlefield, Adams.

Hildebrand, D., Laing, J., & Rosenthal, H. (1977). *Prediction analysis of cross-classifications.* New York: John Wiley.

Kaufmann, A. (1975). *Introduction to the theory of fuzzy subsets.* New York: Academic Press.

McClintock, C. (1978). Social values: Their definition, measurement and development. *Journal of Research and Development in Education, 12,* 121-136.

Nagel, E. (1939). Principles of the theory of probability. *International encyclopedia of unified science* (Vol. 1, No. 6). Chicago: University of Chicago Press.

Parsons, D. (1975). *Directory of popular tunes and musical themes.* Cambridge, UK: Spencer Brown.

Powers, W. (1989). *Living control systems.* Gravel Switch, KY: The Control Group.

Sankoff, D., & Kruskal, J. (Eds.) (1983). *Time warps, string edits, and macromolecules: The theory and practice of sequence comparison.* Reading, MA: Addison-Wesley.

Savage, L. (Ed.). (1962). *Statistical inference.* London: Methuen.

Smithson, M. (1987). *Fuzzy set analysis for behavioral and social sciences.* New York: Springer.

Stinchcombe, A. (1968). *Constructing social theories.* Chicago: University of Chicago Press.

Thorngate, W. (1976). In general vs. it depends: Some comments on the Gergen/Schlenker debate. *Personality and Social Psychology Bulletin, 2,* 404-410.

Thorngate, W. (1986a). Ordinal pattern analysis. In W. Baker, M. Hyland, H. van Rappard, & A. Staats (Eds.), *Current issues in theoretical psychology* (pp. 345-364). Amsterdam: North Holland.

Thorngate, W. (1986b). The production, detection, and explanation of behavioural patterns. In J. Valsiner (Ed.), *The individual subject and scientific psychology* (pp. 71-93). New York: Plenum.

Thorngate, W., & Carroll, B. (1986). Ordinal pattern analysis: A method for testing hypotheses about individuals. In J. Valsiner (Ed.), *The individual subject and scientific psychology* (pp. 201-232). New York: Plenum.

Chance Models and Types of Hypotheses in Evidential Statistics

ALEXANDER VON EYE

Warren Thorngate (Chapter 3) and many other researchers (e.g., Froman & Hubert, 1980; Hildebrand, Laing, & Rosenthal, 1977; von Eye & Brandtstädter, 1988) share a dream. In this dream they elegantly test systems of ordinal—that is, "greater than" or "less than"—hypotheses concerning categorical variables. The testing is free of constraints imposed by such approaches as the General Linear or Log-linear Models; does not make any distributional or other parametric assumptions; nor does it force the researcher to answer questions that no one in his or her right mind would ever ask.

Thorngate proposes an alternative approach, the Ordinal Pattern Analysis (OPA), rather than simply complaining about the Procrustean bed in which, he believes, we poor souls suffer. OPA is a method that is custom tailored for naturalistically minded researchers, that is, researchers emphasizing intuitive observation in natural settings. The typical question asked when applying OPA is a comparative one; for instance, "Does individual A, having reached puberty, experience more social contacts now than before?" (see Table 3.1 in Thorngate's chapter). This type of question can be asked using data pertaining to individuals or to groups of individuals.

Thorngate proposes a Yule-type statistic for evaluating the fit between observed data and theoretical proposition. This statistic is the Index of Observed Fit (IOF):

AUTHOR'S NOTE: Many thanks to Lauren P. Jacobson and Danny Perkins for helpful comments on an earlier draft of this commentary.

$$IOF = (Hits - Misses)/(Hits + Misses) \qquad [1]$$

where "hits" denotes the number of hypothesis-confirming comparisons and "misses" denotes the number of hypothesis-disconfirming comparisons (see Tables 3.1 and 3.2 in Thorngate's chapter). The range of the IOF is $-1 \leq IOF \leq +1$. We obtain $IOF = -1$ if there are no hypothesis-confirming comparisons, and $IOF = +1$ if there are no hypothesis-disconfirming comparisons. If Hits $-$ Misses $= 0$, we obtain $IOF = 0$. Unless specified otherwise, one assumes that half of the comparisons are confirmed by chance.

In this commentary, we ask the question "How does the OPA approach compare to alternative approaches, specifically to Prediction Analysis (PA)?" (Hildebrand et al., 1977; von Eye & Brandtstädter, 1989; Szabat, 1990). Our comparison focuses on the descriptive measures used for evaluating the success of comparisons or predictions, the statistical models on which this evaluation is based, and the type of hypothesis asked in OPA and PA.

The main descriptive statistic in PA is Del. Del is defined as

$$Del = (Expected\ Misses - Observed\ Misses)/(Expected\ Misses) \quad [2]$$

The range of Dels is $-\infty < Del \leq +1$ with Del approaching $-\infty$ as the number of observed misses increases and the number of expected misses decreases. Del $= +1$ if there are no observed misses, that is, if the hypothesized data structure explains 100% of the data. Del $= 0$ if the number of expected misses equals the number of observed misses.

For the following considerations we assume that hits and misses complement each other or, in other words, we assume that Hits + Misses = Number of Decisions Made. If there are more hits than misses the numerator in Equation 1 is positive and the observed number of misses must be smaller than expected by chance. Thus the numerator in Equation 2 must be positive also. In the denominator the coefficients differ in that IOF uses the total number of decisions made whereas Del uses only a subset of that. The two coefficients converge, however, as the number of expected misses approaches N and the numerator is positive.

From this brief comparison we see that OPA and PA are similar to each other as methods for evaluation of prediction success. There are differences, however, between the two methods. These differences become apparent when one compares the chance models that underlie each type of model (cf. von Eye & Sörensen, in press). OPA compares pairs of frequencies in each row, that is, OPA investigates the main effects of the dependent variable separately for each category of the independent variable or conditional on the independent variable. In contrast, when estimating expected frequencies, PA takes main effects of both predictors and criteria into account. It should be noted that, in the present context, we are talking about degree-2 PA. This variant of PA uses pairs of predictor categories as rows and pairs of criterion categories as columns of the matrix under examination. In other words, degree-2 PA compares the observed number of misses with the expected number of misses estimated under the assumption of independence between pairs of predictor events and pairs of criterion events.

This comparison shows that OPA hypotheses are successful if there is a main effect of the dependent variable. In contrast, degree-2 PA hypotheses are successful if the composite predictor and the composite criterion are associated with each other.

When one compares the type of hypotheses analyzed in OPA and PA one realizes that OPA makes ordinal comparisons between criterion categories for each level of the predictor. These comparisons take the following form: "For category i of the predictor it is proposed that the observed frequency in category j of the criterion is greater than the observed frequency in category $j + 1$." In contrast, degree-2 PA focuses on ordinal comparisons that take the following form: "If the observed frequency of predictor category i is greater than the observed frequency of category $i + 1$, then the observed frequency of criterion category j is greater than the observed frequency of category $j + 1$."

From this comparison we see that the type of hypothesis entertained by OPA and PA is different. In addition, as we noted before, the hypotheses are evaluated under different chance models. Another difference between OPA and PA is that the latter allows the researcher to weight misses. This is important if the researcher is to be able to discriminate between more and less grave errors. The last difference to be mentioned here is that PA explicitly includes ties in its analysis.

Summary

Both OPA and PA allow the researcher to analyze ordinal hypotheses. The methods are unique in that they operate under different chance models. OPA tests a conditional main effect model whereas PA tests deviations from independence. In addition, the methods differ in the type of hypotheses that can be tested. For both methods there are both descriptive measures and significance tests available. Warren Thorngate's chapter shows that it may very well be worth our while to pursue the dream mentioned at the beginning of this commentary.

References

Froman, T., & Hubert, L. J. (1980). Application of prediction analysis to developmental priority. *Psychological Bulletin, 97,* 136-146.

Hildebrand, D. K., Laing, J. D., & Rosenthal, H. (1977). *Prediction analysis of cross-classifications.* New York: John Wiley.

Szabat, K. A. (1990). Prediction analysis. In A. von Eye (Ed.), *Statistical methods in longitudinal research: Vol. 2. Time series and categorical longitudinal data* (pp. 511-544). San Diego: Academic Press.

von Eye, A., & Brandtstädter, J. (1988). Evaluating developmental hypotheses using statement calculus and nonparametric statistics. In P. B. Baltes, D. Featherman, & R. M. Lerner (Eds.), *Life-span development and behavior* (Vol. 8, pp. 61-97). Hillsdale, NJ: Lawrence Erlbaum.

von Eye, A., & Brandtstädter, J. (1989). Application of prediction analysis to cross-classifications of ordinal data. *Biometrical Journal, 30,* 651-665.

von Eye, A., & Sörensen, S. (in press). Models of chance when measuring interrater agreement with kappa. *Biometrical Journal.*

4

Modeling Quantitative Developmental Change

FRANÇOISE D. ALSAKER

The focus of this chapter is on the use of hierarchical linear models in the study of intraindividual change over time. New methodological perspectives, or the introduction of new statistical methods as here, often reactivate old questions and debates. This is the case here with the issues of development and quantitative measurement. Using a statistical method that is well suited for the study of intraindividual change is not necessarily equivalent to studying development. Thus before we start praising the advantages of the growth curve approach in hierarchical linear models we want to emphasize the need for clarifying the concepts of development and of quantitative change in psychological research.

Developmental Change

Most definitions of development converge in referring to change (Lerner, 1986) and to time/age (Baltes, Reese, & Nesselroade, 1977).

AUTHOR'S NOTE: The research reported in this chapter was supported by a grant from the Norwegian Council for Medical Research (RMF-HEMIL) to Françoise D. Alsaker, and by grants from the William T. Grant Foundation and from the Norwegian Council for Social Research to Dan Olweus.

The author also acknowledges the valuable comments provided by Dan Olweus and Stephen W. Raudenbush on an earlier draft.

Change in itself, however, is not a developmental event. In actual fact, there has been a great deal of controversy about which changes should be considered developmental and which should not (cf. Reese & Overton, 1970). Attempts at specifying the concept of development have often derived from the fields of cognitive psychology or biology. Adding standards that suited their own theoretical positions, developmental psychologists have generally offered rather restrictive definitions of developmental change, and have used criteria such as increasing differentiation, hierarchic integration, specific sequential ordering of changes, and irreversibility (see Baltes et al., 1977, for an overview). Wohlwill (1970), for example, refused to consider variables that showed consistent age changes in individuals as developmental, if the changes occurred only under specific conditions. Neither did variables qualify as developmental, he said, "which represent dimensions of emergent individual differences, rather than of directional developmental change, such as aggressiveness, attention seeking and the like" (p. 52).

One of the questions that arise from this brief glance at relatively well accepted definitions is whether or not it seems meaningful to apply them to other areas of developmental research than the ones they originally came from. We may note here that Wohlwill's (1970) examples of appropriate developmental variables drew exclusively on the fields of cognitive and biological development. Narrow definitions were probably pertinent when normative development was the major focus of developmental research, but how useful are they today? A scanning of developmental journals shows that the range of issues addressed in this area is clearly broader than the aforementioned definitions of development would allow.

In line with most earlier perspectives, development usually has positive connotations, such as purposefulness, enhancement, or improvement. Nonetheless, developmental psychology exists in a cultural/societal context and cannot, in decency, avoid addressing issues that are relevant for contemporary human development just because they do not match with traditional definitions of developmental change. In actual fact, some of the most central issues we have to face are not necessarily concerned with (normative) age-related changes or "positive" changes. Such issues are for example: Why do some individuals acquire certain types of behavior? Why do they develop in one direction or another (e.g., some becoming more aggressive, some less), or why do they not show any changes at all? What are the specific conditions that facilitate or prevent the development of different types of behavior? Such changes/influences may be of greatest importance for individuals' future life trajectories.

In other words, there seems to be an increasing discrepancy between some theoretical considerations about development on the one hand, and the concerns of developmental psychology on the other hand. In our view, rather than insisting on restrictive definitions and continuing to do research that is clearly beyond the scope of these same definitions, developmental researchers should now devote some attention to conceptualizations of development and developmental research that may be in agreement with what they consider crucial issues of research in this field.

Following the rules of statistical testing, based primarily on whether or not the null hypothesis, H_0, may be rejected, developmental researchers have usually defined the alternative hypothesis, H_1, in terms of *differences* between age groups,[1] or in terms of intraindividual *change*. Doing so, they have often ignored that lack of difference, or change, (i.e., acceptance of H_0, statistically speaking) may be at least as interesting, in a developmental perspective, as presence of age-related differences or change. Questions of *consistency*, on the other hand, have mostly been addressed in terms of consistency of interindividual differences (commonly called stability). In the latter statistical approach H_0 is usually defined as a lack of interindividual stability, which, in fact, also may be central to certain developmental dimensions (see Alsaker & Olweus, 1990b; Asendorpf, this volume; Olweus, 1980, for more detailed discussions of the issue of consistency/stability).

As a consequence of the criticism we have leveled at earlier conceptualizations and practices, we propose that a definition of the tasks of developmental psychology should be motivated by concerns about individuals' life trajectories as well as by the necessity of gaining information about age-related (sequential and normative) phenomena. Concerns about individuals' life trajectories imply that all factors that may have an impact on how persons' lives will be formed, that is, also factors that may lead to interindividual differences in some domains, are of potential interest to developmentalists. Development across the life course may be characterized by periods of change and periods of stability with respect to various variables. Therefore, such a definition should include consistency as well as change and it should take into account that some changes may be irreversible, whereas others may last for longer or shorter periods. In addition, both positive and negative changes should be considered. In sum, our purpose so far has been to propose a basic working definition that should be refined and elaborated to meet the needs of specific areas of research on human development and to take into account the growing knowledge about cultural influences on what we once believed to be universal phenomena (cf. Valsiner, 1989). Such specific definitions should exclude random or idiosyncratic change, and allow for the inclusion of all factors that may significantly affect *individuals' life trajectories*.

Quantitative Change

Modeling quantitative change raises at least one additional major issue that has already been referred to by Bryk and Raudenbush (1987): When are intraindividual quantitative changes meaningful?

It is not the intent of this chapter to deal with the full complexity of this issue. Instead of trying to deliver a "universal solution," we want to encourage researchers in the area of developmental research to address the following questions more explicitly. First, is it meaningful to use a quantitative measure of the phenomenon under study? A quantitative approach to assessment is based on an assumption that a phenomenon (e.g., some aspect of personality) may be conceived of in terms of a dimension. This implies that different levels of a scale measure the same underlying dimension. A quantitative approach to *change* also implies that the same dimension can be used across age/time. A qualitative approach to measurement would be more appropriate if we assume that a phenomenon is best described in terms of categories, as for example, diagnostic categories in psychopathology.

Second, are these measures sensitive enough to assess change? If one assumes that individuals may change on a dimension over time, instruments should be able to depict even small changes, that is, to differentiate between contiguous levels on that dimension.

Third, how large should changes be to qualify as *substantively (not statistically) significant*. This last question is an invitation to depart from the commonly accepted strategy for making decisions about what is worth reporting. The usual decision rule is based on statistical significance. In our view, to rely merely on this rule has two major flaws. One is that interesting "developmental" null results (e.g., lack of change or lack of stability, see above) are underreported in the literature, which may lead to perpetual testing of the same fruitless hypotheses. The other weakness of this strategy is that, given large samples and sensitive tests, even very small changes may reach significance and lead to partly unfounded interpretations and expectations. There is, however, no hard-and-fast rule for deciding when a change is large enough to warrant consideration. Even small differences may have considerable theoretical or practical significance (cf. Rosenthal, 1984; Alsaker & Olweus, 1990a, for a discussion of the use of effect size measures in the study of intraindividual change).

Methods for Assessing Change and the Growth Curve Approach

Once a dimension has been judged appropriate for quantification, sensitive instruments have been constructed, and an adequate design has been adopted, the choice of statistical methods for analyzing data still remains. The choice we make depends on the hypotheses we have about developmental issues in the dimensions under study and how change may occur. At the same time, we should bear in mind that different statistical methods may give different answers to similar questions and are not all interchangeable.

A method like repeated measures ANOVA may be the right choice when normative changes are one's core concern. Use of group means, however, as is the case in such analyses, may mask individual changes that occur in opposite directions and hence cancel each other out. It may well be the case that, in spite of almost constant average levels in a dimension across age/time, marked changes take place at the individual level for certain periods (cf. Alsaker & Olweus, 1990a).

When consistency of interindividual differences is of interest, autocorrelation is often used (i.e., correlation of the same instrument between two points in time, see Asendorpf, this volume). Because this method standardizes the scores to a common mean and variance over time, it does not provide adequate tests of intraindividual change (Bryk & Raudenbush, 1987; Rogosa, Brandt, & Zimowski, 1982).

The methods referred to above all fail to consider the most essential issue in developmental psychology: The individual's own growth/change trajectory. Baltes et al. (1977) included the intraindividual development and the study of interindividual differences in growth parameters in the tasks of developmental psychology. Nonetheless, until recently no statistical method could take on this challenge.

Theoretical and practical developments in the work with hierarchical linear models (HLMs) now enable the study of intraindividual change and its correlates (Bryk & Raudenbush, 1987; see also Laird & Ware, 1982; and Strenio, Weisberg, & Bryk, 1983, for the basic theoretical theory). HLMs permit us to consider each subject as a "group," or "class," of observations. This allows treating the repeated measures within each subject in the same manner as observations from different subjects within a group. Thus considering time/age as one variable and, for example, some behavioral dimension or personality aspect as another variable within subjects, there are as many pairs of observations for each subject as there are measurement occasions. The behavioral dimension may then be regressed on time/age and regression equations are computed for each subject. The parameters for intercept and slope in these regression equations can now be considered and treated as new variables that are added to each subject's data. In a second step, these regression parameters (growth curve parameters) may be entered as outcome variables in a new series of analyses.[2]

In sum, a growth curve approach in HLMs makes it possible to study intraindividual change on an individual level and to examine what other variables may be associated with interindividual differences in intraindividual change. The growth curve approach is presented briefly in the following. For a detailed explanation of theory and methods of estimation in HLMs, the reader is referred to Bryk and Raudenbush (1987), Goldstein (1987), and Raudenbush and Bryk (1986).

Hierarchical linear modeling enables us to pose two models: A within-subject model and a between-subjects model. The first model, the intraindividual change/growth[3] model, may be expressed by the following equation:

$$y_{it} = \pi_{0i} + \pi_{1i} T_{it} + R_{it} \qquad [4.1]$$

where y_{it} is the observed status of individual i at time t, T_{it} represents time since some event (e.g., birth, start of project, or first measurement) for individual i at time t, π_{0i} is the intercept, π_{1i} the linear rate of change, and R_{it} is the error. Estimation of this model gives us information about mean level in the outcome variable at the intercept (which will be the initial status if $T_{it} = 0$ at entry), the average growth trajectory, and deviations of the individual growth curves from the sample mean. The model presented above is a linear growth model, but it can readily be expanded to represent curvilinear growth/change by using quadratic, cubic, or other higher order effects.

In order to predict variation in individual growth/change trajectories, the two growth parameters π_{0i} and π_{1i} are entered in the second model as the outcome variables. The between-subjects model is thus given by two equations, one for the intercept π_{0i} (from Equation 4.1), and one for the slope parameter π_{1i}:

$$\pi_{0i} = \beta_{00} + \beta_{01} X_i + U_{0i} \qquad [4.2a]$$

and

$$\pi_{1i} = \beta_{10} + \beta_{11} X_i + U_{1i} \qquad [4.2b]$$

where X_i represents some between-subject variable influencing both the intercept (π_{0i}) and the slope (π_{1i}) in Equation 4.1. U_{0i} and U_{1i} are the random increments to the individual growth parameters (see Bryk & Raudenbush, 1987).

Equations 4.1 and 4.2 may be combined to give a single linear model,

$$Y_{it} = \beta_{00} + \beta_{01} X_i + \beta_{10} T_{it} + \beta_{11} X_i T_{it} + e_{it} \qquad [4.3]$$

with

$$e_{it} = U_{01} + U_{1i} T_{it} + R_{it} \qquad [4.4]$$

HLM also provides information about the reliability of our measures for studying both level at intercept and growth/change rate. Following classical measurement theory, the reliability of the growth parameters is simply computed as the ratio of estimated "true" parameter variance (e.g., the variance of π_{1i}) to the total observed variance (e.g., the variance of the estimate π_{1i}); see also Bryk and Raudenbush (1987) for more details.

The Case of Global Negative Self-Evaluations

We have chosen to present data on the development of negative self-evaluation (or self-derogation) in early adolescence to illustrate the growth curve approach.

In our view, the process of self-evaluation begins early in life (Alsaker, 1987, 1988). As part of a "construction system," global self-evaluations are expected to have a certain degree of stability, helping us to organize our experiences in a meaningful way. On the other hand, they are also supposed, under normal circumstances; to continue to develop and to change with new experiences across the life span (Alsaker & Olweus, 1990b).

Self-derogation may be meaningfully conceived as a continuum from total lack of negative self-evaluations to extremely high levels of self-deprecation. Furthermore, given the centrality of this dimension for our "construction of the world," quantitative changes, in terms of level of negative self-evaluation, are assumed to be related to general change in well-being and to affect quality of life to a great extent.

Results from two previous studies (Alsaker & Olweus, 1990a, 1990b), addressing issues of normative change and of interindividual stability, have demonstrated that the mean level of self-derogation was not associated with age. Furthermore, the stability of interindividual differences in self-derogation across adjacent years of measurement was relatively high (typically in the .65 to .75 range for disattenuated correlation coefficients). However, stability of global negative self-evaluations decreased fairly rapidly with length of interval between measurements (see also Conley, 1984).

The pattern of stability coefficients combined with the null results concerning age-related changes in the mean level of self-derogation suggested that there were clear intraindividual changes in self-esteem over time, in particular for longer time intervals, but that they obviously occurred in both positive and negative directions and were not especially marked for any particular age period.

In Bowlby's (1969, 1973) theoretical writings on our construction of working models for self and others, these two fundamental working models are assumed to be highly related. On the basis of this conceptualization and of studies on social relations and social support (e.g., Alsaker, 1989; Lewis, Feiring, McGuffog, & Jaskir, 1984; Sarason, Levine, Basham, & Sarason, 1983) we have chosen to consider the relationship between intraindividual changes in the level of negative self-evaluation and two other-related variables: loneliness and relations to parents.

We expected to find self-derogation to be, generally, positively related to loneliness and negatively related to good interaction with parents. Since previous analyses (Alsaker & Olweus, 1990a) have given no grounds for assuming that self-derogation increases with age/time, we expect a small and nonsignificant π_{1i}. On the other hand, we expect individual growth/change trajectories to vary, at least to such an extent that it will be meaningful to look for variables that may explain (predict) this variation.

In this context, we want to examine if changes in self-derogation parallel changes in the two other dimensions over time. Correlation analyses carried out at different points in time would most probably yield coefficients of approximately the same sizes. This would indicate that, independent of time of measurement, individuals who score higher than others on one variable do so to a large extent on the other variable as well. This, however, would not provide time information about a possible parallelism in change in both sets of variables.

The question we want to address here is: Do individuals who experience changes in feelings of loneliness, or a deterioration in their relation to their parents, also experience changes in self-derogation? Is there any parallelism in change in both sets of variables when loneliness and relation to parents at Time 1 are allowed to predict the estimated level of self-derogation at the first measurement occasion?

Method

DESIGN AND SUBJECTS

The subjects participated in a large scale cohort-longitudinal project in Bergen, Norway (see Olweus, 1987, 1990). Data were collected on four large representative samples of school children. The children, who were originally in Grades 4 through 7, came from 112 classes drawn from 28 primary schools and 14 junior high schools. The first time of measurement was in May 1983, when the children's modal ages were 11, 12, 13, and 14, respectively. Data to be presented in this chapter were collected in May 1983, May 1984, and May 1985.

The junior high schools recruited their students to a large extent from the elementary schools represented in the project. A random procedure was used in allocating classes to cohorts and, consequently, the four cohorts should be basically equivalent in most respects (except for possible age-related differences). The cohorts can be considered largely representative of students in the relevant grades and kinds of schools in the community of Bergen, and to a considerable degree also of students in these kinds of schools in "town" communities in the whole of Norway.

The number of students sampled was 2,607, and 2,473 or 94.9% of them participated in the first wave of measurement in May 1983. There were 1,143 girls and 1,330 boys. Students who moved to the project schools after the project had started were also allowed to participate. At Time 2, valid questionnaires were obtained from 86.5% of the original sample of 2,473 students. On the third measurement occasion, 70.6% of the original sample were still participating in the project.

Due to the large-scale nature of the study we had to rely heavily on self-report data. Several questionnaires covering a number of different domains were administered to the subjects in their ordinary classrooms by two research assistants (with the teacher absent).

INSTRUMENTS

Global Negative Self-Evaluations (GSE)

Because we wanted to use the same scale for all students, independent of age, the Global Negative Self-Evaluation Scale (GSE) was constructed (Alsaker & Olweus, 1986). This is a six-item, 6-point Likert scale, with four of the items (with the format somewhat modified) taken from Rosenberg's self-esteem instrument (RSE; Rosenberg, 1965). The following two items can serve as examples:

At times I think I am no good at all.
All in all, I am inclined to feel I am a failure.

As seen from the content of the items, the scale refers to global negative self-evaluation.[4] A high score indicates a high level of negative self-evaluations. Data from this scale were obtained on three occasions, May 1983, May 1984, and May 1985.

As documented in a previous paper (Alsaker & Olweus, 1986), the scale has satisfactory internal consistency and validity. In the present study, Cronbach's coefficient alpha was .80, .88, and .88, respectively, for the three measurement occasions. Separate analyses for girls and boys revealed similar patterns of factor loading for the items, on a one-factor solution, for both sexes and across age (Alsaker &

Olweus, 1986). The constancy of the factorial structure of the items is an indication that students from the various age and sex groups interpreted and responded to the items in essentially the same way. This, in turn, is a prerequisite for assuming that the same concept is measured at different points in time and that possible changes over time reflect changes in the dimension of self-evaluation (see Asendorpf, this volume, for a discussion of the question of continuity).

Loneliness

Feelings of loneliness were assessed with two items tapping loneliness at school, and using the same general format as for GSE. The items were:

I often feel lonely at school.
I often feel lonely, and somewhat isolated, when I am together with peers.

Data on loneliness were obtained on three occasions, as for GSE. The items correlated moderately with each other at the three times of measurement, yielding alpha reliability coefficients of .60 through .63 for girls and .51 through .63 for boys.

Parent-Child Relations

Relationships with parents were assessed with two sets of questions. Four items tapped general negativism and self-report of behaviors that reflected a desire to do the opposite of what parents would wish. The other set of items (six) tapped positive feelings toward parents and a general positive relational climate. The two following items may serve as examples:

I do the opposite of what my parents want me to do.
I usually get on well with my parents.

After some preliminary analyses showing general similarity in the results obtained with both subscales with respect to negative self-evaluations, it was decided to combine all 10 items in order to simplify the presentation in this chapter. Data on this scale were obtained at two points in time. The first occasion was in October 1983, that is, about four to five months after the first measurement of GSE and loneliness. The second measurement occurred in May 1985. Data could not be obtained for subjects who were in the seventh grade in 1985 (modal age 12 in 1983, Time 1). Alpha reliability coefficients varied from .86 through .88 in girls, and were .85 at both occasions in boys.

VARIABLES IN THE GROWTH MODEL

As noted earlier, we were interested in studying the role of (a) loneliness and (b) parental relations in 1983 (May and October) for initial status of self-derogation. In addition, we wanted to relate change over time (from 1983 to 1985) in (c) feelings of loneliness and in (d) experiences of good interaction with parents, to the change parameters in GSE. For this purpose, difference scores[5] were computed for loneliness and parental relationships. In addition, the subjects' actual age at the first time of measurement was also used in the between-subjects model.

The analyses were conducted on a PC version of HLM, developed by Bryk and Raudenbush (cf. Bryk, Raudenbush, Seltzer, & Congdon, 1988). The version used here was compiled to permit the introduction of data for a maximum of 1,200 subjects.

Results

The HLM program we used does not require data for all subjects at each measurement time. On the other hand, at least three measurements are required to compute a regression coefficient (when both the intercept and the slope are to be considered random) and the program cannot handle missing data on between-subject variables. Therefore, the original sample was reduced to some extent, given that not all subjects had GSE scores on all three measurement occasions and that one of the four cohorts did not answer the parent-child relations questionnaire in May 1985 (Time 3). Information about the number of students included in the analyses may be obtained from Table 4.1, together with descriptive statistics on GSE. The correlation matrix for GSE, loneliness, and parental relations is presented in Table 4.2. As

TABLE 4.1   Mean Scores and Standard Deviations in Global Negative Self-Evaluations (GSE), at Three Times of Measurement

| | | | | | *GSE Scores* | | | | |
| | | *Time 1* | | | *Time 2* | | | *Time 3* | |
Gender	*n*	*M*	*SD*	*n*	*M*	*SD*	*n*	*M*	*SD*
Girls	605	2.30	1.01	553	2.27	1.06	605	2.34	1.09
Boys	670	2.10	.96	602	2.13	1.02	670	2.11	.96

we may see, the correlations were in the expected directions and of moderate sizes.

In order to estimate the reliabilities of the growth parameters, that is, intercept (initial status here) and slope (growth/change), the average growth rate, and the variance in the growth parameters, the first analysis of data should be carried out on a model that does not include predictor variables on the between-subjects level. This was done here, using measurement occasion to model growth. Also of note, we could have chosen to model growth/change using the individuals' respective ages at the three measurement occasions. Given previous results (Alsaker & Olweus, 1990a), however, there were no reasons for expecting age to be a more powerful indicator of change than measurement time.

TABLE 4.2   Correlation Matrix for Global Negative Self-Evaluations (GSE), Loneliness (L), and Parent-Child Relations (PCR) at the Different Measurement Times

	GSE1	*GSE2*	*GSE3*	*L1*	*L2*	*L3*	*PCR1*	*PCR3*
GSE1	—	.55	.44	.52	.30	.21	−.26	−.20
GSE2	.50	—	.69	.30	.50	.35	−.29	−.26
GSE3	.47	.62	—	.25	.33	.49	−.27	−.30
L1	.47	.28	.26	—	.34	.22	−.03[a]	−.04[a]
L2	.29	.51	.37	.35	—	.45	−.21	−.15
L3	.21	.30	.49	.27	.43	—	−.17	−.17
PCR1	−.30	−.25	−.27	−.18	−.27	−.23	—	.55
PCR3	−.19	−.26	−.30	−.11[b]	−.17	−.21	.56	—

NOTE: *n* = 543-605 in girls, and *n* = 591-670 in boys. Correlations among girls above diagonal, correlations among boys below diagonal.
a. nonsignificant
b. $p < .001$; all other coefficients $p < .0001$

TABLE 4.3   Fixed and Random Effects for the Estimation of the Within-Subject Model, With Global Negative Self-Evaluations (GSE) as Dependent Variable and Measurement Time as Within-Subject Variable

Fixed Effects β		Parameter Estimate	SE	T
Girls	Initial Status	2.2852	.0395	57.830*
	Growth Rate	.0226	.0221	1.020
Boys	Initial Status	2.1292	.0358	59.399*
	Growth Rate	−.0074	.0185	−.402
Random Effects π		Estimated Variance		
Girls	Initial Status	.6536*		
	Growth Rate	.1216*		
Boys	Initial Status	.5309*		
	Growth Rate	.0300*		

* *p* < .0001

The reliabilities for our measures of initial status and growth rate were .692 and .410 respectively in girls, and .616 and .131 in boys. These figures indicate that estimation of initial status in GSE was moderate but satisfactory. The reliability of the measure of growth rate in girls was judged acceptable, although somewhat low (cf. Bryk & Raudenbush, 1987), and it was even lower in boys. In the latter cases we must conclude that most of the observed variance is due to error rather than to true parameter variance.

Results in terms of average initial status and growth rate are presented in Table 4.3. We can compare the figures for estimated levels of GSE at the intercept (Time 1 here) with the observed means in Table 4.1. We note that the results are very similar. The results concerning growth rate also fit very well with our previous analyses, using repeated measures ANOVA. There was no significant change in GSE over time (Alsaker & Olweus, 1990a).

It should be noted here that the coefficients reported in Table 4.3 (and Table 4.4) may be interpreted in the same manner as unstandardized coefficients from a usual regression analysis. That is, the coefficient for growth rate being .023 in girls, simply indicates that averaged GSE scores are increasing with .023 units for each unit in Time (which is one year here). Descriptive statistics presented in Table 4.1 show that the standard deviations for GSE were generally around 1.00. In other words, the average increase in GSE

Stability and Change in Development

TABLE 4.4   Effects of Age, Loneliness (L1), Parent-Child Relations (PCR1)
at Time 1, Change in Loneliness (DL) and in Parent-Child
Relations (DPCR) on Growth Parameters for Global Negative
Self-Evaluations (GSE) in Girls

Fixed Effects β	Parameter Estimate	SE	T
L1 on Initial Status $\hat{\beta}_{10}$	.6422	.0375	17.124*
PCR1 on Initial Status $\hat{\beta}_{20}$	−.3672	.0394	−9.314*
Age on Growth Rate $\hat{\beta}_{30}$	−.0130	.0124	−1.044
DL on Growth Rate $\hat{\beta}_{40}$	.2625	.0198	13.258*
DPCR on Growth Rate $\hat{\beta}_{50}$	−.0925	.0242	−3.823*
Random Effects π			
Initial Status	.3546*		
Growth Rate	.0720*		

* $p < .0001$

for a one-year period is less than one 40th of a standard deviation (sd)
in girls.

Furthermore, in line with our expectations, we found significant parameter variance in growth rate. On the basis of the estimated variance
for the slope parameter we calculated the standard deviation for this parameter in girls ($\sqrt{.1216}$ = .349) and in boys ($\sqrt{.03}$ = .173). Thus we
found that a girl one standard deviation above average (as regards rate of
change) is changing at a rate of .371 (.023 + .349) per unit time while a
girl one sd below average is changing at a rate of −.326 (.023 − .349).
Examples of such slopes are presented graphically in Figure 4.1, assuming that both subjects had the same GSE score at Time 1. Corresponding
figures for boys were .166 (one sd above average) and −.180 (one sd
below average). That is, in spite of no normative or time/age-related
changes in GSE, subjects did differ fairly substantially in their change
trajectories. The parameter variance in boys was significant but clearly
lower than in girls. On the basis of the rather low reliability of the
growth rate parameter in boys, we decided not to continue the analyses
for the sample of boys. Even with this low reliability coefficient (.131)
some effects could still be found (Raudenbush, personal communication,
October 3, 1990). As noted above, however, the low reliability coefficient indicates that most of the observed variance in GSE scores over
time in boys is due to error. Thus we would take the risk of conducting analyses mainly on error data.

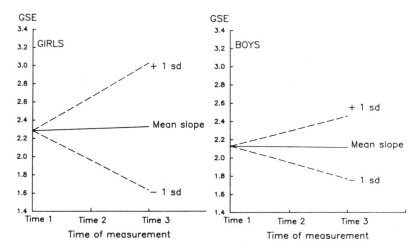

Figure 4.1. Average Growth Curves and Growth Curves One Standard Deviation Above and Below Average in Girls and Boys, Assuming That Subjects Started at the Same Level at Time 1[a]

NOTE: a. The score chosen here for Time 1 corresponds to the estimated mean level in GSE at Time 1.

The next step in our analysis was to introduce possible correlates of initial status and growth rate. As described earlier in this chapter, we chose, originally, four predictor variables. Two variables were entered in the between-model for π_{0i} (intercept), and the two others in the between-model for π_{1i} (slope). In addition, age at Time 1 was entered in the model for π_{1i}, primarily as a matter of demonstration. In previous analyses with repeated measures ANOVAs (Alsaker & Olweus, 1990a), age at Time 1 was entered as a between-subject factor, and the possible interaction between age and time (within-subject factor) was tested as well. The HLM approach is similar to the interaction test in ANOVA, in that age is treated in terms of its interaction with measurement time (see Equation 4.3). On the basis of these arguments, we should not expect age at Time 1 to predict growth rate to any large extent, since we did not find any interaction between age and the within-subject factor in previous ANOVAs. However, since HLM techniques are more sensitive to intraindividual changes than techniques based on averaging scores, we decided to test age at Time 1 as a possible predictive variable of growth rate.

The equations to be estimated were then the within-subject model

$$Y_{it} = \pi_{0i} + \pi_{1i} T_{it} + R_{it} \qquad [4.1]$$

and the between-subject models

$$\pi_{0i} = \beta_{00} + \beta_{10} X_{1i} + \beta_{20} X_{2i} + U_{0i} \qquad [4.5a]$$

where X_1 and X_2 are respectively, loneliness (L1) at Time 1 (May) and parent-child relations (PCR1) at Time 1 (October), and

$$\pi_{1i} = \beta_{01} + \beta_{31} X_{3i} + \beta_{41} X_{4i} + \beta_{51} X_{5i} + U_{1i} \qquad [4.5b]$$

where X_3 is age at Time 1, and X_4 and X_5 are difference scores in feelings of loneliness $(T3 - T1)$ and in PCR $(T3 - T1)$.

The results for the between-subjects model are presented in Table 4.4. A note of caution is in order before we start presenting and discussing the size and significance of the effects. Our design is a correlational one, and although we decided to use growth parameters for self-derogation as the dependent variables, and loneliness and parental relations as independent variables, we are aware of the fact that the causal relationship between the explanatory variables and the dependent variable is much more complex than suggested by this formulation. Therefore, "effects" should primarily be interpreted as an indication of relationships, without any causal connotations.

As expected, feelings of loneliness at Time 1 were highly related to the estimated level of self-derogation (GSE) at the same point in time. GSE was .64 units higher for each unit in feelings of loneliness. The parent-child relationship was also significantly related to the initial status in GSE. The coefficient β_{20} (−.37), however, was clearly lower than β_{10} (.64). It should be noted here that both effects (L1 and PCR1) are controlled for each other in the analysis. That is, individuals' GSE scores were .37 units lower per unit of parent-child relations, when feelings of loneliness at school were controlled for.

Turning to the prediction of growth rate, we can state that age at Time 1 had, as expected, no effect on intraindividual changes in GSE. Changes in feelings of loneliness covaried with changes in GSE. That is, for each increase of one unit in feelings of loneliness between May 1983 and May 1985, the *growth rate parameter* for GSE increased by .26 units. In other words, young adolescents experiencing an increase of one unit in loneliness at school in this period, would typically report an increase of .52 units in GSE (2-year period) as compared to students who did not experience increases in loneliness. An increase of one unit in positive relations to parents was associated with a decrease of .09 units in the growth rate parameter of GSE.

On the random side of the model we see that the variance parameters for both initial status and growth rate are still significantly different from 0. That is, there is still interindividual variance in intraindividual changes that cannot be explained on the basis of the variables entered in the model. Both variances, however, decreased as a consequence of the introduction of the five between-variables in the model (cf. Table 4.3, for initial values). Our model accounted for 45.7% of the parameter variance in initial status and 40.8% of the parameter variance in growth rate.

Discussion

The data presented in this chapter have given support to our hypotheses with regard to prediction of initial status and rate of change in global negative self-evaluations. Some of the results could have been obtained, and had actually been obtained, with other statistical methods. We knew for example, that loneliness and parent-child relations correlated with GSE at Time 1 (Table 4.2). We also knew that there were no significant averaged changes in GSE with time, nor with age. HLM, however, using the individuals' growth parameters, provides a more accurate estimation of these relationships. Moreover, HLM enabled us to *identify* the average growth rate. Doing so, we could give the "null results" a concrete content: Growth rate was .02 units a year in girls, and −.01 in boys.

In addition, the growth curve approach enabled us to answer some essential developmental questions. One of these questions was: Are there interindividual differences in intraindividual changes, even when there is no time-related change on a group level? The answer to this question was yes. The estimated parameter variance (in girls) was clearly significant. In fact, assuming that two girls had the same score at Time 1, a girl changing at a rate of one standard deviation above average and a girl changing at a rate of one sd below average would yield scores that are 1.39 GSE units apart two years later. The difference between these two scores corresponds to 1.73 standard deviation units for the *estimated* initial status of GSE (sd for $\pi_{0i} = \sqrt{.6536} = .808$; see Table 4.3). That is, although most girls probably did not ex-perience crucial changes in GSE in the period under study, we found a substantial variation between individuals' rates of change. This en-abled us to ask the next question: Do changes in GSE over time correlate with changes in loneliness or parental relations? This type of issue, that is, the assumption that there may be relationships between changes in two sets of variables, is fundamental in developmental research.

In this presentation we have used difference scores in between-subject variables to predict growth rate in GSE. Although the differ-ence score can only be considered a rough approximation of growth rate, it enabled us to conduct preliminary tests of the relationship be-tween growth curves. As noted previously, nonlinear change may also be examined in hierarchical linear modeling. This is done by entering different polynomial transformations of the T variable in the equation.

On the substantive side, the relationship between the intra-individual changes in self-derogation, loneliness, and parent-child re-lationships indicates that social-relational variables are closely associated with negative self-evaluations. Bowlby (1969, 1973) pro-posed considering working models of self and of others as comple-mentary. Following this argument, we may assume that changes in one of the two construction systems also imply changes in the other system. The question arises then, which of the two systems does influ-ence the other? It may be hazardous to answer this question by trying to disentangle the effects of both systems on each other empirically, or even theoretically. Instead, we may offer alternative interpretations to these results.

First, aversive experiences in relational dimensions, either among peers or with parents, lead to self-derogation. Subjects who experience rejection, isolation, and the like, interpret these events as indications of their own worthlessness. Therefore, increases in such aversive experi-ences lead to parallel increases in negative self-evaluations.

Second, increases in loneliness or negative changes in the rela-tion to parents may also be due to a large extent to a general lower-ing of mood, as a consequence of a high level of self-derogation. In other words, an increase in self-derogation (causes being un-known) could lead to more *feelings* of loneliness and negativism in parental relationships. In this case, one may propose that a nega-tive change in the working model of self would lead to negative appraisals in the working models of others, independent of what others actually do. This in turn may be detrimental to relations with others, and we may therefore also consider the third possibility that increases in negativism toward self may affect relations to peers and parents negatively, which, in turn, stabilizes negative self-attitudes.

The changes in self-derogation associated with changes of one unit in loneliness over the project period amounted to about 65% of the estimated standard deviation of GSE at Time 1 (.52/.808), which may be characterized as fairly substantial changes. Changes in GSE associated with changes in parental relations were not as high (23% of the estimated sd in GSE for the 2-year period). Even relatively small changes in the level of negative self-evaluations, however, may imply clear qualitative changes, depending on the initial level of negative self-evaluations. That is, the same increase, in absolute terms, may represent a shift from relative absence of negative self-attitudes to a low-to-moderate level of negative self-evaluations (still functional level), but it may also represent a shift from a moderate to a high and pathological level. This underscores the need for considering issues of magnitude of change in relation to the dimensions under study. In addition, we should be aware of the fact that changes in feelings of loneliness at school may be accompanied by changes in parental relations and that both effects may add. That is, a subject experiencing an increase of one unit in feelings of loneliness and a decrease of one unit in parental relations would be likely to experience an increase of .71 GSE units over the project period (.88% of the estimated sd in GSE).

We may conclude that hierarchical linear modeling enabled us to examine and test empirically some fundamental questions about quantitative intraindividual change. As is the case for all other statistical methods, however, it cannot give us the whole answer to the causes of development. So even if this method forces us to define a variable as dependent and the other variables as predictors, we might bear in mind that this remains a deliberate choice, based on theoretical assumptions and earlier empirical findings.

We started this chapter stating that new methods may reactivate old debates. They often start new debates, as well. Hierarchical linear modeling, providing new possibilities for testing developmental hypotheses in terms of a growth curve approach may, hopefully, open up new fields of inquiry in developmental research.

Notes

1. Wohlwill (1970) noted that negative findings as regards the effect of age were rare, "since they are not apt to be reported in print" (p. 56).

2. Hierarchical linear models may be conceived of in terms of the two-step procedure used in this presentation. However, the statistical estimation is entirely simultaneous.

3. The terms *growth* and *change* are used interchangeably here. Growth is often used to describe increases in a dimension, whereas change does not have such a connotation. However, the slope describing intraindividual changes is often referred to as a growth curve, independent of the direction of change.

4. The scale can be considered basically comparable with other scales for this domain, such as Rosenberg's RSE (Rosenberg, 1965) or Harter's Perceived Competence Scales (General Self-Worth) (Harter, 1982).

5. It should be noted that, contrary to widespread beliefs, difference scores are not automatically less reliable than raw scores (see Rogosa et al., 1982).

References

Alsaker, F. D. (1987). *Research on the self: Need for integrative models.* Mimeo.

Alsaker, F. D. (1988). Om utvikling av selvoppfatning [On the development of self-concept]. In O. F. Lillemyr & G. Hyre (Eds.), *Selvoppfatning og sosialisering* (DMMH publikasjonsserie, Nr. 1). Trondheim, Norway: DMMH.

Alsaker, F. D. (1989). Perceived social competence, global self-esteem, social interactions and peer dependence in early adolescence. Preliminary results from a cohort-sequential study. In B. H. Schneider, G. Attili, J. Nadel, & R. Weissberg (Eds.), *Social competence in developmental perspective* (pp. 390-392). Dordrecht, Netherlands: Kluwer.

Alsaker, F. D., & Olweus, D. (1986). Assessment of global negative self-evaluations and perceived stability of self in Norwegian preadolescents and adolescents. *Journal of Early Adolescence, 6,* 269-278.

Alsaker, F. D., & Olweus, D. (1990a). *Global self-evaluations and perceived instability of self in early adolescence: A cohort longitudinal study.* (Manuscript submitted for publication).

Alsaker, F. D., & Olweus, D. (1990b). *Stability of self-evaluations in early adolescence: A cohort longitudinal study.* (Manuscript submitted for publication).

Baltes, P. B., Reese, H. W., & Nesselroade, J. R. (1977). *Life-span developmental psychology: Introduction to research methods.* Monterey: Brooks/Cole.

Bowlby, J. (1969). *Attachment and loss: Vol. 1. Attachment.* New York: Basic Books.

Bowlby, J. (1973). *Attachment and loss: Vol. 2. Separation.* New York: Basic Books.

Bryk, A. S., & Raudenbush, S. W. (1987). Application of hierarchical linear models to assessing change. *Psychological Bulletin, 101,* 147-158.

Bryk, A. S., Raudenbush, S. W., Seltzer, M., & Congdon, R. T. (1988). *An introduction to HLM: Computer program and user's guide.* (Mimeo).

Conley, J. J. (1984). The hierarchy of consistency: A review and model of longitudinal findings on adult individual differences in intelligence, personality, and self-opinion. *Personality and Individual Differences, 5,* 11-25.

Goldstein, H. (1987). *Multilevel models in educational and social research.* London: Charles Friffin.

Harter, S. (1982). The perceived competence scale for children. *Child Development, 53,* 87-97.

Laird, N. M., & Ware, J. H. (1982). Random-effects models for longitudinal data. *Biometrics, 38,* 963-974.

Lerner, R. M. (1986). *Concepts and theories of human development* (2nd ed.). New York: Random House.

Lewis, M., Feiring, C., McGuffog, C., & Jaskir, J. (1984). Predicting psychopathology in six-year-olds from early social relations. *Child Development, 55,* 123-136.

Olweus, D. (1980). The consistency issue in personality psychology revisited—with special reference to aggression. *British Journal of Social and Clinical Psychology, 19,* 377-390.

Olweus, D. (1987). *Bully/victim problems among school children in Scandinavia. Overview.* (Mimeo). University of Bergen, Norway.

Olweus, D. (1990). Bully/victim problems among school children: Basic facts and effects of a school based intervention program. In K. Rubin & D. Pepler (Eds.), *The development and treatment of childhood aggression* (pp. 411-448). Hillsdale, NJ: Lawrence Erlbaum.

Raudenbush, S. W., & Bryk, A. S. (1986). A hierarchical model for studying school effects. *Sociology of Education, 59,* 1-17.

Reese, H. W., & Overton, W. F. (1970). Models of development and theories of development. In L. R. Goulet & P. B. Baltes (Eds.), *Life-span developmental psychology: Research and theory* (pp. 116-149). New York: Academic Press.

Rogosa, D., Brandt, D., & Zimowski, M. (1982). A growth curve approach to the measurement of change. *Psychological Bulletin, 92,* 726-748.

Rosenberg, M. (1965). *Society and the adolescent self-image.* Princeton, NJ: Princeton University Press.

Rosenthal, R. (1984). *Meta-analytic procedures for social research.* Beverly Hills, CA: Sage.

Sarason, I. G., Levine, H. M., Basham, L. R., & Sarason, B. (1983). Assessing social support: The social support questionnaire. *Journal of Personality and Social Psychology, 44,* 127-139.

Strenio, J.L.F., Weisberg, H. I., & Bryk, A. S. (1983). Empirical Bayes estimation of individual growth curve parameters and their relationship to covariates. *Biometrics, 39,* 71-86.

Valsiner, J. (1989). *Human development and culture: The social nature of personality and its study.* Lexington, MA: Lexington.

Wohlwill, J. F. (1970). The age variable in psychological research. *Psychological Review, 77,* 49-64.

COMMENTARY ON CHAPTER 4:

Prerequisites and Advantages of the Growth Curve Approach to Developmental Change

JENS B. ASENDORPF

Chapter 4 by Françoise Alsaker provides a good introduction to the growth curve approach to developmental change as it was originally proposed by Rogosa, Brandt, and Zimowski (1982) and further elaborated by Bryk and Raudenbush (1987). To illustrate her argument, she uses data from a longitudinal study on self-esteem that nicely illustrate the case often found in developmental research on social-emotional characteristics, that strong and interesting differential-developmental change is observed in the absence of universal change.

In her introduction, Alsaker defines developmental psychology as the study of individual life trajectories that may show periods of gains, periods of losses, and periods of stability, and defends this view against more narrow notions of development that focus only on universal gains. It should be clear from the editors' introduction and the two preceding chapters, however, that there is no need to be defensive here; in the social-emotional domain of development, interesting differential-developmental phenomena abound and have always been at the heart of research, and in the cognitive domain, differential-developmental questions (e.g., Weinert, Schneider, & Knopf, 1988) as well as developmental losses (Uttal & Perlmutter, 1989) are increasingly recognized as underresearched areas of investigation.

In my commentary I focus on two aspects of the growth curve approach to developmental change that may need more elaboration: its requirements in terms of the developmental phenomenon under study as well as the quality of the developmental data, and its advantages when it is compared with traditional approaches in terms of analyses of difference scores.

The first fundamental requirement for the applicability of the growth curve approach is the *cross-age comparability* (or *continuity*) of the individual attribute that is supposed to change during development: It must retain a comparable (but not necessarily the same) meaning over the sequence of observations. This requirement also applies to any other approach that is based on individual comparisons across age at least at the ordinal level, such as difference scores, residualized change scores, or Thorngate's ordinal comparisons (see Chapter 3). Whether the developmental phenomenon under study meets this requirement is a matter of theory as well as of the cross-age comparability of the nomological network that encompasses the construct under scrutiny. In Chapter 5, a method is proposed for studying the continuity of a construct empirically. Note that continuity does not imply identity of measurement procedures; it may be necessary to operationalize the same individual attribute at different ages in different ways.

The second fundamental requirement for the applicability of the growth curve approach is the *cross-subject comparability* of the individual developmental functions: They must be of a comparable type (but not necessarily of an identical type). In principle, this appears not to be a strong requirement for the growth curve approach because it rests on polynomial functions that allow a good approximation of any empirical curve. In general, if there are k measurement points, polynomial functions of degree $l \leq k - 1$ should be chosen where l is the smallest possible degree that allows a good approximation of the data of most subjects. In practical applications, problems may arise here when only a few measurement points exist, but many individuals show complicated growth functions. For example, if there are three assessments of the same variable per subject, but many subjects' change is quadratic rather than linear, the reliabilities of the individual change parameters that are based on linear change functions will be low.

One way to reduce the highest degree of the polynomial individual growth functions is to change the scale of the measurements. For example, if there are four assessments of the same variable, and the individual growth functions can be well approximated by quadratic curves, a square root transformation of the variables may allow us to apply linear growth curves with high reliability.

A more technical, but frequently encountered problem is that the interindividual distributions of the variables on some measurement occasions are not normally distributed. As Bryk and Raudenbush (1987, p. 156) point out, such violations of the normality assumption have little influence on the most important estimates of the parameters that describe individual growth (the πs) and the influence of external variables (the βs). They may, however, seriously affect estimates of the reliability of these parameters and of the correlation between initial status and rate of change.

Readers of Chapter 4 may ask why the growth curve approach is superior to traditional methods of data analysis, such as the analysis of difference scores. In fact, the data presented by Alsaker could be analyzed in a traditional way by (a) computing difference scores between the first and the last assessment for each subject, (b) analyzing these difference scores for gender-specific significant change at the sample level, and (c) correlating these difference scores with the initial assessment, the external variables, or their change (again in terms of difference scores) within each gender. Do not difference scores also describe individual growth functions? What do we need these complicated Greek parameters for? In the following I will spell out three major advantages of the growth curve approach as compared to traditional difference scores.

First, the growth curve approach is much more flexible than the difference score method in handling multiple assessments and nonlinear growth functions. If there are more than two assessments, (non)linear average change in the sample can be treated within an ordinary ANOVA approach by testing trends (linear, quadratic, etc.) within a repeated-measures analysis of variance. But when it comes to differential-developmental questions such as "is the quadratic change in variable A related to the linear change in variable B," tricky raw data transformations are needed in order to answer these questions by correlating differences of transformed scores (and these transformations are rarely applied in developmental research). The growth curve approach offers a straightforward alternative of simultaneously answering general- and differential-developmental questions by analyzing individual growth curves that refer to an unlimited number of assessments and to degrees of the polynomial functions that are in principle only limited by the number of assessments. It should be noted, however, that presently there exist few attempts to apply the model to nonlinear growth functions.

Second, the growth curve approach allows testing of the reliability of the *change parameters* if the number of assessments is greater than the highest degree of the fitted polynomial functions, without needing parallel measures. Often, even developmental researchers avoid the analysis of change because they believe that the reliability of difference scores is always much lower than the reliability of the raw scores. As Rogosa et al (1982) have pointed out, this belief is a myth (though a very obstinate one). It is an empirical question whether an assessment procedure is better suited to measure change or status. The critical variable in most cases is the amount of interindividual variance in change scores as compared to the amount of interindividual variance in status scores; the higher the variance of the change scores is, the more reliable measures of change can be.

The growth curve approach offers a straightforward procedure for estimating the reliability of the parameters of initial status as well as those of change by comparing the observed scores with their estimates. The example discussed in Chapter 4 illustrates nicely that the reliability of change parameters is an empirical question (it can even be a function of the sex of the subjects). Because the growth curve approach makes reliability analysis so easy, it safeguards against misinterpretations of results that are due to poor reliabilities of measurement.

Furthermore, the model advocated by Bryk and Raudenbush (1987) entails a particular advantage: The model draws on whatever strengths are available in the data. If within-subject data are precise, the model weights these data heavily; if between-subjects relations are strong, these data are emphasized by the estimation procedures (see Bryk & Raudenbush, 1987, p. 150, formulas 17 and 18).

Last but not least, the growth curve approach motivates researchers to state their model of developmental change explicitly rather than to approximate it by linear two-points-in-time comparisons, and to address the critical issue of the reliability of the individual developmental functions explicitly by incorporating at least one more assessment for this evaluation (as Bryk & Raudenbush, 1987, footnote 4, point out, this is not necessary for an application of their model, but there is no question that it is desirable).

Of course, the growth curve approach is not the ultima ratio of modeling quantitative developmental change. There are alternatives available that may be better suited for particular research questions.

A widespread tradition in biology and sociology is to analyze change by differential equation models (see, e.g., Guire & Kowalski, 1979). A recently emerging approach that seems to have a great and not yet fully exhausted potential is the study of latent growth curves within structural equation modeling such as LISREL (see McArdle & Epstein, 1987). Another alternative is time series analysis (e.g., Gottman, 1981), but because it requires a high number of measurement points, it can rarely be applied to developmental research. Much to be recommended are models of change that are specifically tailored to the phenomenon under study in that they derive the individual developmental functions from a *theoretical model* of the developmental mechanisms, either analytically or by computer simulation. This recently emerging approach may help to bridge the present gap between theory and methods in developmental psychology.

A certain danger of the growth curve approach to the measurement of developmental change results from its wide applicability in terms of fairly good (but perhaps not always optimal) approximations of empirical change data. Although his theory was wrong, Johannes Kepler was able to describe the movement of the planets with great precision by rather complex equations; if he had had a microcomputer at hand, he might have convinced his colleagues even more. Luckily he did not have a microcomputer for simulating star movements easily, and so Galileo Galilei was strongly motivated to search for more parsimonious explanations of the planets' orbits (Loftus, 1985). What we can learn from the growth curve approach is how a straightforward modeling procedure can be derived from rather simple assumptions about the individual developmental functions. What we should not forget, however, is that it depends on our theory of how development proceeds in a particular domain as to which form of function we would predict.

Therefore I would like to invite readers to look at the growth curve approach to developmental change not only as a very flexible tool for approximating data, but also as one viable example of comparing observations of developing nature with theoretical predictions of the nature of development.

References

Bryk, A. S., & Raudenbush, S. W. (1987). Application of hierarchical linear models to assessing change. *Psychological Bulletin, 101,* 147-158.

Gottman, J. M. (1981). *Time-series analysis: Introduction for social scientists.* New York: Cambridge University Press.

Guire, K. E., & Kowalski, C. J. (1979). Mathematical description and representation of developmental change functions on the intra- and interindividual levels. In J. R. Nesselroade & P. B. Baltes (Eds.), *Longitudinal research in the study of behavior and development* (pp. 89-110). New York: Academic Press.

Loftus, G. (1985). Johannes Kepler's computer simulation of the universe: Some remarks about theory in psychology. *Behavior Research Methods, Instruments, and Computers, 17,* 149-156.

McArdle, J. J., & Epstein, D. (1987). Latent growth curves within developmental structural equation models. *Child Development, 58,* 110-133.

Rogosa, D., Brandt, D., & Zimowski, M. (1982). A growth curve approach to the measurement of change. *Psychological Bulletin, 92,* 726-748.

Uttal, D. H., & Perlmutter, M. (1989). Toward a broader conceptualization of development: The role of gains and losses across the life span. *Developmental Review, 9,* 101-132.

Weinert, F. E., Schneider, W., & Knopf, M. (1988). Individual differences in memory development across the life span. In P. B. Baltes (Ed.), *Life-span development and behavior* (Vol. 9, pp. 39-85). Hillsdale, NJ: Lawrence Erlbaum.

5

Continuity and Stability of Personality Traits and Personality Patterns

JENS B. ASENDORPF

In the preceding chapters, the focus of analysis has always been on describing intraindividual change—qualitative, ordinal, or quantitative change. If interindividual differences were discussed from a differential-psychological perspective, they were conceptualized as interindividual differences in intraindividual change—developmental change was primary, and interindividual differences were secondary. This chapter is different. It treats developmental change from the perspective of the personality psychologist who is primarily interested in personality differences and only secondarily in the change of these differences during development.

Personality differences are most often conceptualized as differences on one continuous dimension, for example, intelligence. This approach reduces a person to a point on some continuum. If it can be demonstrated that the interindividual differences on that dimension show a high short-term stability, for example, that most persons change only very little in their position on that continuum, the continuum is called a *personality trait*. From a developmental perspective

AUTHOR'S NOTE: The section on trait stability draws heavily upon an article in press in the *European Journal of Personality* (Asendorpf, in press a), and the section on the differential stability of Q-sort upon an article in press in the *Journal of Personality* (Asendorpf & van Aken, in press).

we can then ask whether the continuum has the same meaning at different ages (the question of *continuity*), and whether the rank-order of the members of a population remains the same between different ages (the question of *stability*).

This chapter carries the analysis beyond traditional notions of trait stability by demonstrating that continuity and stability are confounded in present notions of trait stability but can be empirically investigated independently of each other. Furthermore, stability is not only treated at the aggregate level in terms of the mean stability of the interindividual differences in a sample of individuals but also in terms of *differential stability,* that is, interindividual differences in the stability of the individual trait scores.

Recently, a second approach to personality differences has found increasing interest among personality psychologists. Individuals are not described by a point on a continuum but by a *personality pattern.* This pattern can consist of the individual's profile in many personality traits that are separately measured, for example, an intelligence profile. Or it can be constructed in a more idiographic way by ranking different traits for one individual in terms of their saliency for that person (Q-sort procedure). In the latter case, the short-term stability of the Q-sort profiles must be demonstrated before they can be considered personality patterns. This pattern approach, better than the variable-oriented approach, respects the fact that personality is not the sum of unrelated traits but a system of interrelated traits: the "individual organization of behavior" (Allport, 1937).

From a developmental perspective we can then again ask questions of continuity and stability. Does such a personality pattern have the same meaning at different ages (the question of *continuity*), and do the personality patterns remain the same between different ages (the question of *stability*). This chapter shows that the notion of profile stability confounds the continuity and the stability of personality patterns, and that the *differential stability* of personality patterns can be profitably studied empirically.

Two Approaches to Personality Differences

J. Block (1971) and again Magnusson (1988) have criticized the "variable-orientation" of mainstream personality psychologists who reduce individuals to points on some continuum (see above), and have

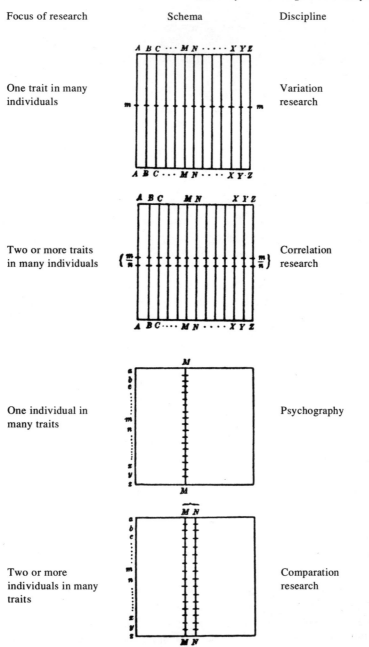

Focus of research   Schema   Discipline

One trait in many   Variation
individuals   research

Two or more traits   Correlation
in many individuals   research

One individual in   Psychography
many traits

Two or more   Comparation
individuals in many   research
traits

Figure 5.1. A Conceptual Framework for the Study of Personality Differences
SOURCE: Adapted from Stern, 1911.

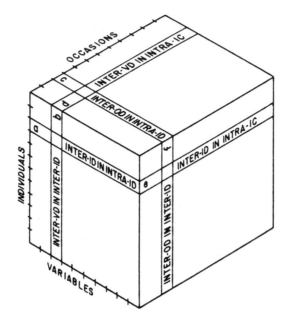

Figure 5.2. A Conceptual Framework for the Study of Personality Development
SOURCE: Buss, 1974, Figure 2. Reprinted with permission of the American Psychological Association.

advocated a "person-oriented view" that treats individuals as complex organized systems. These two perspectives on personality can be traced back to the seminal work of Stern (1911) on the methodological foundation of differential psychology. Stern (1911) proposed a common conceptual framework for the study of personality differences that treats both views as complementary (see Figure 5.1).

Stern (1911) assumed that individuals A, B, . . . , Z can be each assigned to traits a, b, . . . , z. Stern (1911) then distinguished between four "disciplines of differential psychology." *Variation research* studies the interindividual variation of one trait in many individuals. *Correlation research* compares two traits among many individuals. *Psychography* studies the variation of many traits within one individual. And *comparation research* compares two individuals in terms of many traits. Thus, Stern (1911) treated individuals and traits in a completely symmetric fashion. The first two variable-oriented "disciplines" can be transformed into the last two person-oriented disciplines by interchanging individuals and traits. Later, Cattell (1946) extended this schema to a three-dimensional "covariation chart" by adding another dimension of "occasions" (situations or time points). This model was used by Buss (1974) in his discussion of different developmental questions (see Figure 5.2).

Within this three-dimensional model, two nondevelopmental and four developmental questions can be asked that are visualized in Figure 5.2:

(a) Interindividual differences in intraindividual differences (this is Stern's comparative research);

(b) intervariable differences in interindividual differences (this is Stern's correlation research);

(c) interoccasion differences in intraindividual differences (e.g., the cross-age stability of the personality profile of one person);

(d) intervariable differences in intraindividual changes (e.g., the correlation between two variables over time within one individual);

(e) interindividual differences in intraindividual changes (e.g., the correlation between two individuals' change patterns in one variable);

(f) interoccasion differences in interindividual differences (e.g., the cross-age stability of one trait).

Although the schema of Buss (1974) can be further extended by incorporating situational variations (e.g., Ozer, 1986), it suffices as a framework for describing the development of personality both from a variable- and a person-oriented point of view. In this chapter, we will discuss questions of the type (c), (e), and (f) because these involve both interindividual differences and developmental change.

In empirical applications of this approach to personality differences, data of many individuals are sampled for many variables. It is important to note, however, that this is not sufficient for a study of *personality* differences. Before a variable qualifies as a personality trait, the *short-term stability* of the measurement must be demonstrated. Within the variable-oriented view, the interindividual differences within the variable under study must be stable over an interval of some days or weeks (correlation research sensu Stern), and within the person-oriented view, the intraindividual differences within persons must also show a high short-term stability (comparative research sensu Stern). If this requirement is not met, the assessments tap fluctuating psychological states rather than traits, and the long-term stability of inter- and intraindividual differences must be low simply because of their low short-term stability (see Asendorpf & Weinert, 1990, for a more detailed discussion of this requirement).

In the remainder of this chapter the questions of continuity and stability are separately discussed from a variable-oriented and from a person-oriented point of view.

The Variable-Oriented Point of View

CONTINUITY OF TRAITS

Traditionally it is assumed without empirical investigation that a certain operationalization of a trait in terms of ratings or behavioral observation refers to the same underlying *construct* at different ages (behavior is observable but personality traits are not; they are always inferred from judgments or behavioral observations, see MacCorquodale & Meehl, 1948, for the distinction between constructs and empirical indicators, and Cronbach & Meehl, 1955, for the construct validity of the operationalization of a construct). Thus it is assumed that the operationalization at both measurement points refers to the same construct.

Recent advances in the measurement of intelligence have made psychologists painfully aware of the fact that this is an assumption that is not always met and that merits more careful investigation. Traditionally, intelligence among infants and very young children has been operationalized by a battery of tests in which the subject's reactions to certain stimulating situations are observed (e.g., the Bayley Scales of Infant Development; Bayley, 1969). The correlations between these early IQ tests and preschool children's IQ tests such as the Stanford-Binet have been significant but very low (around .30, see Kopp & McCall, 1980). Recently, however, studies have found surprisingly high correlations between highly aggregated measures of infants' visual attention and preschool IQ (e.g., .60 between visual attention at 6 months of age and the Stanford-Binet IQ at 3 years; Bornstein & Sigman, 1986; Rose, Feldman, & Wallace, 1988).

This discrepancy between the old and the new stability data for tests—that all are considered to measure the same underlying intellectual capacity—suggests that the old tests of early intelligence were less valid operationalizations than the new ones. Therefore it would be misleading to interpret the low stability of interindividual differences found in the earlier studies of intelligence as indicating that intelligence is an unstable trait in infancy and very early childhood. Instead, the old infant intelligence tests measured *a different construct* than the Stanford-Binet test. Although correlations of .60 are very respectable, even the new operationalization of infants' IQ could perhaps be improved by other testing procedures that might lead to even higher stabilities.

The measurement of early intelligence is particularly difficult because intelligence in infancy cannot be operationalized in the same way as intelligence in childhood or adulthood. Kagan (1980) draws an important distinction between the "homotypic" and the "heterotypic" continuity of a trait. A trait is characterized by homotypic continuity if it can be operationalized by the same empirical indicators at different ages, whereas heterotypic continuity of a trait requires different operationalizations at different ages. Intelligence is an example for heterotypic continuity. Kagan (1980) also distinguished heterotypic continuity from discontinuity where a construct applies to one point in time but not to the other. The distinction between heterotypic continuity and discontinuity is a matter of theoretical decision rather than of empirical investigation because in empirical studies constructs are always operationalized in terms of some observables.

But even if it seems to make sense to operationalize a trait in the same way at different ages, this may be an erroneous assumption. I have recently suggested a new method by which the (homotypic) continuity of a trait can be empirically studied independently of its stability (Asendorpf, in press b). First, the trait is defined by some criterion measure that is based on judgments or on behavioral observations. This criterion measure is then correlated with the frequency or intensity of many behaviors that are sampled from a relevant behavioral domain. For example, if we are interested in aggressiveness, we should sample behavior in social-interactional situations where some people react aggressively and others not. A crucial point is that these behaviors are not exclusively selected for high correlations with the criterion measure. Instead, behaviors are sampled "representatively," that is, in a way that represents the whole continuum from very valid to completely invalid behaviors. Because it is often difficult to define the domain of behaviors from which a representative sample is to be obtained, the behaviors should be sampled at least systematically by criteria that are independent of the target trait as well as of the age of the target persons.

TABLE 5.1 Behavioral Correlates of Shyness in Children and Adults (adapted from Asendorpf, in press a)

	88 Children Age 4 yrs		70 Students Age 19–32 yrs	
Behavioral measures	r^a	*rank*[b]	r^a	*rank*[b]
Latency to first spontaneous utterance	.64***	1	.46***	1
Percent speaking alone	−.55***	17	−.40***	17
Mean lenght speaking alone	−.14	10	−.11	10
Percent listening	−.21	14	−.09	9
Mean length listening	.17	5	.07	5
Percent silence	.55***	3	.41***	2
Mean length silence	.59***	2	.38**	3
Percent double talk[c]	−.40***	16	−.33**	15
Mean length double talk	−.15	13	−.14	14
Percent gazing during speaking	−.09	8	−.13	13
Mean length gazing during speaking	−.01	7	−.07	8
Percent gazing during silence	−.35**	15	−.35**	16
Mean length gazing during silence	−.11	9	.04	7
Mean length gaze aversion during speaking	−.15	12	.05	6
Mean length gaze aversion during silence	.39***	4	.31*	4
Percent self-adaptors	−.14	11	−.11	12
Mean length self-adaptors	.16	6	−.11	11

NOTE: a. Spearman correlations with parental scale (children) or with shyness scale (students).
b. Rank of correlation among all behaviors.
c. Percentage of observation time when both partners were speaking at the same time.
* $p < .05$ ** $p < .01$ *** $p < .001$

In this way we obtain for each point in time a rank-order of the validity coefficients of the various behaviors for the trait criterion. The temporal stability of this rank-order reflects the (homotypic) continuity of the trait. If it is high, the trait refers to the same behaviors at both points in time. If the stability of the rank-order is low, the operationalization of the trait refers to different behaviors. In this case, the operationalization of the trait might be improved by changing it in a way that increases continuity (see Asendorpf, in press b, for a more detailed discussion).

In a first application of this method I have demonstrated a high continuity for the trait of shyness between preschool age and adulthood (see Asendorpf, in press b, for details). Shyness was operationalized for 4-year-olds by a parental scale and for university students by a self-rating scale. These criterion measures of shyness were correlated with children's or students' behavior in an encounter with an unfamiliar stranger. The same 17 behaviors were coded for both children and adults, and each behavior was correlated with the criterion measure of shyness in each age group. Table 5.1 presents the rank-order of the validity coefficients of the 17 behaviors for 4-year-olds and for university students.

The rank-orders were highly similar; a Spearman correlation of .84 was found between the two rank-orders. This high correlation could have been inflated, however, if the differences between the short-term stabilities of the behaviors were also stable between the two age groups. But the rank-orders of the short-term stabilities of the behaviors were not significantly stable between childhood and adulthood, and when the validity coefficients of Table 5.1 were each corrected for their age-specific short-term stability (correction for attenuation), the rank-orders of the corrected validity coefficients still correlated .84 between childhood and adulthood. Thus preschool children and university students expressed their shyness toward strangers by a very similar pattern of conversational behavior. This finding provides a firm empirical base for an operationalization of shyness by the same behavioral criteria at different ages.

STABILITY OF TRAITS

When trait continuity has been demonstrated, we can ask the question: Are the interindividual differences in the trait stable between different ages? Personality psychologists have a tendency to expect high stabilities because in this case they can ignore developmental considerations. From a developmental perspective, instability is the more interesting case because then some people of the population under consideration have changed their relative rank-order which, in turn, indicates that *differential development* has taken place: Some people have developed differently from others.

Mean Stability

Traditionally, trait stability has been assessed in terms of the *mean stability of the individual deviation scores* in a sample of persons. The deviation score of a person is obtained by subtracting the person's trait score from the sample mean of the trait and by then dividing this difference by the standard deviation in the sample. These z

scores have per definition a sample mean of 0 and a standard deviation of 1. After this transformation, all information about the mean and the variance of the trait scores in the sample at a given point in time is lost. This procedure guarantees that any comparison of the individual deviation scores across age is completely independent of change phenomena that affect all persons, such as an increasing mean or an increasing variance with increasing age.

Mean stability between Time 1 and Time 2 is in most cases assessed by a Pearson correlation between the trait scores at Time 1 and 2. If the trait scores show odd distributional characteristics, such as extreme outliers or very skewed distributions, Pearson correlations may be severely biased, however. For example, if the distributions are skewed in the same direction at both time points, Pearson correlations overestimate the degree of stability, and if the distributions are skewed in different directions at the two points in time, Pearson correlations will underestimate the degree of stability in the sample. In this case, it is better to compute rank-order Spearman correlations that measure the stability of the rank-order of the trait scores. They are robust against skewness or outlier problems.

Mean stability is high if most persons do not change in their deviation from the sample mean; it is zero if the deviation scores at Time 1 show no linear relation to the deviation scores at Time 2; and theoretically there could be "negative mean stability" in the sense that persons systematically "switch around the sample mean" (high scorers become low scorers and vice versa); negative stabilities are rarely found, of course. Thus mean stability is identical with the absence of differential change in the sample.

It is important to note that mean stability is a characteristic of a *sample,* not of a trait. Therefore, mean trait stability is quite sensitive to the sampling of individuals. The critical variable here is the interindividual variance of the trait. If it is increased by selecting only individuals with very high or very low scores, mean stability is also increased, and the mean stability of the trait in the whole population of interest is overestimated. On the other hand, if high scorers or low scorers are systematically omitted in the sample, the mean stability in the population will be underestimated. If the interindividual variance in the population is known, it is possible to correct statistically the stability coefficient (Thorndike's range correction procedure; Thorndike, 1947).

In developmental studies, sometimes bottom or ceiling effects seriously distort stability coefficients. Imagine that we are interested in the question whether mathematical ability is a trait that is stable between kindergarten and Grade 2. We operationalize mathematical ability by a test that contains items such as "how much is 5 + 9?" In kindergarten we will very likely find a bottom effect, that is, children will rarely solve any item correctly. In Grade 1 the test may be quite appropriate to distinguish between children. But in Grade 2 we will very likely find a ceiling effect, that is, most children will solve all items correctly. Because of the restriction in range and because the distributions in kindergarten and in Grade 2 are skewed in opposite directions, the stability of the test scores will be very low between kindergarten and Grade 2. The test was not adequate as a measure of interindividual differences in mathematical ability both for kindergarten age and Grade 2 although it may be quite appropriate for Grade 1. There are no statistical tricks to circumvent this problem.

Two principles of the mean long-term stability of traits. In recent years, longitudinal studies of adult personality have reported impressively high correlations between self- or other-ratings of personality that were assessed after long retest intervals (up to 45 years; see, e.g., J. Block, 1977; Conley, 1984, 1985; Costa & McCrae, 1988; West & Graziano, 1989). For example, Conley (1984) reported stabilities of .65 for extraversion and .62 for neuroticism over a 19-year period; over a 45-year period during which the assessment instrument was changed, correlations of .26 for extraversion and of .33 for neuroticism were found.

The results of these longitudinal studies of adults' personality traits suggest a first principle: The longer the retest interval is between assessments, the less stable are the observed interindividual differences. Conley (1984) has demonstrated that this rule of thumb can be expressed more precisely. In a meta-analysis of 60 longitudinal studies of personality and self-opinion he showed that the decreasing stability coefficients with increasing retest intervals could be well approximated by power functions of the type $C = Rs^n$, where C is the observed stability coefficient, R the reliability of the measuring instrument, s the annual stability, and n the number of years between the two assessments on which C is based.

For example, the 19-year and 45-year stabilities of .62 and .33 for neuroticism can be approximated by the function $C = 0.90 \cdot 0.98^n$ that yields estimates of .61 and .36, respectively. Thus the true annual stability of neuroticism would be estimated as .98 by this method.

This formula rests upon the assumption that *systematic* instability (the instability that remains if the unreliability of measurement has been controlled) is due to the continuous accumulation of small changes of personality that occur with a constant rate throughout the whole observation period.

This is quite a bold hypothesis at the individual level, but at the sample level it leads to fairly good approximations of mean stability over retest intervals of varying lengths because mean stability applies to aggregates of individuals. Of course there exist strong interindividual differences in personality changes for certain periods of time, but they appear to cancel each other out to a great extent. What remains observable at the sample level is a rather robust index of mean stability that—if standardized for a certain retest interval such as one year—characterizes personality traits. For example, on the basis of 60 longitudinal studies of adults' personality, Conley (1984) estimated the annual true stability of intelligence as measured by IQ tests as .995, of self-rated extraversion and neuroticism as .98, and of self-opinion (mainly measures of life satisfaction) as .93.

A second principle concerning stability stems from studies of the development of interindividual differences during infancy, childhood, and adolescence: The younger subjects are, the lower is the stability of interindividual differences over a retest interval of a constant length (see, e.g., Brim & Kagan, 1980; Digman, 1989; Giuganino & Hindley, 1982). Stability is low during infancy and increases progressively until it reaches its maximum in adulthood. For example, predictions of preschool children's IQ from traditional measures of infants' IQ have rarely overcome a .30 barrier (Kopp & McCall, 1980), whereas Wilson (1983) found a continuous increase of the uncorrected one-year stabilities of IQ from .74 (age 2-3) to .90 (age 8-9).

Many different factors contribute to this *stabilization* of interindividual differences during development. A first factor that should always be controlled is the increasing reliability of measurement with increasing age. Particularly in infancy it is difficult to assess behavior with a high short-term reliability although this problem can be solved by aggregation over many observations (see Epstein, 1979, 1986, for the merits of aggregation). But even if age differences in the reliability of measurement are controlled by correction for attenuation, in most cases the corrected stability coefficients will still increase with increasing age.

A second factor that may sometimes contribute to the stabilization of interindividual differences is often neglected in discussions of stability: an *increasing construct validity* of the operationalization of the trait. An example has been already discussed above: the increasing stabilization of intelligence. After the new infant IQ tests were introduced that measure intelligence in terms of attention to visual stimuli, the stabilization effect was found to be much smaller than before; instead of an increase of the three-year stabilities from roughly .30 (1-4 years) to .80 (5-8 years), the new data show only an increase from .60 to .80. This difference suggests that the strong stabilization effect found in the older studies of early intelligence was to a great extent due to the fact that the old infant IQ tests measured something different from the preschool IQ tests, that is, that the operationalization of intelligence was not continuous. It may well be that construct validity increases with increasing age for most traits, and that this factor contributes to the increasing stabilization of traits.

A third, also often neglected factor contributing to the increasing stability of interindividual differences is an increasing *continuity* of the *construct* underlying the observed behaviors. Many personality traits refer to differences in the functioning of neural systems or to differences in acquired knowledge. Before these systems have begun to function or before this knowledge has been acquired during development, the trait simply does not exist, and it makes no sense to assess it. And if the nature of the trait changes due to changes in gene activity, experience, or their interactions, this discontinuity of the construct will severely limit stability.

Very often increasing stabilization is explained by the differential accumulation of experience. Different people learn different things; they gain different knowledge that, in turn, influences their personality in different ways. For example, differences among children's achievement in intelligence tests may stabilize with increasing age because different children grow up in environments that vary in terms of intellectual stimulation.

Less often it is recognized that this line of reasoning rests on the implicit assumption that either the environmental differences themselves are stable, or that they are stable at least during the first years of life and that later instabilities are no longer very important because the early environmental influences on personality have become crystallized in traits that are highly resistant to change. These assumptions are questionable, though, and have rarely been studied empirically. So far studies of stability have focused too much upon individuals and have neglected to study the differential *development of environments* (see, however, Chapter 6, this volume).

Another factor that may contribute to increasing stability is based on the same accumulation principle but is less often considered by personality psychologists. Differential genetic activity also accumulates during ontogeny and is crystallized in stable neuroanatomical structures and neurophysiological functions (see Plomin, 1986, for an excellent overview of human developmental behavioral genetics). Many personality psychologists nowadays still appear to share the naive view that if genotypes affect behavior they do this "directly" and "continuously." But it is not the genotype that affects behavior, it is the genes' *activity* that sets in motion a long process leading from the regulation of protein synthesis via enzymatic regulation via neuronal system functioning to behavior. There is no simple, direct causal link between genes and behavior.

Furthermore, many genes of the human genome seem *never* to be active during the life course, and consequently do not affect behavior, and many genes are "switched on" and "switched off" during ontogeny and hence may give rise to interindividual differences if these genes or the timing of their activity differ among individuals (see Plomin, 1986). Despite the fact that the genotype is constant throughout life, gene activity, and hence genetic effects on behavior, are highly variable across the life span. Therefore it is not surprising that estimates of genetic influence on interindividual differences vary widely according to the age of the subjects under study (see Plomin, 1986, for empirical evidence). The influence of gene activity on personality is as complex and as long a process of accumulation as the influence of differential experience on personality.

A last factor contributing to the stabilization of individual differences has been *en vogue* among personality psychologists for many years now: The active selection and shaping of environments by individuals according to their personality. Different people approach and avoid different situations, and if they can they also try to change their environment according to their needs and interests (see Scarr & McCartney, 1983; Snyder & Ickes, 1985; Sternberg, 1985). With increasing age, people become more able to control their environment according to their individual preferences, and this increasing personality-environment fit may contribute to the stability of interindividual differences.

The problem with these interpretations of the observed increasing stabilization of personality is that they are based on principles that may also account for a *decreasing* stability with increasing age. When children grow older, they leave their family and make new experiences; this change might destabilize experience-based interindividual differences. The effects of genotypic differences do not always accumulate smoothly because new genes may be switched on differentially during development, thereby destabilizing interindividual differences. Finally, when people are suddenly freed of environmental pressures and become able to control their environment to at least some extent, this may also destabilize interindividual differences. Thus it remains essentially an *empirical question* how much each of these possible mechanisms, and their interactions, contribute to the stabilization of personality traits.

Differential Stability of Traits

So far our discussion of the long-term stability of personality traits has been concerned only with the aggregate level: How high is the *average* stability in a sample of individuals? In this section we ask the question whether *interindividual differences in the stability of the individual deviation scores* exist, how these differences can be measured, and whether these differences reflect meaningful psychological characteristics. Only if stability equals +1 or −1 will no interindividual differences in intraindividual change exist; in the realistic case of medium stability, individuals may vary widely in terms of the stability of their deviation scores. As personality psychologists we should therefore move beyond mean stability by asking how *differential stability* comes about.

For example, when we try to explain an observed instability at the sample level by the principles of an unstable environment, differential gene activity, or limited opportunities of controlling one's environment, we may carry the analysis one step further by asking questions about the differential stability in the observed sample. Did subjects differ in the degree to which their environment was stable, and does the stability of their environment predict the amount of their individual stability? Did subjects differ in their gene activity, and do these differences predict the amount of their individual stability? Could subjects control their environment to different degrees, and do these differences predict the amount of their individual stability?

Thus if we want to *explain* instability we must relate some external variables (e.g., the stability of the environment) to the *individual stabilities themselves,* not only to a summary score such as a correlation. But how can we properly measure these individual stabilities? How can the correlation be decomposed into the individual contributions to this overall measure of stability?

Personality psychologists as well as developmental psychologists interested in differential development have devoted surprisingly little attention to this question, probably because so far research has been more concerned with describing stability than with explaining instability. But even a decent description of stability needs more than a correlation.

I have proposed to regard the score

$$i_{12} = 1 - \frac{(z_1 - z_2)^2}{2}$$

as a measure of *individual stability,* where z_1, z_2 are the individual deviation scores at the two measurement points. Simple computation shows that the population mean of these scores is *identical with the correlation r_{12} between the two assessments.*[1] Furthermore, the individual stability of a person is identical with the *intra*individual variance of that person between the two z-transformed assessments subtracted from 1. Thus this approach is consistent with the notions of both the correlation and the intraindividual variance. The statistical properties of this coefficient of individual stability are delineated in Asendorpf (1990b), and the major assumptions underlying this approach and possible alternatives are discussed in Asendorpf (in press a).

This coefficient of individual stability has the undesirable property that its distribution tends to be strongly skewed to the left. This skewness poses a problem if we want to correlate the individual stability scores with some external variable. This problem can be solved in two different ways. Either the individual stability scores are transformed in a way that yields a fairly normal distribution in most cases (see Asendorpf, 1990b, in press a, for details). Or the individual stability coefficients are treated at the level of an ordinal scale. In this case, the individual stability score is simply the absolute difference between the two deviation scores: $i_{12} = |z_1 - z_2|$. Spearman correlations can then be computed between these individual stability scores and external variables. So far, applications of these two approaches to the measurement of individual stability have yielded very similar results.

The following example illustrates how the individual stability scores can be used in empirical studies of personality development (see Asendorpf, in press a, for more details). Children's individual stability in their inhibition to peers was related to the stability of their extrafamilial social network and—as a control condition—to the stability of their family. It was expected that major changes in children's extrafamilial social relationships would destabilize their inhibition toward peers. In some cases, inhibition might increase because of the confrontation with new, unfamiliar peers, but other children's inhibition might decrease if their inhibition had been primarily due to the social rejection or neglect by particular peers in their former extrafamilial environment. On the other hand, a change in the composition of children's family was not expected to have an impact on their inhibition toward peers (see Asendorpf, 1990a, for empirical evidence for the existence of different, domain-specific kinds of inhibition among children).

Every year from age 5 to 8, children's main caregiver was asked to check a list of major critical life events if these had happened to the child during the last year. Three of these events indicated major changes in children's extrafamilial social network: change of school, the family moved into a new home at least 5 km away from the old one, and close friends of the child moved away from town. Three other events indicated a change in the family environment: a person living together with the child in the same household died, such a person left the household (e.g., father left after divorce), and birth of a sibling. Furthermore, children's main caregiver rated the child's inhibition toward peers on four 7-point scales. Because these four ratings per child were highly consistent (Cronbach *alpha*s varied between .86 and .94), they were averaged, yielding one parental inhibition rating per year.

Table 5.2 contains the correlations between the number of critical life events of either type for a particular year of assessment and the individual stability scores of children's inhibition as judged by their caregiver for this one-year period.

Table 5.2 indicates that changes in children's extrafamilial environment were associated with unstable inhibition scores whereas changes in children's family did not affect the stability of their inhibition toward peers.

These correlational analyses were supported by one-tailed *t* tests comparing the (transformed) individual stability scores of children

TABLE 5.2 Correlations Between Individual Stability in Inhibition and the Stability of the Extra- and Intrafamilial Environment (adapted from Asendorpf, in press b)

		Change of environment			
		Extrafamilial		Intrafamilial	
Age interval	N	i [a]	ti [b]	i [a]	ti [b]
4-5 years	83	−.18	−.23*	.07	.06
5-6 years	94	−.24*	−.19*	−.08	−.10
6-7 years	90	−.23*	−.27*	−.04	−.00

NOTE: The change of either type of environment was assessed by the number of environmental changes (0-3 for each age interval).
a. Spearman correlations with individual stability scores $i_{1\,2}$.
b. Pearson correlations with transformed individual stability scores $ti_{1\,2}$ (see Asendorpf, 1990b, for the transformation).
* $p < .07$.

whose environment changed with those whose environment did not change. For all three intervals of observation, children with a stable extrafamilial environment had significantly higher transformed individual stability scores for inhibition than children whose extrafamilial environment did change. Furthermore, a comparable analysis of effects of the stability of children's family did not reveal any significant effects.

All in all, these analyses demonstrate that we can go beyond correlations if we are interested in the longitudinal stability of personality traits. The individual stability of particular persons can be assessed and can be related to external variables such as the stability of the environment.

BEYOND STABILITY

Psychologists interested in personality development can move beyond the analysis of the stability of traits by asking questions about the *direction* of change. Analyses of stability at the level of the sample or at the level of the individual are insensitive to differences in the direction of change. They only provide information about the *amount* of change. In some cases this is quite appropriate because the amount of change is more important than its direction (e.g., when environmental instability is correlated with the individual instability of subjects' traits). In other cases it is not appropriate because clear hypotheses exist about the direction of change (e.g., when children's inhibition in class is related to preceding experiences of being re-jected by peers; in this case, it is to be expected that more frequent re-jection leads to more inhibition—a directional hypothesis).

If directional hypotheses exist about interindividual differences in intraindividual change, analyzing individual stabilities is not appro-priate. Instead, *individual change scores* should be analyzed. Simple difference scores are to be preferred to residualized change scores in most cases (see Rogosa, Brandt, & Zimowski, 1982, for a discussion). If more than two measurement points exist, the reliability of the indi-vidual change scores can be evaluated without a parallel measure-ment, and if more than three measurement points exist, nonlinear individual patterns of change can be analyzed (see Alsaker, this volume).

The Person-Oriented Point of View

CONTINUITY OF PROFILES

In analogy to the discussion of the stability of traits we can first ask whether a personality profile in terms of the intraindividual differences in many traits has the same meaning at different ages. One approach to this continuity question is to trace the continuity of profiles back to the continuity of the correlational structure of the traits upon which the profile is based. For example, if the vari-ous subtests of an intelligence test show the same intercorrelations at different ages, intraindividual differences between subtests can be considered to convey the same meaning. If, on the other hand, two subtests that were only loosely correlated at Time 1 show a very high correlation at Time 2, intraindividual differences be-tween these two subtests are likely to be much smaller on average at Time 2 than at Time 1. In this case, the stability of the individ-ual profiles will be attenuated because of the change in the correla-tional structure of the subtests.

This approach to the continuity of personality was first presented by Emmerich (1964), who defined continuity as the temporal con-stancy of the factorial structure of a large item pool. Emmerich (1964) interpreted changes in the percentage of variance accounted for by a particular factor as evidence for the emergence or decline of this factor during development. More straightforward are recent approaches of testing the temporal constancy of a factor structure by confirmatory factor analysis or structural modeling techniques (see Hertzog & Schaie, 1986, for an application of LISREL to the continuity of the factor structure of intelligence in adulthood).

In the case of intelligence profiles the continuity question is rather easy to handle because the means and standard deviations of the various subtests are identical per definition (usually expressed in terms of the IQ norm, that is, a mean of 100 and a standard deviation of 15). If individual profiles are based on trait measures that differ in their means or standard deviations, age differences in these means or standard deviations can seriously affect the stability of these profiles (see Epstein, 1983). Thus if we are interested in the stability of interindividual differences in the organization of personality and if we want to study these differences by an analysis of profiles based on many trait measurements, we should first standardize all trait measures (e.g., by a z-transformation). If we do not do this, we will confound universal developmental trends in the various traits with the stability of the interindividual differences in the personality profiles.

More complicated is the case of the Q-sort method. In the Q-sort method, judges rank-order many traits in terms of their saliency (typicality) for a particular person (Stephenson, 1953). For example, in applications of the California Child Q-set of J. H. Block and J. Block (1980), judges sort 100 personality traits of children into nine categories of saliency for a particular child ("least characteristic"-"most characteristic"). This "idiographic" sorting procedure results in an intraindividual profile. This profile is usually standardized by asking judges to assign the same number of traits to each category of saliency (forced equal distribution, for example used in the California Child Q-set) or by asking them to produce a quasi-normal distribution with more traits in the middle categories than in the extreme categories (forced quasi-normal distribution, for example used in the California Adult Q-set; J. Block, 1971). A forced equal distribution has the advantage of maximizing the intraindividual variance.

This *intraindividual standardization* of the Q-sort profiles causes two problems. First, the mean and the variance of each profile is identical across persons or ages but the means and the standard deviations of the various traits vary across traits and ages. Therefore the stability of individual profiles over time confounds necessarily universal developmental changes in the saliency of certain traits in the organization of personality with the stability of the individual deviation from the average organization of personality. This problem could be solved by z-transforming the saliency scores of each trait in the sample (the same strategy was discussed above for profiles based on non-standardized traits). However, this procedure appears to be odd because the Q-sorts were generated from an intraindividual perspective in the first place.

The second problem caused by the forced distribution of Q-sorts is that the various traits of the Q-sort item pool are intrinsically negatively related (placing one item in a category of saliency makes it less likely that another item is placed in the same category). Therefore the temporal constancy of the factor structure of a Q-sort item pool will be inflated, and analyses of continuity that rest upon a factor-analytic approach will overestimate continuity.

Because of these two problems—caused by the forced intraindividual distribution—the stability of the profile of a particular person or the mean profile stability in a sample is affected by the continuity of the average personality pattern in the sample. If, however, we are interested in *interindividual differences* in the stability of Q-sort profiles, no problems arise because these interindividual differences are independent of the mean level of stability.

STABILITY OF PROFILES

Mean Stability of Profiles

Besides the problem of confounding continuity and stability, the interpretation of the mean level of profile stability is affected by the problem that the short-term stability of the profiles is often rather low; therefore no high longitudinal stability can be expected. If profiles are based on trait measures, the short-term individual profile stabilities are often much lower than the retest correlations of the traits because they are attenuated by positive intercorrelations of the traits. In fact, the short-term profile stability R is $R = (r_{ii} - r_{ij})/(1 - r_{ij})$ where r_{ii} is the mean short-term stability of the traits upon which the profile is based, and r_{ij} is the mean intercorrelation of all these traits. For example, if the subtests of an intelligence test have a mean short-term stability of .70 and a mean intercorrelation of .30, the short-term stability of the intelligence profile is .57.

If Q-sort profiles are investigated, the short-term stability of the individual profiles is also usually quite low. For teacher Q-sorts of a German short version of the California Child Q-set (Göttert & Asendorpf, 1989) I found 3-week retest correlations that varied between .28 and .86 in a sample of 45 5-year-old children, with a median of .64. The short-term stability of Q-sort profiles can be increased if the sorts of many raters per child are averaged.

The long-term stabilities of intelligence profiles are rather poor because the long-term stabilities of the various IQ subtests are much lower than the long-term stability of the overall IQ score. For Q-sort profiles respectable long-term stabilities have been found, given the rather low short-term stabilities. Asendorpf and van Aken (in press) reported median 2-year stabilities of .43 for 151 German children who were judged at ages 4 and 6 by their teachers, .47 for 80 Dutch children who were judged by their teachers at ages 10 and 12, and .61 for the same stabilities based on Q-sorts of the mothers. Ozer and Gjerde (1989) reported 3- or 4-year stabilities that varied between .52 for children and .71 for adults. In this study, the Q-sorts of at least three different judges were averaged per person, yielding a more reliable profile.

Differential stability of Q-sort profiles. More interesting than these average stabilities in a sample is the fact that in all Q-sort studies great *interindividual differences* in the profile stability were found. Asendorpf and van Aken (in press) found individual profile stabilities that varied between at least −.09 and .83, and Ozer and Gjerde (1989) found for four age comparisons and both genders individual stabilities that varied at least between −.01 and .80. What factors contribute to this high variability of the stability of individual Q-sort patterns?

Some of the variance reported by Asendorpf and van Aken (in press) and Ozer and Gjerde (1989) may be due to differences among observers rather than to differences among the judged individuals. These differences in perception may be related to the accuracy of observers, but they may also reflect meaningful differences in the situational context in which the behavior is observed, or in the focus on particular aspects of behavior. If a person is evaluated by different observers at different points in time, differences among observers will necessarily cause some variation in the consistency of the personality descriptions of that person. If individuals are evaluated by the same observers at both points in time, a similar though probably somewhat smaller effect stems from temporal changes in the accuracy of the observers' perception of the individual. Thus the variability of stability will be overestimated in both cases by observer effects. These effects can be minimized by aggregating the personality descriptions of many observers for each individual.

Because Ozer and Gjerde (1989) used at least three observers per subject, it is very likely that much of the variance of the stability coefficients in this study could not be attributed to different perceptions. Instead, it reflects differences among subjects' stability of personality. Ozer and Gjerde (1989) tried to approach these differences by a gender-specific cluster analysis of the four stability coefficients obtained from each subject. These clusters describe different patterns of stability through the 3-18-year age range (e.g., always stable or increasingly stable). For both males and females, the largest cluster consisted of subjects with a continual high stability of personality. These subjects differed from the rest of the sample in terms of their most characteristic and least characteristic traits. Although these typical traits changed from age to age and were somewhat different for males and females, stable subjects were always described as having more culturally desirable traits (e.g., high intellectual capacity), and less undesirable traits (e.g., fearfulness); see Hampson, Goldberg, and John (1987), for a discussion of the cultural desirability of personality traits. J. Block (1971) reported a similar finding for another sample followed from junior through senior high school.

Asendorpf and van Aken (in press) replicated this finding by a somewhat different methodology. They compared extreme groups of very stable and very unstable children with a control group of children with average profile stability. All traits that were significantly more typical of stable children than for control children were culturally desirable traits, whereas all characteristics that were significantly more typical of unstable children were undesirable ones.

This finding suggests that children who deviate from societal expectations of what a "good child" is, meet a continual pressure to change, whereas children who confirm to the prototype of a desirable child meet less pressure. Thus the relation between cultural desirability and stability of personality seems to reflect the socialization pressure that children meet during their development.

Furthermore, Asendorpf and van Aken (in press) demonstrated that the individual stability of Q-sort profiles could also be predicted by the child's *ego-resiliency,* that is, the ability of flexibly responding to

TABLE 5.3 Prediction and Retrodiction of the Stability of Q-Sort Profiles by Ego-Resiliency (Adapted from Asendorpf & van Aken, in press)

Stabilities	N	Ego-resiliency score			
		T1	*M1*	*T2*	*M2*
Teacher, age 4-6	151	.57***	—	.29***	—
Teacher, age 10-12	80	.38***	.23*	.47***	.33**
Mother, age 10-12	87	.25*	.49***	.31**	.36***

NOTES: Reported are Pearson correlations between Pearson correlations.
T1 = Teacher Q-sort, first assessment
M1 = Mother Q-sort, first assessment
T2 = Teacher Q-sort, second assessment
M2 = Mother Q-sort, second assessment
$* p < .05$ $** p < .01$ $*** p < .001$

environmental demands as well as the ability of controlling one's environment to some extent (see J. H. Block & J. Block, 1980, for a discussion of this construct). A child's ego-resiliency was measured by correlating the child's Q-sort profile with the profile of a "prototypical ego-resilient child" (see J. H. Block & J. Block, 1980). A high positive correlation indicated that the child's overall personality pattern was similar to the personality of an ego-resilient child; a high negative correlation indicated that the child's personality was very different from that prototype. Table 5.3 presents the correlations between these ego-resiliency scores and the stability of the Q-sort profiles.

In all cases, significant positive correlations were found between children's ego-resiliency and the stability of their Q-sort profile, even if one of these two measures was obtained from the child's teacher and the other one from the child's mother. Thus the relation between ego-resiliency and stability cannot be a judgment artifact. Instead, it seems to reflect the fact that ego-resilient children can buffer their personality against environmental influences by selecting and shaping their environment according to their needs whereas nonresilient children are more a victim of their environment.

Trying to explain stability differences by differences in cultural desirability or ego-resiliency is not the whole story, though. Stability of Q-sort profiles always means consistency of the view that important referent persons (parents, teachers) have. It is not unlikely that a high consistency of this view promotes ego-resiliency because the social environment is more predictable.

Finally, an important hidden variable may simultaneously increase profile stability, cultural desirability of personality, and ego-resiliency: the stability of the overall environment. Children who grow up in a generally stable, predictable environment may find it easier to adapt to particular changes in environmental demands. Consequently, they may act more resilient, may be more stable in their personality, and may be better able to keep up with cultural expectations of what a good child is like.

These recent findings about the nature of interindividual differences in the stability of personality patterns as well as about the link between environmental stability and the individual stability of single traits (see above) suggest that the differential stability of personality is an interesting although largely unexplored area of psychological investigation. The lack of a high stability of interindividual differences in a trait or a personality profile is not, as Mischel (1968) has suggested, a problem for personality psychology. Instead, meaningful interindividual differences in intraindividual change seem to exist that provide a valuable source of information about personality development.

Note

1. The mean of the individual stabilities is only identical with the correlation if the correlation is computed with n as a denominator in the formula $r = 1/n \cdot \Sigma z_1 \cdot z_2$. Statistical packages use the formula for the best sample estimate of the correlation in the population (with $n - 1$ as a denominator). In this case, the mean individual stability deviates slightly from the correlation depending on the proportion $n/(n - 1)$.

References

Allport, G. W. (1937). *Personality: A psychological interpretation.* New York: Holt & Co.

Asendorpf, J. B. (1990a). Development of inhibition during childhood: Evidence for situational specificity and a two-factor model. *Developmental Psychology, 26,* 721-730.

Asendorpf, J. B. (1990b). The measurement of individual consistency. *Methodika, 4,* 1-23.

Asendorpf, J. B. (in press a). Beyond stability: Predicting interindividual differences in intraindividual change. *European Journal of Personality.*

Asendorpf, J. B. (in press b). A Brunswikean approach to trait continuity: Application to shyness. *Journal of Personality.*

Asendorpf, J. B., & van Aken, M. (in press). Correlates of the temporal consistency of personality patterns in childhood. *Journal of Personality.*

Asendorpf, J. B., & Weinert, F. E. (1990). Stability of patterns and patterns of stability in personality development. In D. Magnusson & L. R. Bergman (Eds.), *Data quality in longitudinal research* (pp. 181-197). Cambridge, UK: Cambridge University Press.

Bayley, N. (1969). *Bayley Scales of Infant Development*. New York: Psychological Corporation.

Block, J. (1971). *Lives through time*. Berkeley, CA: Bancroft Books.

Block, J. (1977). Advancing the psychology of personality: Paradigmatic shift or improving the quality of research. In D. Magnusson & N. S. Endler (Eds.), *Personality at the crossroads: Current issues in interactional psychology* (pp. 37-63). Hillsdale, NJ: Lawrence Erlbaum.

Block, J. H., & Block, J. (1980). The role of ego-control and ego-resiliency in the organization of behavior. In W. A. Collins (Ed.), *Minnesota Symposia on Child Psychology* (Vol. 13, pp. 39-101). Hillsdale, NJ: Lawrence Erlbaum.

Bornstein, M. H., & Sigman, M. D. (1986). Continuity in mental development from infancy. *Child Development, 57,* 251-274.

Brim, O. G., Jr., & Kagan, J. (Eds.) (1980). *Constancy and change in human development*. Cambridge, MA: Harvard University Press.

Buss, A. R. (1974). A general developmental model for interindividual differences, intraindividual differences, and intraindividual changes. *Developmental Psychology, 10,* 70-78.

Cattell, R. B. (1946). *The description and measurement of personality*. Yonkers, NY: World Book.

Conley, J. J. (1984). The hierarchy of consistency: A review and model of longitudinal findings on adult individual differences in intelligence, personality, and self-opinion. *Personality and Individual Differences, 5,* 11-25.

Conley, J. J. (1985). Longitudinal stability of personality traits: A multitrait-multimethod-multioccasion analysis. *Journal of Personality and Social Psychology, 49,* 1266-1282.

Costa, P. T., & McCrae, R. R. (1988). Personality in adulthood: A six-year longitudinal study of self-reports and spouse ratings on the NEO Personality Inventory. *Journal of Personality and Social Psychology, 54,* 853-863.

Cronbach, L. J., & Meehl, P. E. (1955). Construct validity in psychological tests. *Psychological Bulletin, 52,* 281-302.

Digman, J. M. (1989). Five robust trait dimensions: Development, stability, and utility. *Journal of Personality, 57,* 195-214.

Emmerich, W. (1964). Continuity and stability in early social development. *Child Development, 35,* 311-332.

Epstein, S. (1979). The stability of behavior: I. On predicting most of the people much of the time. *Journal of Personality and Social Psychology, 37,* 1097-1126.

Epstein, S. (1983). A research paradigm for the study of personality and emotions. In M. M. Page (Ed.), *Personality: Current theory and research: 1982 Nebraska Symposium on Motivation* (pp. 91-154). Lincoln: University of Nebraska Press.

Epstein, S. (1986). Does aggregation produce spuriously high estimates of behavior stability? *Journal of Personality and Social Psychology, 50,* 1199-1210.

Giuganino, B. M., & Hindley, C. B. (1982). Stability of individual differences in personality characteristics from 3 to 15 years. *Personality and Individual Differences, 3,* 287-301.

Göttert, R., & Asendorpf, J. (1989). Eine deutsche Version des California Child Q-Sort, Kurzform [A German short version of the California Child Q-set]. *Zeitschrift für Entwicklungspsychologie und Pädagogische Psychologie, 21,* 70-82.

Hampson, S. E., Goldberg, L. R., & John, O. P. (1987). Category-breadth and social-desirability values for 573 personality terms. *European Journal of Personality, 1,* 241-258.

Hertzog, C., & Schaie, K. W. (1986). Stability and change in adult intelligence: 1. Analysis of longitudinal covariance structures. *Psychology and Aging, 1,* 159-171.

Kagan, J. (1980). Perspectives on continuity. In O. G. Brim, Jr., & J. Kagan (Eds.), *Constancy and change in human development* (pp. 26-74). Cambridge, MA: Harvard University Press.

Kopp, C. B., & McCall, R. B. (1980). Stability and instability in mental performance among normal, at-risk and handicapped infants and children. In P. B. Baltes & O. G. Brim, Jr. (Eds.), *Life-span development and behavior* (Vol. 4, pp. 33-61). New York: Academic Press.

MacCorquodale, K., & Meehl, P. E. (1948). On a distinction between hypothetical constructs and intervening variables. *Psychological Review, 55,* 95-107.

Magnusson, D. (1988). *Individual development from an interactional perspective: A longitudinal study.* Hillsdale, NJ: Lawrence Erlbaum.

Mischel, W. (1968). *Personality and assessment.* New York: John Wiley.

Ozer, D. J. (1986). *Consistency in personality: A methodological framework.* New York: Springer.

Ozer, D. J., & Gjerde, P. F. (1989). Patterns of personality consistency and change from childhood through adolescence. *Journal of Personality, 57,* 483-507.

Plomin, R. (1986). *Development, genetics, and psychology.* Hillsdale, NJ: Lawrence Erlbaum.

Rogosa, D., Brandt, D., & Zimowski, M. (1982). A growth curve approach to the measurement of change. *Psychological Bulletin, 92,* 726-748.

Rose, S. A., Feldman, J. F., & Wallace, I. F. (1988). Individual differences in infants' information processing: Reliability, stability, and prediction. *Child Development, 59,* 1177-1197.

Scarr, S., & McCartney, K. (1983). How people make their own environments: A theory of genotype → environment effects. *Child Development, 54,* 424-435.

Snyder, M., & Ickes, W. (1985). Personality and social behavior. In G. Lindzey & E. Aronson (Eds.), *Handbook of social psychology* (Vol. 2, pp. 883-947). New York: Random House.

Stephenson, W. (1953). *The study of behavior.* Chicago: University of Chicago Press.

Stern, W. (1911). *Die differentielle Psychologie in ihren methodischen Grundlagen* [Methodological foundations of differential psychology]. Leipzig: Barth.

Sternberg, R. J. (1985). *Beyond IQ: A triarchic theory of human intelligence.* Cambridge, UK: Cambridge University Press.

Thorndike, R. L. (1947). *Research problems and techniques* (Report No. 3). Washington, DC: Government Printing Office.

West, S. G., & Graziano, W. G. (1989). Long-term stability and change in personality: An introduction. *Journal of Personality, 57,* 175-193.

Wilson, R. S. (1983). The Louisville twin study: Developmental synchronies in behavior. *Child Development, 54,* 298-316.

COMMENTARY ON CHAPTER 5:

Studying Change in Variables and Profiles: Some Methodological Considerations

LARS R. BERGMAN

A Person-Oriented Approach

The considerations and comments that follow have their root in a person-oriented framework for the study of individual development. This framework has been described elsewhere (see e.g., Bergman & Magnusson, 1983; Magnusson & Bergman, 1988) and is briefly summarized here.

It is fair to say that research on individual development has been dominated by an interest in *variable-oriented* approaches where the variable is the main conceptual and analytical unit (Wohlwill, 1973). From an interactional perspective, however, where the focus is on the structures and processes involved in the total functioning of an individual, this approach to the study of individual development has clear limitations (Magnusson, 1985, 1988).

Viewing individual functioning as a multidetermined, stochastic process partly unique to the individual leads to the conclusion that a variable-oriented approach has to be complemented with a *person-oriented* approach in which the person as a gestalt is the central object of interest. Empirically, such a person orientation often implies that individuals' patterns of values in relevant variables are studied and that, consequently, patterns or configurations of values become the basic units of analysis. An example of this approach within the adjustment problem field is given by Bergman and Magnusson (in press).

A person-oriented approach has implications for the choice of methodology and for how concepts like stability, change, continuity and so on are interpreted. Some of these implications are viewed against the background of Asendorpf's discussion in Chapter 5.

Continuity and Stability

In Chapter 5 Asendorpf discusses the problem that the same operationalized measure can tap different constructs for different ages from a variable-oriented perspective. It is interesting that this issue can be viewed quite differently from a person-oriented perspective. Within this approach there is no need to measure exactly the same constructs at different ages. What is important instead is to compile a set of variables for a given age range that as truly as possible reflects the individuals as gestalts within the area of interest; this set of variables can differ from age to age. For instance, if the focus is on the growth of extrinsic adjustment problems during school age, it is not sensible to attempt to measure exactly the same problems at different ages. One should instead take great care to include at each age the important problem areas within that age range (Bergman & Magnusson, in press). Continuity and discontinuity, as they are defined and discussed in relation to traits, may then be less relevant when a person-oriented approach is adopted.

Continuity- and discontinuity-related issues could, however, be studied in terms of relations between *patterns* at different ages. For instance, cluster analysis could be used at each age for the classification of the patterns of variable values into a small number of (hopefully) homogeneous clusters. The cluster solutions for the different ages are compared and a high degree of similarity between the solutions could be interpreted as a sort of continuity in a multivariate sense. Another approach to the study of the continuity of profiles is discussed by Asendorpf in which the correlation matrices for the variables constituting the profiles are compared between the different ages. High continuity is implied if they are similar and this could be tested using factor analytic techniques. This, however, is a variable-oriented and not a person-oriented approach since the wholeness of the profile is not retained in the analysis.

The cluster solutions for the different ages can also be related by ordinary contingency table analysis. A high degree of individual stability is implied if individuals' longitudinal streams are generally located between clusters that are theoretically similar; correspondingly, a high degree of individual change is implied if individuals' longitudinal streams generally lie between clusters that are not similar.

Measurement and Standardization

In my opinion, data quality issues and, especially, measurement issues can be very difficult to handle both in developmental and nondevelopmental settings. An extensive discussion of these issues in relation to the study of individual development is given in Magnusson and Bergman (1990); only some measurement and standardization issues will be discussed here.

It was mentioned above that the same operationalized measure can tap different constructs at different ages thus creating serious interpretational problems. It was also claimed that the situation in this respect may be more favorable when a person-oriented approach is adopted. However, even when attention is confined to one point in time, difficult problems of measurement can, of course, still arise. Unfortunately, these measurement problems for a specific age can be more difficult to handle using a person-oriented approach than when a variable-oriented approach is adopted. This has to do with the fact that the different measures constituting an individual's profile must all be comparable—in the sense that they must be interpretable in relation to one another. Consider the following two examples of profile approaches:

(1) The focus is on the development of interindividual profile differences in adjustment problems, which first are measured separately at each age. It is considered desirable that the profile for a given age should take into account the fact that different adjustment problems have different prevalences. This implies, for instance, that the profiles should be more heavily influenced by adjustment problems having a large variation at a given age than by adjustment problems that might scarcely occur at all at that age and for which the variation is trivial. In this situation, to standardize the variables involved would be disastrous, and some other way of scaling the variables must be found. One such way is to construct quasi-absolute scales, as discussed by Bergman and Magnusson (in press). They argue for the importance of a *multivariate* scaling in which all the variables are scaled using

uniform and comparable procedures. Of course, for other purposes standardization of the variables involved can be appropriate as Asendorpf points out.

(2) The focus is on the development of intraindividual profiles of personality traits formed at each age separately. Here, an approach based on the Q-sort technique (Block, 1971) has been developed by Asendorpf and Weinert (1990). The method is briefly described in Chapter 5 where some scaling problems are also discussed. A special problem with the technique is the dependency of the scores on the pool of items. If a personality trait is added or subtracted from the set, the scores on some of the other traits are affected.

A related problem that is shared by (1) and (2) is that a pattern analytic approach based on the profile of values sometimes can give very different results if just a single variable is added or subtracted (Milligan, 1981). Extreme care must be taken in the selection of an appropriate set of variables to constitute the individual's profile. It is also important to include only indicators with a high reliability since, otherwise, both the analysis for a given age and the longitudinal analyses can be appreciably affected. Light is also shed on this issue by Asendorpf's discussion of the stability of profiles.

Coming back to the variable-oriented approach, it is well-known that the measurement of change poses many difficult methodological problems (Bergman, 1972; Rogosa, Brandt, & Zimowski, 1982); in particular—as Asendorpf points out—residual scores should normally be avoided. Sometimes, the difference between the Time 2 and Time 1 scores is used as the change measure that, for instance, is then correlated with other variables; alternatively, group means are compared. Difference scores, however, should be used with great care (for instance, it has been shown that the results can be influenced by transformations of the scores; Bergman, 1972). When relations between change and other variables are to be studied, it can be a sensible strategy to control for the Time 1 measurement, and then study the relation between the Time 2 measurement and the other variables (Cronbach & Furby, 1970).

In Chapter 5 Asendorpf suggests a measure of individual stability that is a function of the squared difference score between the Time 2 and Time 1 measurements. The attempt to measure individual stability and not just change is an interesting approach. However, the measure is not problem-free. For instance, in the presence of errors of measurement the measure will tend to underestimate stability, and its correlation with another variable will tend to underestimate the size of the true correlation. Asendorpf also points out that its distribution will tend to be strongly positively skewed.

Some Concluding Comments

It is interesting to observe that theory and method often borrow concepts from each other. Obviously, methods should match the problem or theory that is the focus of investigation and, from this perspective, it is both natural and proper that the methodology used includes concepts related to those contained in the theory. Quite frequently, however, the reverse is also true: Theoretical concepts borrowed from the world of methodology are employed. For instance, the term *relationship* is often interpreted as something like a "Pearson correlation" even in theoretical thinking. Compare also the interpretation of concepts like "stability," "change," "continuity," and so on as used, for instance, in a variable-oriented factor analysis setting and in a person-oriented cluster analysis setting. Again, one can say that this state of affairs is only natural and proper, that theoretical thinking starts from empirical observations and that the language of describing data contains methodological terms like the ones mentioned above. Viewed from another perspective, however, it is discomforting: One starts to wonder to what extent theoretical thinking is shackled by the methodology of the day. Methodology provides the window to reality through which we look to see if our theory is supported or rejected. But should methodology also provide the building blocks we should use when thinking about reality, and about where the next window should be erected?

For good reasons, there is a consensus on the importance of sound theorizing and hypothesis testing. For instance, linear structural modeling in longitudinal settings has grown into an important avenue of research for testing different developmental models. The important first step of thoroughly observing and describing data sets in a new field before formulating theories has, however, sometimes been neglected. From this perspective, Asendorpf's chapter is instructive in that it pays attention to basic methodological issues in the description of continuity, stability, and change. The danger of theorizing before observing and describing in areas where knowledge is highly incomplete has been emphasized many times (Bergman & Magnusson, in press; Cronbach, 1975); it can easily lead to academic sectarianism and the establishment of research traditions testing and investigating theories that careful observation could have ruled out from the very beginning (Greenwald, Pratkanis, Lieppe, & Baumgardner, 1986). The extremely complex phenomena under study and a highly incomplete level of knowledge in many developmental fields underscore the importance of careful observation and description as a precursor to sound theorizing.

Finally, a few words on the use of linear structural modeling as a method for testing/constructing developmental theories. When used with good judgment it can, of course, be a highly useful approach; but not infrequently it is employed as a (nonrecognized) exploratory device—a procedure that is encouraged by the automatic parameter modification mechanisms in some of the statistical packages. This is all right provided that the descriptive and exploratory nature of the study is recognized. A model, however, is often successively modified using a sort of quasi-testing procedure. The fit of the final model is then "tested" (overall fit or fit in relation to a more general model). If the fit is good (which it almost always is), a strong belief sometimes arises in the generalizability of the result obtained—since "it is a model that has been tested." What one has in essence, of course, is *one* model that describes the data—rather like an explorer going into a forest armed with a rifle and with the vague notion of finding out what kind of rabbits there are in the forest. The outcome of his model hunt is that he shoots a white rabbit; and it should be recognized that this does not provide very strong support for the theory that all rabbits are white. The issue of model testing versus exploration is further discussed in Bergman (1988).

References

Asendorpf, J. B., & Weinert, F. E. (1990). Stability of patterns and patterns of stability in personality development. In D. Magnusson & L. R. Bergman (Eds.), *Data quality in longitudinal research* (pp. 181-197). Cambridge, UK: Cambridge University Press.

Bergman, L. R. (1972). *Change as the dependent variable.* Unpublished doctoral dissertation. Department of Psychology, Stockholm University.

Bergman, L. R. (1988). Modeling reality: Some comments. In M. Rutter (Ed.), *Studies of psychosocial risk: The power of longitudinal data* (pp. 354-366). Cambridge, UK: Cambridge University Press.

Bergman, L. R., & Magnusson, D. (1983). *The development of patterns of maladjustment: The IDA project* (Research Report No. 50). Stockholm: Stockholm University, Department of Psychology.

Bergman, L. R., & Magnusson, D. (in press). Stability and change in patterns of extrinsic adjustment problems. In D. Magnusson, L. R. Bergman, G. Rudinger, & B. Törestad (Eds.), *Problems and methods in longitudinal research.* Cambridge, UK: Cambridge University Press.

Block, J. (1971). *Lives through time.* Berkeley, CA: Bancroft Books.

Cronbach, L. J. (1975). Beyond the two disciplines of scientific psychology. *American Psychologist, 30,* 116-127.

Cronbach, L. J., & Furby, L. (1970). How we should measure "change"—or should we? *Psychological Bulletin, 74,* 68-80.

Greenwald, A. G., Pratkanis, A. R., Lieppe, M. R., & Baumgardner, M. H. (1986). Under what conditions does theory obstruct research progress? *Psychological Review, 93,* 216-229.

Magnusson, D. (1985). Implications of an interactional paradigm for research on human development. *International Journal of Behavioral Development, 8,* 115-137.

Magnusson, D. (1988). *Individual development from an interactional perspective: A longitudinal study.* Hillsdale, NJ: Lawrence Erlbaum.

Magnusson, D., & Bergman, L. R. (1988). Individual and variable-based approaches to longitudinal research on early risk factors. In M. Rutter (Ed.), *Studies of psychosocial risk: The power of longitudinal data* (pp. 45-61). Cambridge, UK: Cambridge University Press.

Magnusson, D., & Bergman, L. R. (Eds., 1990). *Data quality in longitudinal research.* Cambridge, UK: Cambridge University Press.

Milligan, G. W. (1981). A review of Monte Carlo tests of cluster analysis. *Multivariate Behavioral Research, 16,* 379-407.

Rogosa, D., Brandt, D., & Zimowski, M. (1982). A growth curve approach to the measurement of change. *Psychological Bulletin, 92,* 726-748.

Wohlwill, J. F. (1973). *The study of behavioral development.* London: Academic Press.

COMMENTARY ON CHAPTER 5:

Going Beyond Correlations: Parameter Specificity of Stability and Change

ALEXANDER VON EYE

Jens Asendorpf (Chapter 5) discusses developmental stability and change from the perspective of a personality psychologist primarily interested in personality differences. Of secondary interest are changes in these differences over time. In terms of the framework provided by Baltes, Reese, and Nesselroade (1977) the author is interested in *interindividual differences* rather than in changes in intraindividual differences. More specifically, Asendorpf investigates *interindividual differences that are stable over time*. The author shows elegantly, both theoretically and empirically, that present concepts of trait stability confound continuity and stability. The author also shows, however, that continuity and stability can be investigated independently of each other.

Asendorpf's chapter touches upon a number of interesting topics that can be taken up in a commentary. For instance, it seems worthwhile to discuss the meaning of the term *stability*. Does it describe a continuum? If yes, is it uni- or bipolar? Where on this continuum does high stability begin? Is low stability the same as lack of stability or instability? Can personality characteristics be both trait-like and state-like, that is, be both stable and unstable (see Costa & McCrae, 1980; Nesselroade, 1988; Nesselroade, Pruchno, & Jacobs, 1986)? Are there stable patterns of change? Do individuals differ in these patterns? Do item selection strategies bias empirical results toward

AUTHOR'S NOTE: The author is indebted to Mike Rovine and Patty Mulkeen for critical comments on an earlier draft of this commentary.

more (or less) stability? Is it meaningful and desirable to base statements concerning stability and change on such assumptions as "dimensional identity" (Schmidt, 1977) or temporal constancy of the factor structure of an item pool (Emmerich, 1964)? Do modern methods for data analysis provide new approaches to concepts of stability and change (see Asendorpf, 1990, in press; von Eye, 1990a, 1990b)?

This commentary focuses on the following key statement made in Asendorpf's chapter in the section on differential stability of traits: "We can go beyond correlations if we are interested in the longitudinal stability of traits." This statement allows for the following explication, which is not elaborated in the chapter: *longitudinal stability is parameter specific.* Thus such parameters as autocorrelations, individual change scores à la Asendorpf, and test-retest-correlations are just sample cases of stability parameters. In other words, time series of behaviors can have many parameters. Stability in one parameter can go hand in hand with either stability or instability in others, where stability implies that parameters remain unchanged across the whole observation period, and instability implies that parameters that apply to one time segment do not apply to another.

For example, suppose a researcher talks about mean trends and proposes that the mood of a patient has been trendless over a lengthy observation period. This statement may only refer to the average value of the mood measures that may have a zero slope.

The variability around this average, however, may have undergone drastic changes. The patient may have developed to show virtually no variation in the later observation phases while he or she had displayed great variations at the beginning of the observations.

In the following sections I discuss two types of parameters. Specifically, I discuss parameters that describe the determination of constancy and change and parameters of change functions. For the first type of parameter I propose that a time series is determined the following way:

$$y_i = f(P, T, L, \dots) \tag{1}$$

where i is the location within the time series; P denotes person variables such as age, gender, race, intelligence, patterns of personality characteristics, and psychiatric status; T denotes time-related variables such as time of the day, season of the year, pattern of observation points, and years of education; L denotes location-related variables such as home game, away game, laboratory versus natural environment, bedroom, torture chamber, or Caribbean island. In other words, Equation 1 states that time series of observation, or measurement variables, depend on a number of parameters of independent or *selection variables* (Nesselroade, 1983).

In addition, each time series is described by a number of parameters. For instance, univariate time series can be described using polynomials. A polynomial is given by

$$y_i = a_0 x_{0,i} + a_1 x_{1,i} + a_2 x_{2,i} + \ldots = \sum_{j=0}^{t-2} a_j x_{j,i} \qquad [2]$$

The parameters a_j in this time series can be estimated such that they are independent of each other. This is guaranteed if we use orthogonal polynomials or, in other words, if the x_j are polynomials that are orthogonal to each other.

With the parameters of the time series being independent, the following parameter patterns can be observed (the following are sample cases; there is no space in this commentary for an exhaustive treatment):

(1) There is a linear trend and all other trends that describe deviations from the grand mean are zero;
(2) There is a quadratic trend and all other trends are zero;
(3) There is both a linear and a quadratic trend and all other trends are zero.

If any of the above-noted effects applies to the whole observation period we consider the phenomenon stable. Thus we can talk about stability in terms of trends. Alternatively, we can talk about changes in trends when trends are different across segments of an observational period. Examples of changing trends include shifts in slope that may necessitate estimation of piecewise regression parameters (see Neter, Wasserman, & Kutner, 1990), that is, separate parameters for each segment of an observational period.

In addition, in regard to Equation 1 both stable and unstable parameters may vary depending on selection variables. Furthermore, when estimating parameters we implicitly assume that other parameters— such as the variation around the polynomial of measured values—do not follow any systematic pattern not captured by the polynomial. In brief: *When operating with one type of parameter we assume that other parameters are either zero or irrelevant.*

For multivariate time series we can define stability and change along the same lines as before, for univariate time series. In addition, we can describe stability and change in terms of parameters that relate variables to each other. Examples of such parameters include correlational patterns and factor structures. In most instances, items for tests and questionnaires are selected so that correlational patterns and factor structures remain stable across time. Such methods generate *change-insensitive tests* that may lead to descriptions of change patterns biased toward stability. In addition, we have to assume that changes in parameters not used for item selection do not matter. For example, it is well-known that the magnitude of correlations is not affected by differences in means and standard deviations. Thus constant factor structures may (or may not) go hand in hand with changes in means and variability.

Summary

Jens Asendorpf did a commendable job showing that stability and change have more facets than standard retest correlation. This commentary attempts to generalize from Asendorpf's results and outlines a framework for the notion that longitudinal stability is parameter specific. Two sets of parameters were discussed. The first refers to selection variables, the second refers to the parameters of developmental or change functions. Examples show that (1) changes in one parameter may or may not coincide with changes in other parameters, and (2) focusing on one parameter presupposes strong assumptions concerning other parameters.

References

Asendorpf, J. B. (1990). The measurement of individual consistency. *Methodika, 4,* 1-23.

Asendorpf, J. B. (in press). A Brunswikean approach to trait continuity: Application to shyness. *Journal of Personality.*

Baltes, P. B., Reese, H. W., & Nesselroade, J. R. (1977). *Life-span developmental psychology: Introduction to research methods.* Monterey, CA: Brooks/Cole.

Costa, P. T., Jr., & McCrae, R. R. (1980). Still stable after all these years: Personality as a key to some issues in adulthood and old age. In P. B. Baltes & O. G. Brim,

Jr. (Eds.), *Life-span development and behavior* (Vol. 3, pp. 65-102). New York: Academic Press.

Emmerich, W. (1964). Continuity and stability in early social development. *Child development, 35,* 311-332.

Nesselroade, J. R. (1983). Temporal selection and factor invariance in the study of development and change. In P. B. Baltes & O. G. Brim, Jr. (Eds.), *Life-span development and behavior* (Vol. 5, pp. 59-87). New York: Academic Press.

Nesselroade, J. R. (1988). Some implications of the trait-state distinction for the study of development over the life-span: The case of personality. In P. B. Baltes, D. F. Featherman, & R. M. Lerner (Eds.), *Life-span development and behavior* (Vol. 8, pp. 163-189). Hillsdale, NJ: Lawrence Erlbaum.

Nesselroade, J. R., Pruchno, R., & Jacobs, A. (1986). Reliability versus stability in the measurement of psychological states: An illustration with anxiety measures. *Psychologische Beiträege, 28,* 255-264.

Neter, J., Wasserman, W., & Kutner, M. H. (1990). *Applied linear statistical models* (3rd ed.), Homewood, IL: Irwin.

Schmidt, H. D. (1977). Methodologische Probleme der entwicklungspsychologischen Forschung [Methodological problems of developmental research]. *Probleme und Ergebnisse der Psychologie, 62,* 5-27.

von Eye, A. (Ed.) (1990a). *Statistical methods in longitudinal research: Vol. 1. Principles and structuring change.* San Diego, CA: Academic Press.

von Eye, A. (Ed.) (1990b). *Statistical methods in longitudinal research: Vol. 2. Time Series and longitudinal data.* San Diego, CA: Academic Press.

6

Modeling Environmental Development:
Individual and Contextual Trajectories

THOMAS A. KINDERMANN

ELLEN A. SKINNER

It is almost impossible to find a developmental psychologist today who would argue against a contextualized understanding of individual development. Development is widely viewed as a joint function of organismic and environmental forces and as proceeding within a frame of organizing contexts. Nevertheless, there is considerable variation in the specifics of models constructed to conceptualize the nature and characteristics of those contexts that are assumed to be influential for individual development (Bronfenbrenner, 1989; Bronfenbrenner & Crouter, 1983; Wohlwill, 1983). One feature almost all of them share, however, is that they rarely include the notion that environments, like individuals, themselves develop.

This chapter explores the idea that the explanation of individual development is closely tied to an understanding of how contexts change across time. Predicated on the assumptions that individual trajectories are the targets to be explained, that individuals and environments

AUTHORS' NOTE: We extend our thanks to Jens B. Asendorpf, Dale Dannefer, Zilma Moraes de Oliveira, Maria Clotilde Rossetti-Ferreira, and Jaan Valsiner for their helpful critiques of an earlier version of this chapter.

influence each other reciprocally, that multiple and changing processes of influence are the rule, and that these processes construct
both normative and differential change and stability, we propose three
models of environmental development. We try to specify the methodological implications of each model and provide empirical examples
of how each model can be used in research. These models are built on
current conceptualizations of kinds and levels of contexts, and so we
begin this chapter with a selective overview of current models of context in psychology.

CONTEXTUAL MODELS IN THE STUDY
OF HUMAN DEVELOPMENT

Because an exhaustive discussion of models of context is beyond
the scope of this chapter (but see Bronfenbrenner, 1989; Bronfenbrenner & Crouter, 1983; Sameroff, 1983), we will focus on four recent
changes in conceptions of contexts in the developmental disciplines:
(1) a shift in focus from monolithic conceptions to a consideration of
multiple dimensions and levels of contextual influences on individuals; (2) a move from descriptive to more explanatory models of context; (3) an increasing "agent-ization" of the social and material
context, including for example the recognition that contexts largely
consist of other individuals who may have their own agendas; and (4)
renewed interest in the dynamics of reciprocal shaping between individuals and environments. All of these emerging features are important elements in the present models of environmental development.

Multiple Dimensions and Levels

In an extensive overview, Bronfenbrenner and Crouter (1983) present a taxonomy of environmental models in developmental psychology (see also Bronfenbrenner, 1989). In their view, contextual models
can be classified according to the level of complexity or the number
of factors that are included in theory and research on environmental
influences. Four kinds of contextual systems are proposed. In the
study of contexts as *microsystems,* environmental influences are examined within single settings or across ecological (setting) transitions. The study of *mesosystems,* composed of systems of
microsettings, involves ascertaining the relations between different

developmental settings a person is affiliated with at a certain point in time. With even higher complexity, the *exosystem* contains micro-systems, mesosystems, and larger social structures that influence the characteristics of lower level systems and individuals. In studying ex-osystems, linkages and processes between two or more settings are examined. At least one of these settings does not ordinarily contain the developing person, but is the stage for events that influence pro-cesses within the immediate setting of the developing person. Finally, *macrosystems* describe the structure of society at large, in terms of values, norms, and political systems.

Historically, Bronfenbrenner and Crouter (1983; Bronfenbrenner, 1989) depict the evolution of contextual models in multiple dis-ciplines as well as in developmental psychology as a progression in the complexity. Concomitant features of this process were, for exam-ple, the advent of multifactorial theories and methods of data analy-sis, and an emerging appreciation for variables of social structure. The recognition of multiple levels of contextual influences has led psychologists to reach out to such disciplines as sociology and history for help in conceptualizing institutions and social systems.[1] Accord-ing to such models, a full consideration of contextual influences re-quires teams of multidisciplinary researchers. One remaining issue that our models will attempt to address is how the multiple levels of contextual influences can be focused and coordinated, in order to pro-duce manageable programs of research.

From Description to Explanation

Bronfenbrenner and Crouter (1983) describe the evolutionary pro-cess in the development of context understanding as a branching-off process of conceptions from basically two ancestors: the model of so-cial addresses and the nature-nurture model. Based on these, more theory-based models first emerged, focusing on the effects of social structure on individual development. From these again, more recent conceptions are beginning to focus on questions about the specific processes by which environments and individuals reciprocally influ-ence each other.

The recent interest in explanatory models of environments (see also Scarr's 1985 discussion of the use of proximal, behavioral, versus dis-tal, background variables) is not restricted to developmental psychology.

In the domain of sociology, an approach has been proposed by Dannefer (in press) to distinguish models of contexts with regard to their relevance for developmental processes. Dannefer criticizes traditional conceptions of contexts for their lack of theoretical grounding, resulting in depictions of the environment as an "amorphous, haphazard, and unpredictable set of circumstances" (p. 14). In his view, environments need to be distinguished with regard to the influences they exert on individual development. This would entail differentiating among models in which context is assumed to be irrelevant for producing or explaining developmental outcomes; in which context is viewed as presumably important for developmental outcomes, but has random effects; in which contexts are static themselves, but lead to orderly developmental effects in individuals; and finally models in which contexts are understood as comprising an active system of social relations, in which individual development is an outcome.

This progression from the use of descriptive markers toward the inclusion of explanatory hypotheses in the understanding of environments may be characterized as a process of moving beyond a focus on classifications of contexts as "unitary" and "monolithic entities" (Wohlwill, 1983) toward increasingly more theory-based and multifaceted conceptualizations. This pertains to all levels of complexity of context conceptualizations. New questions focus on the exact components of contexts that are relevant for development at different points in time, the processes that might be involved in context-individual and individual-context transmissions, and the specifics of what contexts and individuals actually "do to each other." The concern with explanations of the processes of individual-environment interchanges across time will be the focus of the present chapter.

Agent-ization

At first glance, the question of what environments and people "do to each other" seems to be crucial with regard to social environments only. There is, however, similar concern growing with respect to the influence of physical contexts. Researchers have been increasingly dissatisfied with conceptualizations of the environment that simply reference the presence or absence of specific features or objects; Wohlwill (1983) criticizes them as "passive exposure" conceptions (p. 113). These "monolithic" feature models have given way to theoretical and empirical attention to the *processes* by which physical contexts exert influence on individuals' behavior and development (for examples, see Green, Gustafson, & West, 1980; Gustafson, 1984; Valsiner, 1984; Valsiner & Mackie, 1985; Yarrow, Rubenstein, & Pedersen, 1975).

Overall, increasing attention has been paid to the psychologically relevant characteristics and functions that contexts possess in contributing to individual change across time. This includes efforts to recognize the "psychological structure" of environments (cf. Sameroff, 1983), the "affordances" that environments provide for individuals' actions (Gibson, 1982), and the mechanisms by which environments influence psychological development (cf. Wohlwill, 1983).

This trend toward agent-ization or personalization has many consequences for the conceptualization of environmental functions. Social contexts are becoming recognized as created by or consisting largely of persons themselves, of persons who have personality characteristics, belief systems, and behavior tendencies. This can be seen in microsystems, where people in interactions are assumed to serve as contexts for each other (Laboratory of Comparative Human Cognition, 1983), or in contexts of higher complexity (Bronfenbrenner, 1989), where modes of context-individual transmission are assumed to be less direct. Again, we will build on this trend of analyzing the "psychological features" of the environment.

Reciprocal Context-Individual Influences

Finally, recent developments in conceptualizations of contexts have pointed out the role of individuals as "active agents" who participate in their own development within contexts. The influences that environments exert on individuals are assumed to feed back into the environment and to influence further environmental change; influences that individuals exert on their contexts are expected to feed back into the pathway of individual development. Through processes of selection, initiation, avoidance, interaction, selective perception, and interpretation, contexts are influenced by the individuals who reside within them (R. M. Lerner & Busch-Rossnagel, 1981; Wohlwill, 1983). Although environments are typically treated as independent variables, the outcomes of which are observed in the change of individuals, increasingly, individuals and contexts are viewed as parts of dynamic systems, which reciprocally influence each other.[1] This is one assumption that is common to the models for contextual development described in this chapter.

In sum, we are encouraged by new models of context that focus on multiple levels of environmental influences, that move from description toward explanation of individual development, that assume that contexts have many "psychological" features of their own, and that view context-individual influences as dynamic and reciprocal. Building on such conceptions, we hope to contribute a serious consideration of development or systematic change to emerging models of context. We also attempt to examine the usefulness of our models of environmental development in planning programs of empirical research.

BASIC REQUIREMENTS FOR DEVELOPMENTAL MODELS OF THE PSYCHOLOGICAL ENVIRONMENT

A thorough consideration of models of environmental development rests squarely on a description of the psychological target to be explained. We focus on three crucial features of target phenomena in developmental research. First, we argue that conceptualizations of the contextual aspects that should be studied depend on the *target psychological phenomenon* under study. For example, different aspects of the very same physical context may be examined, depending on whether changes in an individual's emotions, cognitions, behaviors, or motivations are of interest. Second, consistent with a life-span perspective on human development, we assume that the "dependent variables" in developmental research are *intra-individual trajectories* and inter-individual differences in such trajectories (P. B. Baltes, Reese, & Nesselroade, 1977). Third, we argue that a *developmental frame* or window is needed to identify those points in time during which a target phenomenon should be open to the influence of environmental factors. What are the implications of this position for views of the developing context?

Specification

The first, and simplest, implication is that the dimensions, components, and levels of the environment that are of interest will vary depending on the target phenomenon. In general, this means that any theory that attempts to outline *the* dimensions of a context, such as the dimensions of parenting behavior, will be of only limited use. Such a theory provides a menu of choices; however, researchers will use theories about the causal antecedents of their target phenomenon in selecting among potential dimensions.

Two examples may illustrate this point. Recent reviews of research on the consequences of critical life events have attempted to identify the dimensions upon which such events can differ, for example, their severity and age-normative prevalence (e.g., Brim & Ryff, 1980; Reese & Smyer, 1983). These reviews are very useful for pointing out the variety of dimensions underlying nonnormative life events. No conclusions can be drawn, however, about which of these contextual elements are the most important. This depends completely on the target phenomenon: Those dimensions critical in predicting development of coping, for example, might be totally different from those that explain subsequent personality development. A second example can be taken from the research on parenting. Discussions of whether the critical dimensions of parenting are warmth, control, permissiveness, or structure are bound to be inconclusive. The dimensions that are "critical" will depend on the child outcome; for example, the parent behaviors contributing to children's perceived competence will be different from those contributing to their behavioral compliance.

Hence, decisions about the proximal (microsystem) dimensions of context to study will depend on explanatory theories about the antecedents of the target phenomenon of interest. In turn, all subsequent decisions about higher levels of complexity will build on these decisions: The particular dimensions or components at the mesosystem level will be those theorized to influence the microsystem components. For example, in the study of the development of children's intrinsic motivation, several dimensions of teacher behavior have been found to be influential. Specifically, student intrinsic motivation remains stable (as opposed to decreasing across time) in classrooms in which teachers provide more choice and latitude in selection of learning activities, explain the relevance of the activities to children's goals, and do not try to control or coerce children through threats, sanctions, or rewards (Deci & Ryan, 1985). In studying the origins of such teacher behavior, typical measures of classroom structure, teacher beliefs, student behavior, or teacher-parent relationships will not be useful unless researchers have identified which of these antecedents should predict relevant aspects of teacher behavior. For example, there probably exist hundreds of dimensions of teacher expectations or parent-teacher relationships that do not (and theoretically, should not be expected to) predict teachers' autonomy-supportive behaviors. Using explanatory theories of the target phenomenon in order to identify proximal antecedent dimensions of the context, and then using (or constructing) explanatory theories of these proximal dimensions in order to identify more distal antecedent dimensions, researchers can include the potentially most powerful predictors of the target phenomenon from several levels of contextual complexity in a single study.

When one gives an "anchoring" role to the target developmental trajectory, then the decision about which individuals (or characteristics) to study as target subjects and which individuals (or characteristics) to study as contextual elements may result in entirely different research programs. For example, when studies show that parental sensitivity predicts subsequent child attachment better than earlier child attachment predicts later parental sensitivity, such studies are clearly testing theories in which children are the target individuals and the target to be explained is child attachment. These studies would not be fair tests of the potential child antecedents of parental sensitivity. If parental sensitivity were the target phenomenon, then a different set of child antecedents would be needed. The inclusion of infant characteristics that were theoretically linked to sensitivity, such as clarity of signals and soothability, would allow a more thorough examination of reciprocal parent-child influences in this area.

Developmental Trajectories and Interindividual Differences Therein

The second implication follows from the assumption that the target phenomena to be explained are developmental trajectories and interindividual differences in these trajectories. In empirical terms, this means that the dependent outcomes are not, as traditionally assumed, a distribution of scores at Time n. Instead, the target variable can be either a single growth function, described by a particular intercept and shape, or a set of these functions. Hence, interindividual differences at any point in time have to be regarded as the endpoints of differential trajectories of change. With regard to individuals' environments, we

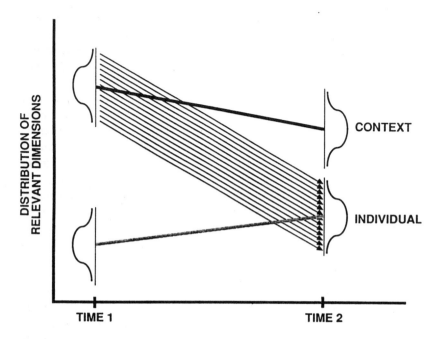

Figure 6.1. The Study of Individual-Context Development: Examining Interindividual and Intercontext Covariation Across Time Versus Examining the Covariation of Trajectories

have to be aware that differences in *their* developmental trajectories may similarly exist and these different patterns of change may produce differential impact on individuals. Thus when the possibility of context development is acknowledged, the task of examining its influences on individuals can be characterized as finding the differences in individuals' environmental changes that are responsible for differences in individuals' developmental trajectories.

An example is given in Figure 6.1; for reasons of simplicity, both interindividual and inter-environmental differences are assumed to be stable across time. The traditional method of empirically examining "context effects," by correlating outcome scores at Time n with context scores at Time $n - 1$ (or relating intercontext differences to interindividual differences at any time), cannot reveal information about the connection between changing contextual characteristics and the development of the outcomes. In fact, it would be possible to find a correlation of +1.0 between context and outcome variables even when the correlation between individual and environmental *changes* was negative. As Figure 6.1 shows, this could occur when the context decreases across time and the individual increases.

Developmental Frame

Can we assume that contextual influences on individual trajectories will trigger the same effects for all individuals in the same way, at any time in the development of an individual? Probably not. At specific times, individuals and microsystems, for example, might be immune to radical changes in the outer environment; at other times, individuals might be very sensitive to even minor contextual changes. For example, Stewart and Healy (1989) provide arguments for assuming that socio-historic events have differential impact on individuals, depending on the stage of life when they experience the event.

The frame issue addresses the likelihood that points of measurement in a study are timed so as to capture theoretically interesting processes of context-individual influences. Unless one makes the assumptions that processes are very global, regular, frequent, cross-situationally stable, and dominant, a developmental frame would be needed from which points in time can be derived that should be central for emerging change, and that takes into account the pace of change in these processes. This metric could then be used to localize times for measurement when the impact of the context on the individual should be present.

Although these windows of susceptibility to contextual influences exhibit a close similarity to the concept of "sensitive periods," they address a much broader and more general issue. The notion of sensitive periods usually entails three restrictive criteria: (1) the window of influence is open at one developmental period only and is subsequently permanently closed; (2) the developmental consequences are significant and permanent; and (3) the resulting developmental pathway is unchangeable (e.g., Bornstein, 1989). In contrast, time frames are useful for the study of any phenomenon for which the magnitude of contextual impact differs as a function of the individual's developmental level. They refer to any time in development at which an individual is differentially open to outside influences or "ready to be socialized" (Maccoby & Martin, 1983). As opposed to sensitive periods, time frames during which windows of influence are open can reoccur; their developmental consequences may be minor and temporary; and the resulting developmental pathways may be modifiable by subsequent contextual influences. In this general sense, sensitive periods are a special case of time frames. Hence, psychological theories are needed for determining (1) at what times those "windows" are likely to be "open" with regard to which developmental phenomenon, (2) which individuals will be susceptible to environmental changes, and (3) for what length of time these influences will have an impact on the individual.

An example can be provided by mothers' use of discipline techniques in interactions with their children. It could reasonably be argued that these techniques become most salient at those times in development when new competencies emerge in children and need to be shaped to conform with cultural or social standards. Each time new competencies emerge, concurrent child-rearing techniques would again be expected to have a strong impact on child behavior.

Models Indifferent to Environmental Development

On a large scale and historically, there may be no doubt that contexts change across time. Theoretical accounts of contextual change are typically found in the domains of history or sociology (Cain, 1987; Elder, 1985; Featherman, Spenner, & Tsunematsu, 1988; Riley, Johnson, & Foner, 1972). In developmental psychology, interest in contextual change mainly emerged out of a life-span perspective (cf. Baltes, 1987). Here, these notions became widely accepted when research on the history-graded changes of social environments showed that changing developmental conditions for different birth cohorts could be related to marked change in psychological functioning across time (P. B. Baltes, Cornelius, & Nesselroade, 1979; Nesselroade & Baltes, 1984; Schaie, 1965).

With regard to the span of human life, however, we have to ask ourselves whether the pacing of contextual change can be considered important for intraindividual development—as historically short-lived as we are—or only for explanations of cross-cohort differences. Traditionally, developmental psychology seems to rely on assumptions that contexts are stable and exert quite stable influences on individuals. As Hetherington and Baltes (1988) state, "much developmental research still presents a picture of the child developing within rather static ecosystems. Certainly more attention is focused on individual change than on contextual change" (p. 12). For example, in child psychology, child-rearing styles, qualities of the family home, teaching styles, or sociodemographic marker variables have traditionally been employed to study socialization effects in children's development. All of these do not, by and large, seem to be regarded as phenomena captured at certain points in time, but as features that are stable and exert relatively constant and long-lasting influences on the individual.

TRADITIONAL CONCEPTIONS OF
ENVIRONMENTAL INFLUENCES: THE LAUNCH MODEL

The methodological model most commonly used to study contextual influences on individual development ignores contextual change; we refer to it as the *launch model.* We will briefly describe and illustrate it (see also Connell & Skinner, 1990) to provide a basis of comparison for models that allow the examination of environmental change. We do not hold that this model cannot characterize many phenomena. We simply argue that its usefulness is more restricted than its current widespread application would imply and that researchers should consider a variety of other models of context-individual development relations before choosing the model appropriate to their target of study.

The launch model depicts a time-lagged influence from variation in contextual antecedents to variation in subsequent developmental outcomes. Specifically, it uses the (interindividual) distribution of context variables at Time 1 to predict the (interindividual) distribution of outcomes at Time 2 (usually controlling for outcomes at Time 1) (see Figure 6.2). This model does not necessarily assume environmental stability; contextual variables may change from Time 1 to Time 2. It does, however, assume that such contextual change, if it does occur, is irrelevant to the prediction of Time 2 outcome scores (or of change in outcome scores from Time 1 to Time 2). The causal process represented by this model is analogous to a catapult, in which the initial forces of the contextual antecedent are the major determinants of the shape of the curve of the outcome.

Phenomena for which launch models may be useful representations are those that are open to influence from the environment at one point

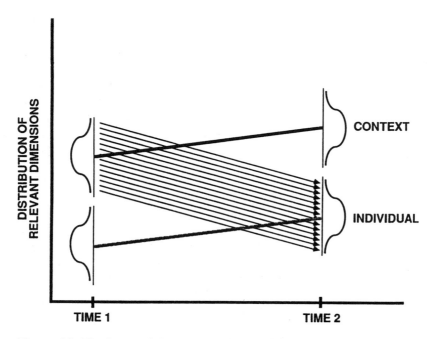

Figure 6.2. The Study of Context-Individual Influences Within the "Launch Model": Using Variations in Contextual Antecedents to Predict Subsequent Interindividual Differences

and subsequently become "sealed off." Examples include, but are not restricted to, research on sensitive periods (Bornstein, 1989). For example, according to learned helplessness theories, children who are exposed to initially high levels of noncontingency between their actions and outcomes subsequently show a variety of affective, cognitive, and motivational deficits (Seligman, 1975). These deficits appear even in environments that have changed and are characterized by high action-outcome contingencies. The initial context "launched" a behavioral trajectory that (by definition) is impervious to changing environmental conditions. Intervention researchers sometimes refer to programs designed to prevent helplessness deficits (for example, by exposing children to high doses of contingency) as "inocculation" programs. Again, this implies that early experiences will determine later behavior, even in the face of changing environmental conditions.

Constructs or Methods

The launch model, which assumes that contextual change is irrelevant to the prediction of the target outcomes, has up to now accounted for a large portion of the research on environmental influences on individual development. If, in fact, this is the most prevalent model used to study contextual influences, how is it that it has been so successful in informing us about the antecedents of development? Does its success justify ignoring models of contextual change in future research?

We would argue that most developmental research, although using this model, has nevertheless attempted to incorporate notions of environmental development. Where? In the constructs: Under the rubric of developmental equivalence, researchers have often changed the operational definitions of contextual constructs as a function of the developmental level of the target. For example, the specific behavioral referents of the construct "parental sensitivity" differ for parents of 18-month-olds and 5-year-olds. Hence, parents who display "sensitive parenting" when their children are 18 months and 5 years old, are not producing a constant environment; instead, they are showing parental adjustment of their behaviors to the developmental level of their children. In our view, changing construct referents to be "developmentally appropriate" is not a measurement issue. Instead, these changes should be the target of empirical inquiry. Specifically, we argue for removing contextual changes from constructs and analyzing them using appropriate methodologies. As alternatives to the launch model, we suggest four models that differ with regard to the nature and role of environmental change in the development of individuals.

SYSTEMATIC AGE DIFFERENCES IN ENVIRONMENTS: THE DEVELOPMENTAL TRANSITION MODEL

Traditionally, when changes of contexts were included in our picture of influences on individuals, these were conceived as processes of transitions across contexts (Bronfenbrenner & Crouter, 1983; Whiting, 1980). For individuals at different ages, different contextual influences are at work; the notion that contexts actually change themselves is not entailed in the conceptualization of individual development.

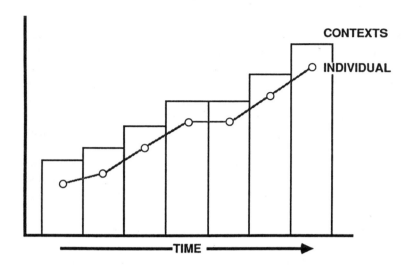

Figure 6.3. The Study of Individual-Context Influences With the "Developmental Transition Model": Individual Development Proceeding Across Multiple Contexts

According to the *developmental transition model,* individual development takes place within a changing environment: Individuals experience systematic changes in environments, not because environments are developing, but because people are moving across different age-graded contexts (see Figure 6.3). For these transitions to be able to explain systematic age changes, the context transitions must themselves be organized or stratified according to age. Is there evidence that contexts are age-graded? And if so, according to what features does age-gradation occur?

Age-Graded Environments

In our everyday experience, examples are widespread for contexts that are culturally designed as explicitly age-graded or age specific. There are, at early times, families, schools, and orphanages, which are designed for children. Schools, most clearly, are cultural institutions that exhibit a strong age stratification (Minuchin & Shapiro, 1983). On the other end of the life-span, there are retirement homes and other institutions for the care of the elderly. Similarly, certain contexts exhibit features of age segregation, which may be due to cultural rules (laws) or processes of self-selection: There are movies or kinds of bars that are explicitly reserved for adults only; there are hang-outs or restaurants that are typically frequented by adolescents.

Two kinds of contexts will be distinguished: culturally designed or institutionalized contexts (e.g., families, schools, institutions), and spontaneous (Dannefer & Perlmutter, 1990) or self-selected contexts (e.g., peer groups, friendships, partnerships). Culturally designed environments are designed for specific individuals, in our case for individuals of specific ages. Age is a necessary condition for the individuals to be there and age of inhabitants is one of the constituting factors of the ecology. In contrast, within self-selected environments, individuals are the creators of any age-specificity, and to some extent the designers of the environment's characteristics.

The prevalence of these two kinds of contexts for individuals across their ages can be age-graded in itself. In early childhood, children's small range of mobility largely limits their access to a wide range of contexts; the major contextual agents are mothers, fathers (or other caretakers), and siblings. These contextual agents are culturally or biologically assigned. In childhood, the environment's effect on children's development may be effectively captured in the assignment of the child to the family setting and its socializing impact (Whiting, 1980). With increasing age, however, the relative importance of family-determined settings decreases. Which contexts are experienced and which are not will more and more become a matter to be decided by the individual him- or herself. For example, a first major step in acquiring self-determination regarding which contexts to join is the onset of being able to walk.

With further increments in independence, individuals become increasingly able to determine for themselves those micro-contextual influences to which they will be exposed. For example, during early childhood, the context of schooling includes a large number of potential socializing agents from which individuals can select (e.g., Cairns, Neckerman, & Cairns, 1989; Strayer & Noel, 1986). Objectively defined are, of course, the boundary conditions in which these self-selection processes take place (classrooms, schools, neighborhoods, etc.).

Further age-related changes in developmentally relevant contexts can be noted in adolescence and adulthood, when contexts can be selected according to the options they provide for further development of individuals (jobs, university training programs, mentors, religious affiliations). The selection of a constant primary partner and the legalization of this partnership leads to institutionalization of a self-selected context. And, the ability to reproduce allows adults to produce contexts that then actually feed back into their own further development.

Finally, old age presents new changes in environments. Processes of biological decline are likely to set limits to individuals' mobility and power in handling contexts; these are accompanied by cumulative losses of contexts and contextual agents that were self-selected across time—important friends, mentors, and family members are lost. Successful aging is assumed to depend largely on how individuals manage to cope with these age-related transitions (cf. P. B. Baltes & M. M. Baltes, 1990). In the extreme case of living in institutions for the elderly, an individual's context might be restricted to a number of professional caretakers (cf. M. M. Baltes & Reisenzein, 1986).

The distinction between self-selected and culturally assigned contexts might be helpful for examining interindividual differences in contextual transitions. The focus would be on the relative amount of variability in these transitions. Thus higher diversity can be expected with regard to transitions across self-selected contexts (especially after childhood), whereas individuals' transitions across culturally assigned contexts may appear quite age-normative (especially at younger ages). Even for these, however, interindividual differences may be substantial. Gifted children, for example, can experience developmental transitions, even in terms of culturally assigned contexts, that are quite different from those of their average agemates.

In sum, the developmental transition model describes one way in which individuals experience different contexts at differing points in development. In this model, environmental change is experienced by the individual while moving across different contexts. Although the explication of developmental transitions may require cultural and sociological theories of age stratification (Cain, 1987; Riley et al., 1972), the model does not necessarily involve conceptions of a changing or developing environment. We turn next to three models in which this is attempted.

Models Incorporating Environmental Development and Change

The three models we discuss in this section have in common the notion that the environment itself is changing as the individual develops within it. According to each, a correlation would be expected between individual and contextual trajectories of change; however, each posits a different explanatory scenario. The first, termed *weather model,* describes systematic environmental change that impacts on individual development but is not initiated or shaped by the individual. The second, the *developmental co-adaptation model,* depicts individual-context influences in which changes in individual and environment feed back into each other reciprocally (cf. dynamic interactionism, R. M. Lerner, 1979). The third, the *developmental attunement model,* describes reciprocal individual-context development in which the changes of the environment are calibrated to the development of the individual (cf. apprenticeship or scaffolding: Bruner, 1982; Kaye, 1982). We will illustrate each model using existing research when possible. Because some of the models are not yet used widely, however, we will also speculate about the empirical questions they might generate. Throughout, we will discuss the models as if the target variables were interindividual differences in individual trajectories.

UNIDIRECTIONAL INFLUENCES OF ENVIRONMENTS ON INDIVIDUALS: THE WEATHER MODEL OF CO-DEVELOPMENT

The individual-context relations described by this model are analogous to the weather: Although changes in contextual factors are essential in influencing individual trajectories, they are not initiated or steered in any way by a target individual (see Figure 6.4). This conception of environmental change differs from subsequent models in that changes in the context are in no way calibrated or significantly determined by the developing individual him- or herself.

Within such models, theories would be needed that identify significant global changes in the environments of individuals, determine the environmental dimensions that are changing, and the interindividual differences in these patterns of changes, and then suggest the consequences such changes may have for the development of target individuals of different ages. Two examples will be provided from research on siblings and on critical life events.

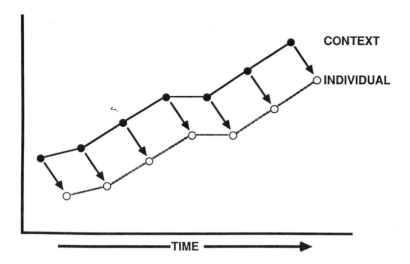

Figure 6.4. The Study of Individual-Context Co-Development With the "Weather Model": Individual Development Influenced by Contextual Change

Birth of a Sibling as a Significant Contextual Change

Although one of the biggest normative shifts in a child's early life occurs when a new sibling is brought home (Kreppner, 1989; Kreppner, Paulsen, & Schuetze, 1982), rarely do children have any influence over the advent of this change. A wide variety of individual differences would be expected in the environmental changes brought about by a sibling's arrival, depending on a host of factors, including, for example, the temperament and health of the new child (e.g., a premature sibling may result in radical changes for the older child), and the child-care arrangements (extended family care may have already added younger children to the child's daily life). The most common dimensions of the environment that this global change affects include changes in parents' energy level, patience, amount of attention, and responsiveness to requests/bids from the older child; for the older child, especially affected seems to be the amount of time available with the mother. Potential changes could also range from the amount of private space the child is allowed to the level and frequency of parental conflict.

Each of the dimensions of environmental changes suggests target developmental phenomena that could be influenced by the birth of a sibling. Especially critical in identifying the consequences would be the age of the older sibling. For example, decreases in amount of time and responsiveness of mothers may have an impact on their children's attachment to them, especially for younger children (the age from 6 to 18 months is hypothesized to be important for attachment formation). Likewise, if decreases in interactions with mothers are accompanied by increases in time spent with fathers (Kreppner et al., 1982), then corresponding increases in attachment with fathers might be expected. Conceptualizing the birth of a sibling within weather models allows us to focus on "events" as a series of shifts in the environment, over which the child has little control, but which may nevertheless have important consequences for the child's development in a variety of domains.

Parents' Critical Life Events
as Environmental Changes for Their Children

The weather model might also provide an organizing framework for researchers studying the effects of parents' critical life events on their children. The occurrence of a critical life event can be used as a marker to locate the advent of a contextual shift. An illustration can be found in the work on the effects of parental divorce on children's development, conducted by Hetherington and her colleagues (Hetherington, 1989; Hetherington & Camara, 1984; Hetherington, Cox, & Cox, 1982). Parental divorce, leading to the partial loss of one socializing agent in the child's ecology, at the same time seems to be associated with a high likelihood for family income loss, shift in residence, social isolation, and disruptions in parenting behavior. It seems that these shifts in the environment (along with more salutary shifts, such as decreases in parental conflict and increases in independence) might account for the effects of divorce on individual development. To test a weather model of co-development, the trajectories of the contextual factors (e.g., decreases in time spent with parents, increases in independence support) would be assessed and then examined for the effectiveness in accounting for corresponding trajectories of individual change (i.e., decreases in attachment security and increases in independence, respectively).

Critical life events of adults could also be seen as environmental shifts for their other important social partners. For example, an older person's illness may produce significant changes in the lives of his or her grown children; a teenager's pregnancy could change the lives of all other family members; loss of a wife's job would shift the context for a husband. In fact, some of the most stressful changes in women's lives appear to be the result of critical life events in the other members of their social network (Belle, 1982). The weather model attempts to highlight the dynamic nature of "events" (for review, see Sugarman, 1986, chapter 6), which often produce multiple environmental changes in the lives of those who experience them as well as for their social partners. The analysis of these changes, their dimensions and variations in their trajectories, may contribute to our understanding of their effects on individuals' development and on the interindividual differences therein.

RECIPROCAL INDIVIDUAL-ENVIRONMENT CHANGE: THE DEVELOPMENTAL CO-ADAPTATION MODEL

This model, like that described previously, depicts environments that are changing. Unlike in the one described above, however, in the current model the changes and developments of the context are reciprocally linked to the target individual (Bell, 1979; R. M. Lerner & Busch-Rossnagel, 1981). These models have in common that the explanation for environmental changes involves how the target individual's behaviors or characteristics produce contextual change. Although these environmental changes include reactions to the individual (see Figure 6.5), they are not calibrated to the target individual's development, nor produced by a developmental agenda of the context.

Changes in the environment that are the product of individual influences are easiest to imagine when social partners are the contextual elements of interest. More difficult is tracing the link from the individual to changes in aspects of the social micro-ecology that should feed back to the developing target individual. Theories of two explanatory links are needed: (1) how the social contextual antecedents influence individual development; and (2) how the individual antecedents produce changes in the relevant aspects of the social context. Two general functions that these reciprocal influences could

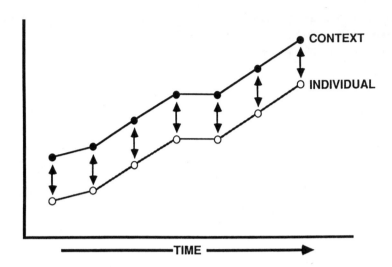

Figure 6.5. The Study of Individual-Context Co-Development Within the "Developmental Co-Adaptation Model": Reciprocal Exchanges Between Developing Persons and Changing Environments

perform over time can be imagined: one in which individual or environmental changes compensate for changes in the other; and one in which individuals and environments magnify each other's changes. Over time, the first would result in a picture of a relatively flat developmental trajectory, with low stability of interindividual differences; the latter would produce steeper developmental trajectories with relatively high stability of interindividual differences. Three illustrations of the developmental co-adaptation model are described: mutual socialization in peer groups, coping with critical life events (an example of compensation), and motivational dynamics in the classroom (an example of magnification).

Individual-Context Reciprocity in Peer Groups

In tracing mutual socialization in children's peer relations, the first step would be to assess a child's own individual characteristics as well as those of his or her peer group, and to chart changes in both child and peer group members over time (on methodological issues, see Cairns, 1983; Cairns, Gariepy, & Kindermann, 1990). As the second step, it would be a challenge to make a theoretically coherent case for whether and how these two sets of developments would mutually interact to shape the developmental outcomes of the target child (Hartup, 1983).

The initial way in which children influence their peer groups is by selecting social partners among available candidates. Beyond this, each child participates in the group dynamics of relatedness and influence (Lynch & Wellborn, 1988). For example, the more a child cares for and about her individual peer group members, the more influence she allows those members to have on her. At the same time, children play differentially active roles in constructing changing patterns of peer group norms and activities, which will in turn shape the individual child's experiences and subsequent development (e.g., Cairns et al., 1989; Dunphy, 1963; Furman, 1989; Kindermann & Belmont, 1990; Ladd, Price, & Hart, 1990). When organized by the co-adaptation model, a study of such processes would include an assessment of changing group norms and activities, of the target child's role in co-constructing the norms and activities, and of the impact of those on the child's subsequent behavior and development.

Coping as Compensation for
Changes Produced by Stressful Life Events

Developmental co-adaptation models might provide an organizing frame for researchers who study coping processes. Researchers argue that coping processes (as well as the stressful life events that invoke coping) consist not merely of an episode but are comprised of a series of events that take place over time (Folkman, 1984; Skinner & Wellborn, in press). Individuals cope with environmental changes through processes of appraisal, reframing, and active attempts to compensate for or restore loss. For example, the loss of a job encompasses many changes, including perhaps the loss of a social network, a source of self-esteem, respect of others, financial support, and so on, down to loss of a reason to get up in the morning. Over time, the effects of the loss on the individual's developmental trajectory will depend, among other things, on the extent to which these losses are compensated for by changes in the individual and other social partners. Hence, the pattern of change in these contextual elements will influence the individual and the individual will in turn, through his or her coping responses, influence the rate and nature of contextual changes (including the probability of getting a new job). Together, these reciprocal changes will predict the developmental effects of the loss.

School Motivation as an Example of Magnification of Individual-Context Influences

Patterns of mutual adaptation may evolve into a process in which individual and contextual development reciprocally magnify each other over time. For example, researchers studying the development of children's motivation in school have identified a range of teacher behaviors that are hypothesized to promote or undermine student motivation (Connell & Wellborn, 1990; Skinner, 1990). These behavioral dimensions, which are derived from a theory of psychological needs, include structure versus chaos, autonomy support versus control, and involvement versus neglect. The theory holds that when teachers meet students' basic psychological needs, the students will show optimal behavioral and emotional engagement in learning activities (Connell & Wellborn, 1990).

Recent research has focused on the reciprocal side of these student-teacher interactions, namely, on the effects of student motivation on teacher behavior. According to this research, one major determinant of whether teachers are, for example, autonomy supportive or controlling, is student motivation (Deci & Ryan, 1985). Over time, students who show signs of emotional alienation from learning (e.g., rebelliousness or boredom) are responded to by teachers with increasingly more noncontingent and controlling behaviors (Skinner & Belmont, 1990). It is tempting to speculate that, over time, dynamic systems of mutual influence are constructed in which motivated students are treated by teachers in such a way that their motivational development is optimized, and disaffected students are dealt with in ways that further undermine their commitment to school (Skinner, 1990).

DEVELOPMENTALLY ADJUSTED ENVIRONMENTAL CHANGE: THE DEVELOPMENTAL ATTUNEMENT MODEL

The attunement model describes individual-context relations in which the development of the individual is an *agenda* item for the

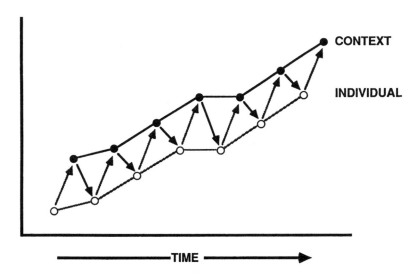

Figure 6.6. The Study of Individual-Context Co-Development Within the "Attunement Model": Reciprocal Exchanges Between Developing Persons and Changing Environments With a Developmental Agenda

context. This model would be a contender for accounts of any context that is entrusted by the culture with nurturance or (re-)socialization activities, such as parents, schools, orphanages, self-help groups, hospitals, prisons, or institutions for the elderly (even though many of these contexts may not actually show such attunement to their charges). This model might also characterize relations in which the context elects to assume these duties; examples include relationships with mentors, coaches, siblings, or grandparents.

Models of developmental attunement are characterized by a pattern of environmental change that is calibrated according to the target individual's development and is guided by the contexts' goals to shape the individual's trajectory (see Figure 6.6).

In these models, complex theories are required that would include explanations of (1) the agenda of the context; (2) the impact of the contextual agenda on what the context actually does; (3) how the resulting socializing interaction patterns shape the development of the target individual; and (4) how developmental change of the individual feeds back onto changes in the agenda and behavior of the context.

Environmental Agendas

Consistent with the conceptualizations of contexts that are increasingly personalized, attunement models view contextual influences as provided by people that carry specific motives and goals for developing individuals (cf. Bronfenbrenner, 1989). The parent-child relationship is the easiest context-individual relation to view in this light. In general, parents can be assumed to have an investment in children's development. In any given culture, parents' opinions about the "right" developmental trajectory in early childhood are presumably quite strong. Even the child's physical environment is "set by parental choices" (Maccoby & Jacklin, 1983, p. 75), which may reflect parental expectations and goals for the child; socialization goals are often "coded" into the objects that serve as material contexts for children (Valsiner, 1987).

During the last decade, research has examined parents' beliefs about and expectations for their children's development (Sigel, 1985). Regarding their children, mothers carry more or less explicit timetables or curricula for achievements and developmental changes (Goodnow, 1984; Goodnow, Cashmore, Cotton, & Knight, 1984). Recently, research has focused on the impact of these beliefs on parental behavior, which, in turn, shapes children's subsequent development (Sigel, 1990).

Havighurst's (1972) conceptualization of developmental tasks may be useful to capture those culture-specific systems of guidance for individual development, which are arranged according to more or less explicit age-specific timetables (Reinert, 1980). Children's timely and successful development can be considered a developmental task for parents (Duvall, 1971). In conceptualizing the environment's agenda for individuals within the family, the concept may be helpful for resolving two issues: (1) the provision of a theoretical frame to specify the aspects around which individuals and their contexts show reciprocal attunement (the agenda that the context holds); and (2) the provision of a metric for these processes (the time frame for the context's agenda). In other words, the concept may provide a base for determining when processes of attunement occur, how long they will last, and what behavior domains they will be focusing on.

Localizing Contextual Change

For the task of framing individual-context attunement, again, the individual's developmental trajectory is used as the anchoring feature, but, within this model, in conjunction with the context's agenda regarding the individual's trajectory. As indicated above, the concept of developmental tasks may be a helpful tool to pinpoint those times in an individual's development when marked changes occur within the individual, and corresponding adjustments of the contextual agents reflect their developmental agenda for the individual (Kindermann & Skinner, 1988). In general, knowledge of normative developmental pathways can be employed for determining windows during which socializing agents are expected to adjust their socializing behaviors.

With regard to later childhood, the school setting provides a paradigmatic case of an ecology in which individual-context relations are age- and competence-stratified. Curricula can be understood as contextual prescriptions of when students are expected to master specific tasks. These prescriptions specify at what ages which competencies are to be fostered by what kind of teaching strategies, and for what period of time. Teachers, as contextual agents, are trained to behave differently with students of different competence levels and to adjust their teaching behavior toward children's changing competence. Thus a developmental schedule of context-individual attunement is built into the design of the ecology.

An important feature of contextual agendas is that they may differ for children of differing ages, sexes, or races. Within the school system, teachers have clearly different expectations of pace, abilities, and optimal level of accomplishment for different children (cf. Jussim, 1989; Rosenthal & Jacobson, 1968). These are institutionalized in all forms of tracking, including programs of special education and giftedness. Similar features of a developmental agenda of contexts for individuals might characterize a large variety of individual-context relationships in later life, for example, in apprenticeship, mentoring, or counseling relationships.

Adjustment of Socializing Interactions

The notion of developmental adjustment in socializing ecologies is not new to developmental psychology. An early example is William Stern's (1930) principle of "convergence" of caretakers' demands and individual's developmental tendencies. Currently, approaches that actually propose that processes of contextual attunement are one of the driving forces of individual development are gaining attention in research on children's development.

To some extent, this trend to include parental adjustment in the picture of children's developmental change can be attributed to the recent popularity of the work of Vygotsky (1978; see also Rogoff, 1990; Rogoff & Lave, 1984; Rogoff & Wertsch, 1984; Valsiner, 1984; Valsiner & van der Veer, in press). Similar frameworks refer to concepts as "scaffolding" (Bruner, 1982), "apprenticeship" (Kaye, 1982), or "readiness to be socialized" (Maccoby & Martin, 1983). These notions are encompassed, for example, in studies examining changes in instruction and support when mothers interacted with their children in games (e.g., Hodapp, Goldfield, & Boyatzis, 1984) or worked jointly with them on laboratory tasks (e.g., Heckhausen 1987; Rogoff, Ellis, & Gardner, 1984).

An illustration of natural processes of individual-context attunement can be found in a study that examined everyday mother-child interactions in basic developmental tasks of early childhood. The focus was on changes in the contingencies mothers provided for children's behaviors in developmental tasks, specifically in the tasks of learning to walk, learning to eat, and learning to dress alone (Kindermann, 1991). In a short-term longitudinal time frame, mothers' perceptions of children's progress in these developmental tasks were assessed, along with in vivo observations of mother-child interactions. The results showed that maternal adjustments in behavior contingencies (behavior consequences following children's independent and dependent task related behaviors) occurred in attunement to mothers' changing perceptions of their children's competence in the tasks.

Two key characteristics of contextual attunement to individual's change should be highlighted. First, in terms of the theoretical frame, the target phenomenon (children's growing competence in the developmental tasks) was theoretically linked to what the context "does" in fostering children's mastery of the tasks—in this case, the supportive behavior of the parental caretaker. Second, the target phenomena were conceived as the developmental trajectories of individuals and their contexts. Hence, the focus of an attunement framework is not on how differences between individuals relate to differences in contexts across time, but on how changes within individuals relate to changes within developing contexts that are assumed to hold an agenda for these individuals.

What are the consequences of adopting an attunement model for developmental research on interindividual differences across development? Clearly, the focus is on the relation of intraindividual and intracontextual change. First, processes of contextual attunement need to be distinguished with regard to the agendas contexts hold for different individuals. For example, for several of their children, parents can have quite different developmental goals.

Second, studies could focus on interindividual differences in the extent to which contexts are attuned to individuals' development. For example, consider that teachers' classroom teaching may be calibrated to the mean level of ability in a group of children. The rate of teachers' environmental change will then be attuned to average children only; children of higher and lower ability will not experience the teachers' change as attuned to their own state of development.

Third, differences in attunement processes can be understood as consequences of differential environmental trajectories of change. That is, attunement differences can be related to differences in the environment's capacity to calibrate its own influences to specific individuals' state of development. For example, according to J. V. Lerner and R. M. Lerner's (1983) formulation of a model of "goodness of fit" between parents and their developing children, parents can differ in their adjustment to changing needs of children who show different characteristics; in this case, to children with an easy versus difficult temperament. The focus would be on states of mismatch between parental demands and children's temperament across time. Inter-context differences in how parents are able to attune to their children's development may have long-term consequences for further individual development.

It might not be too speculative to argue that similar features of attunement between contexts and individuals might characterize a large variety of individual-context relationships in later life. For example, apprenticeship, mentoring, or counseling relationships may exhibit patterns of change in reciprocal individual-context influences that appear compatible with an attunement framework. Again, differential consequences of these relationships would be expected to be based not only on what individuals and contextual agents bring into the situation and how they interact, but also on how contexts and individuals manage to adjust to each other's change across time.

Discussion

This chapter is based on the premise that the study of the processes of individual development will be enriched by a careful consideration of models of developmental contexts: what their components are, what their functions may be, and to what extent they develop themselves. As researchers, our ability to explain the sources and outcomes of individual development will depend on our conceptualization of context-individual relations. First, it will depend on our theories about those contextual characteristics that are influence for specific target developmental phenomena and the nature and timing of the context's influencing impact. Second, it will depend on the position we take on the issues of contextual change and stability. Are individual-context relations best envisioned as movements of individuals across relatively stable "envelopes," or as individual development within developing contexts? Third, it will depend on how we deal with the issue of contextual change methodologically. Do we want to center, as is typical, on the relations of interindividual and inter-context differences across time, or, as is rarely done, on the relations of individual and contextual trajectories across time?

With regard to the issue of differential stability and change, the notion of environmental development requires us to differentiate individuals' change and stability according to the extent to which individual development occurs within environments that are themselves stable or changing. Furthermore, we have to include notions of reciprocal influences between individuals and contexts. The degree to which changes in environments are open to influences from individuals might vary from no control (as depicted in the weather model) to processes of mutual calibration (as in the co-development and attunement models). Hence, interindividual differences in developmental change can possibly occur within (or despite) environments that are stable, as well as within environments that are changing.

We conclude by briefly addressing two questions. First, what does one gain by understanding contexts as stable entities, which affect individuals like a constant frame? And second, what does one lose? The major advantage of assuming a stable set of contextual influences is that it is simpler. Theories of individual development within stable contexts have only one parameter that changes: the individual. Multiple levels of context may be involved as sources of individual development, but their structure and impact on individuals remain constant. Only one explanatory theory is needed, namely, of individual development; the impact of contextual development can remain an issue for historians and sociologists. Most importantly, we can continue to use familiar methods to capture context-individual influences, as summarized by the launch model. Finally, we still can incorporate one notion of contextual variation across time: Individuals can experience environmental change by moving across contexts as described by the developmental transition model.

What do we lose by assuming that the context is relatively stable or that whatever changes are occurring are irrelevant to our understanding of individual development? We would argue that we lose as much by assuming that contexts are stable as we would lose if we assumed that individuals are not developing. First, we would lose track of that part of individual development that is the result of adaptation to changing contextual demands (as opposed to new contextual demands). Second, we would underestimate the potential individuals have to instigate and shape change in the contexts in which they find themselves. Third, we would not take seriously theories that hold that the most powerful contexts are *social*. If contexts are comprised of other people, then development of the social context can never be ruled out a priori. Finally, we would not learn about the contexts' capacities to attend and adjust to the developmental rhythms of individuals.

Many subdisciplines of psychology argue that the most interesting questions center on how individuals *differ* from each other and on how stable these differences are, but do not regard as equally important the question of how individuals *change*. The same distinction can be applied to questions of context differences and contextual change. Developmentalists have argued vigorously about how fundamental the issue of change is to an understanding of individuals, but have tended to take a largely "nondevelopmental" stand with respect to contextual factors.

Our goal in writing this chapter was not to attempt to reconfigure the landscape of research on individual-context influences. Neither do we regard our arguments for contextual development as being radical or new. Rather, we see notions of contextual change and development as an emerging field of interest for developmentalists, deeply rooted within many developmental disciplines. With this chapter, we only wished to encourage theorists to consider the theoretical and methodological ramifications of the notion that the contexts in which individuals develop are developing as well. If some researchers decide to re-examine this possibility for some target developmental phenomenon, for some features of the context, at some key points in development, the purpose of this chapter will have been achieved.

Note

1. The defining characteristics of systems in the social sciences are currently a matter of intense debate (see, for example, Bronfenbrenner, 1989; Dannefer, in press); we use the term in its most general meta-theoretical sense.

References

Baltes, M. M., & Reisenzein, R. (1986). The social world in long-term care institutions: Psychosocial control toward dependency? In M. M. Baltes & P. B. Baltes (Eds.), *Aging and the psychology of control* (pp. 315-344). Hillsdale, NJ: Lawrence Erlbaum.

Baltes, P. B. (1987). Theoretical propositions of life-span developmental psychology: On the dynamics between growth and decline. *Developmental Psychology, 23,* 611-626.

Baltes, P. B., & Baltes, M. M. (1990). *Successful aging: Perspectives from the behavioral sciences.* New York: Cambridge University Press.

Baltes, P. B., Cornelius, S. W., & Nesselroade, J. R. (1979). Cohort effects in developmental psychology. In J. R. Nesselroade & P. B. Baltes (Eds.), *Longitudinal research in the study of behavior and development* (pp. 61-87). New York: Academic Press.

Baltes, P. B., Reese, H. W., & Nesselroade, J. R. (1977). *Life-span developmental psychology: Introduction to research methods.* Monterey, CA: Brooks/Cole.

Bell, R. Q. (1979). Parent, child, and reciprocal influences. *American Psychologist, 34,* 821-826.

Belle, D. (1982). The stress of caring: Women as providers of social support. In L. Goldberger & S. Breznitz (Eds.), *Handbook of stress: Theoretical and practical aspects* (pp. 496-505). New York: Free Press.

Bornstein, M. H. (1989). Sensitive periods in development: Structural characteristics and causal interpretations. *Psychological Bulletin, 105,* 179-197.

Brim, O. G., Jr., & Ryff, C. D. (1980). On the properties of life-events. In P. B. Baltes & O. G. Brim, Jr. (Eds.), *Life-span development and behavior* (Vol. 3, pp. 368-388). New York: Academic Press.

Bronfenbrenner, U. (1989). Ecological systems theory. In R. Vasta (Ed.), *Annals of child development* (pp. 187-249). Greenwich, CT: JAI Press.

Bronfenbrenner, U., & Crouter, A. C. (1983). The evolution of environmental models in developmental research. In W. Kessen (Ed.), *Handbook of child psychology* (Vol. 1, pp. 357-414). New York: John Wiley.

Bruner, J. (1982). The organization of action and the nature of the adult-infant transaction. In E. Tronick (Ed.), *Social interchange in infancy: Affect, cognition, and communication.* Baltimore, MD: University Park Press.

Cain, L. D. (1987). Theoretical observations on applied behavioral science. *Journal of Applied Behavioral Science, 23,* 277-294.

Cairns, R. B. (1983). Sociometry, psychometry, and social structure: A commentary on six recent studies of popular, rejected, and neglected children. *Merill-Palmer Quarterly, 29,* 429-438.

Cairns, R. B., Gariepy, J.-L., & Kindermann, T. A. (1990). Identifying social clusters in natural settings. Unpublished manuscript, University of North Carolina, Social Development Laboratory, Chapel Hill.

Cairns, R. B., Neckerman, H. J., & Cairns, B. D. (1989). Social networks and shadows of synchrony. In G. R. Adams, T. P. Gullota, & R. Montemayor (Eds.), *Advances in adolescent development* (pp. 275-305). Newbury Park, CA: Sage.

Connell, J. P., & Skinner, E. A. (1990, April). *Predicting trajectories of academic engagement: A growth curve analysis of children's motivation in school.* Paper presented at the annual meeting of the American Educational Research Association, Boston.

Connell, J. P., & Wellborn, J. G. (1990). Social and psychological influences on engagement and disaffection across the life span: A motivational analysis. In M. Gunnar & L. A. Sroufe (Eds.), *Minnesota Symposium on Child Psychology* (Vol. 22, pp. 43-77). Minneapolis: University of Minnesota Press.

Dannefer, D. (in press). On the conceptualization of context in developmental discourse: Four meanings of context and their implications. In D. L. Featherman, R. M. Lerner, & M. Perlmutter (Eds.), *Life-span development and behavior* (Vol. 10). New York: Academic Press.

Dannefer, D., & Perlmutter, M. (1990). Development as a multidimensional process: Individual and social constituents. *Human Development, 33,* 108-137.

Deci, E. L., & Ryan, R. M. (1985). *Intrinsic motivation in human behavior.* New York: Plenum.

Dunphy, D. C. (1963). The social structure of urban adolescent peer groups. *Sociometry, 26,* 230-246.

Duvall, E. M. (1971). *Family development.* Philadelphia: J. B. Lippincott.

Elder, G. H. (Ed.) (1985). *Life course dynamics: Trajectories and regressions.* Ithaca, NY: Cornell University Press.

Featherman, D. L., Spenner, K. I., & Tsunematsu, N. (1988). Class and the socialization of children: Constancy, change, or irrelevance? In E. M. Hetherington, R. M. Lerner, & M. Perlmutter (Eds.), *Child development in life-span perspective* (pp. 67-90). Hillsdale, NJ: Lawrence Erlbaum.

Folkman, S. (1984). Personal control and stress and coping processes: A theoretical analysis. *Journal of Personality and Social Psychology, 46,* 839-852.

Furman, W. (1989). The development of children's social networks. In D. Belle (Ed.), *Children's social networks and social supports* (pp. 151-172). New York: John Wiley.

Gibson, E. (1982). The concept of affordances in development: The renascence of functionalism. In W. A. Collins (Ed.), *Minnesota Symposium on Child Psychology: The concept of development* (pp. 55-81). Hillsdale, NJ: Lawrence Erlbaum.

Goodnow, J. J. (1984). Parents' ideas about parenting and development: A review of issues and recent work. In M. E. Lamb, A. L. Brown, & B. Rogoff (Eds.), *Advances in developmental psychology* (pp. 193-242). Hillsdale, NJ: Lawrence Erlbaum.

Goodnow, J. J., Cashmore, J., Cotton, S., & Knight, R. (1984). Mothers' developmental timetables in two cultural groups. *International Journal of Psychology, 19,* 193-205.

Green, J. A., Gustafson, G. E., & West, M. J. (1980). Effects of infant development on mother-infant interactions. *Child Development, 51,* 199-207.

Gustafson, G. E. (1984). Effects of the ability to locomote on infants' social and exploratory behaviors. *Developmental Psychology, 20,* 397-405.

Hartup, W. W. (1983). Peer groups. In E. M. Hetherington (Ed.), *Handbook of child psychology* (Vol. 4, pp. 103-196). New York: John Wiley.

Havighurst, R. J. (1972). *Developmental tasks and education.* New York: McKay.

Heckhausen, J. (1987). Balancing for weaknesses and challenging developmental potential: A longitudinal study of mother-infant dyads in apprenticeship interactions. *Developmental Psychology, 23,* 762-770.

Hetherington, E. M. (1989). Family relations six years after divorce. In K. Pasley & M. Ihinger-Tallman (Eds.), *Remarriage and stepparenting today: Research and theory* (pp. 185-205). New York: Garland.

Hetherington, E. M., & Baltes, P. B. (1988). Child psychology and life-span development. In E. M. Hetherington, R. M. Lerner, & M. Perlmutter, (Eds.), *Child development in life-span perspective* (pp. 1-19). Hillsdale, NJ: Lawrence Erlbaum.

Hetherington, E. M., & Camara, K. A. (1984). Families in transition: The process of dissolution and reconstitution. In R. D. Parke (Ed.), *Review of child development research: The family* (Vol. 7, pp. 398-439). Chicago: University of Chicago Press.

Hetherington, E. M., Cox, M., & Cox, R. (1982). Effects of divorce on parents and children. In M. E. Lamb (Ed.), *Nontraditional families: Parenting and child development* (pp. 233-288). Hillsdale, NJ: Lawrence Erlbaum.

Hodapp, R. M., Goldfield, E. C., & Boyatzis, C. J. (1984). The use and effectiveness of maternal scaffolding in mother-infant games. *Child Development, 55,* 772-781.

Jussim, L. (1989). Teacher expectations, self-fulfilling prophecies, perceptual biases, and accuracy. *Journal of Personality and Social Psychology, 57,* 469-480.

Kaye, K. (1982). *The mental and social life of babies: How parents create persons.* Chicago: Harvester Press.

Kindermann, T. A. (1991). *Fostering independence in everyday mother-child interactions: Intra-dyad changes in contingency patterns as children grow competent in developmental tasks.* Unpublished manuscript, Free University Berlin, FRG.

Kindermann, T. A., & Belmont, M. J. (1990, April). *The power of peer groups.* Paper presented at the annual meeting of the American Educational Research Association, Boston.

Kindermann, T. A., & Skinner, E. A. (1988). Developmental tasks as organizers of children's ecologies: Mothers' contingencies as children learn to walk, eat, and dress. In J. Valsiner (Ed.), *Child development within culturally structured environments: Social co-construction and environmental guidance in development.* Vol. 2, (pp. 66-105). Norwood, NJ: Ablex.

Kreppner, K. (1989). Linking infant development-in-context to the investigation of life-span family development. In K. Kreppner & R. M. Lerner (Eds.), *Family systems and life-span development* (pp. 33-64). Hillsdale, NJ: Lawrence Erlbaum.

Kreppner, K., Paulsen, S., & Schuetze, Y. (1982). Infant and family development: From triads to tetrads. *Human Development, 25,* 373-391.

Laboratory of Comparative Human Cognition. (1983). Culture and cognitive development. In W. Kessen (Ed.), *Handbook of child psychology* (Vol. 1, pp. 357-414). New York: John Wiley.

Ladd, G. W., Price, J. M., & Hart, C. H. (1990). Preschooler's peer networks and behavioral orientations: Relationship to social and school adjustment. In S. R. Asher & J. D. Coie (Eds.), *Peer rejection in childhood: Origins* (pp. 90-115). New York: Cambridge University Press.

Lerner, R. M. (1979). A dynamic interactional concept of individual and social relationship development. In R. L. Burgess & T. L. Huston (Eds.), *Social exchange in developing relationships* (pp. 271-305). New York: Academic Press.

Lerner, J. V., & Lerner, R. M. (1983). Temperament and adaptation across life: Theoretical and empirical issues. In P. B. Baltes & O. G. Brim, Jr. (Eds.), *Life-span development and behavior* (Vol. 5, pp. 197-231). New York: Academic Press.

Lerner, R. M., & Busch-Rossnagel, N. A. (Eds.) (1981). *Individuals as producers of their development: A life-span perspective.* New York: Academic Press.

Lynch, M. D., & Wellborn, J. G. (1988, April). *Peer influences, student engagement, and disaffection.* Paper presented at the annual meeting of the American Educational Research Association, New Orleans.

Maccoby, E. E., & Jacklin, C. G. (1983). The "person" characteristics of children and the family as environment. In D. Magnusson & V. L. Allen (Eds.), *Human development: An interactional perspective* (pp. 75-91). New York: Academic Press.

Maccoby, E. E., & Martin, J. A. (1983). Socialization in the context of the family: Parent-child interaction. In E. M. Hetherington (Ed.), *Handbook of child psychology* (Vol. 4, pp. 1-101). New York: John Wiley.

Minuchin, P. P., & Shapiro, E. K. (1983). The school as a context for social development. In E. M. Hetherington (Ed.), *Handbook of child psychology* (Vol. 4, pp. 197-274). New York: John Wiley.

Nesselroade, J. R., & Baltes, P. B. (1984). Sequential strategies and the role of cohort effects in behavioral development: Adolescent personality (1970-1972) as a sample case. In S. A. Mednick, M. Harway, & K. M. Finello (Eds.), *Handbook of longitudinal research* (Vol. 1, pp. 55-87). New York: Praeger.

Reinert, G. (1980). Educational psychology in the context of the human life span. In P. B. Baltes & O. G. Brim, Jr. (Eds.), *Life-span development and behavior* (Vol. 3). New York: Academic Press.

Reese, H. W., & Smyer, M. A. (1983). The dimensionalization of life-events. In E. J. Callahan & K. A. McCluskey (Eds.), *Life-span developmental psychology: Nonnormative life-events* (pp. 1-33). New York: Academic Press.

Riley, M. W., Johnson, M., & Foner, A. (1972). *Aging and society: Vol. 3. A sociology of age stratification.* New York: Russell Sage.

Rogoff, B. (1990). *Apprenticeship in thinking.* New York: Oxford University Press.

Rogoff, B., & Lave, J. (1984) (Eds.). *Everyday cognition: Its development in social context.* Cambridge, MA: Harvard University Press.

Rogoff, B., & Wertsch, J. V. (1984) (Eds.). *Children's learning in the "zone of proximal development": New directions for child development.* San Francisco: Jossey-Bass.

Rogoff, B., Ellis, S., & Gardner, W. (1984). Adjustment of adult-child interaction according to child's age and task. *Developmental Psychology, 20,* 193-199.

Rosenthal, R., & Jacobson, L. (1968). *Pygmalion in the classroom.* New York: Holt, Rinehart & Winston.

Sameroff, A. J. (1983). Developmental systems: Contexts and evolution. In W. Kessen (Ed.), *Handbook of child psychology* (Vol. 1, pp. 237-294). New York: John Wiley.

Scarr, S. (1985). Constructing psychology: Making facts and fables for our times. *American Psychologist, 40,* 419-512.

Schaie, K. W. (1965). A general model for the study of developmental problems. *Psychological Bulletin, 64,* 92-107.

Seligman, M.E.P. (1975). *Helplessness: On depression, development, and death.* San Francisco: Freeman.

Sigel, I. E. (1985). *Parental belief systems: The psychological consequences for children.* Hillsdale, NJ: Lawrence Erlbaum.

Sigel, I. E. (1990). *Parental belief systems: Consequences for children's development.* Hillsdale, NJ: Lawrence Erlbaum.

Skinner, E. A. (1990). Development and perceived control: A dynamic model of action in context. In M. Gunnar & L. A. Sroufe (Eds.), *Minnesota symposium on child psychology* (Vol. 22, pp. 167-216). Minneapolis: University of Minnesota Press.

Skinner, E. A., & Wellborn, J. G. (in press). Coping during childhood and adolescence: A motivational perspective. In M. Perlmutter, D. L. Featherman, & R. M. Lerner (Eds.), *Life-span development and behavior* (Vol. 12). New York: Academic Press.

Skinner, E. A., & Belmont, M. J. (1990, April). *A longitudinal study of motivation in school: Reciprocal effects of teacher behavior and student engagement.* Paper presented at the annual meetings of the American Educational Research Association, Boston.

Stern, W. (1930). *Psychologie der frühen Kindheit bis zum sechsten Lebensjahre* (6th ed.). Leipzig: Quelle & Meyer.

Stewart, A. J., & Healy, J. M. (1989). Linking individual development and social changes. *American Psychologist, 44,* 30-42.

Strayer, F. F., & Noel, J. M. (1986). The prosocial and antisocial functions of preschool aggression: An ethological study of triadic conflict among young children. In C. Zahn-Waxler, E. M. Cummings, & R. Ianotti (Eds.), *Altruism and aggression: Biological and social origins* (pp. 107-131). New York: Cambridge University Press.

Sugarman, L. (1986). *Life-span development: Concepts, theories and interventions.* London: Methuen.

Valsiner, J. (1984). Construction of the zone of proximal development (ZPD) in adult-child joint actions: The socialization of meals. In B. Rogoff & J. V. Wertsch (Eds.), *Children's learning in the "zone of proximal development": New directions for child development* (pp. 65-76). San Francisco: Jossey-Bass.

Valsiner, J. (1987). *Culture and the development of children's action.* Chichester, UK: John Wiley.

Valsiner, J., & Mackie, C. (1985). Canalization of climbing skills through culturally organized physical environments. In T. Gaerling & J. Valsiner (Eds.), *Children within environments: Toward a psychology of accident prevention* (pp. 165-192). New York: Plenum.

Valsiner, J., & van der Veer, R. (in press). The encoding of distance: The concept of the "zone of proximal development" and its interpretations. In R. R. Cocking & K. A. Renninger (Eds.), *The development and meaning of psychological distance.* Hillsdale, NJ: Lawrence Erlbaum.

Vygotsky, L. S. (1978). *Mind in society.* Cambridge, MA: Harvard University Press.

Whiting, B. B. (1980). Culture and social behavior: A model for the development of social behavior. *Ethos, 8,* 95-116.

Wohlwill, J. F. (1983). Physical and social environment as factors in development. In D. Magnusson & V. L. Allen (Eds.), *Human development: An interactional perspective* (pp. 111-129). New York: Academic Press.

Yarrow, L. J., Rubenstein, J. L., & Pedersen, F. A. (1975). *Infant and environment: Early cognitive and motivational development.* New York: John Wiley.

COMMENTARY ON CHAPTER 6:

Modeling Environmental Development: Some Comments From a Developmental Task Perspective

MARCEL A. G. VAN AKEN

The relation between the development of individuals and their environment has been the subject of study and discussion for quite some time. In their chapter, Kindermann and Skinner describe different models of how individual and contextual change can be studied, either separately or in conjunction with each other. In a short overview of current models in the study of human development, the authors describe four recent changes in developmental psychologists' thinking about the effects of context on individual development.

First, they direct attention to an increasing complexity in dimensions and levels that are relevant in human development. The authors suggest that this increasing complexity led psychologists to draw on disciplines such as history and sociology in order to find a multidisciplinary approach. One of the goals of their chapter is described as examining the coordination of multiple levels of contextual influences into manageable research programs.

The second recent change is an increasing interest in explanatory (theory-based) models of environment, which raises new questions concerning components and processes of mutual effects between persons and environment.

The third change mentioned in the chapter is the increase toward "personalization" of the environment: an active role of the environment that is especially relevant in the case of the social context (as opposed to the physical context).

The last trend Kindermann and Skinner refer to is a shift toward the recognition of the active role of a person in influencing the environmental context.

Kindermann and Skinner formulate a number of requirements for constructing models that describe the relation between the development of person and context.

The first requirement is that a clear target phenomenon for study needs to be specified, as theoretical conclusions often depend on this specification. For example, critical life events may have differential effects, depending on certain dimensions on which these events differ, or "critical parental dimensions" depend on the specific competences to which these dimensions refer.

The second requirement is that developmental trajectories and interindividual differences in these trajectories should be studied. Dependent outcomes should therefore be growth curves, not static distributions of scores at a given time point. In more sophisticated models (presented later in the chapter) "differences in individuals' environmental change that are responsible for differences in individuals' developmental trajectories" should be analyzed.

The third requirement refers to the timing in individual development, and in assessing this development. The authors use the term *developmental frame* to broaden the notion of "sensitive period" into a less time-specific (i.e., important periods can reoccur) and less fatalistic construct (i.e., consequences may also be relatively minor, and may be modified by subsequent influences).

Based on these recent trends and requirements, Kindermann and Skinner describe five models in which the development of a person in an environmental context can be studied. Two of these models are said to assume that contexts are stable and nonchanging, and three models incorporate environmental development.

The goal of the Kindermann and Skinner chapter is to draw more attention to developing contexts. In particular, they formulate the premise "that the study of the processes of individual development will be enriched by a careful consideration of models of developmental contexts." This attention will have to be guided by (1) theories about the nature and timing of influential contextual characteristics, (2) issues of change and stability, and (3) methodological considerations of change.

The first point I want to discuss in this commentary is the description given by Kindermann and Skinner of traditional models for developmental research as relying on the assumption of stable contexts. In my opinion, in the models that are described under the heading of "models indifferent to environmental development," the claim of the authors that contexts are perceived here as being stable and nonchanging does not withstand closer analysis. The problems that may arise regarding this claim are already present in the examples provided by the authors.

In their description of the launch model, in which a time-lagged influence of contextual antecedents on developmental outcomes is assumed, the authors already indicate that environmental changes may be more present in the research described under this model than suspected at first glance. As they say, the success of this model is a result of the fact that these models *do* take environmental changes into account. By assuming that higher order constructs remain the same, whereas concrete behaviors change, environmental changes are described under the heading of developmental equivalence. In fact, this practice is not uncommon (see, e.g., the idea of attachment as an organizational construct [Sroufe & Waters, 1977], or competence as a developmental construct [Waters & Sroufe, 1983]). Researchers pursuing this line of research probably will agree with Kindermann and Skinner that this is not a measurement issue. Studies of the behavioral equivalents of attachment or of behavioral manifestations of competence suggest that these approaches may be more sophisticated than Kindermann and Skinner assume.

The developmental transition model, according to the authors, includes changes in contexts. But these changes refer to static differences in contextual influences, like age-graded environments. The question then is whether in this case one can really say that the environment does not develop. Higgins and Parsons (1983), for example, describe similar mechanisms in terms of age-related subcultures, with each phase having its specific concerns, expectations, rules, and so on. In addition, the distinction made by Kindermann and Skinner between institutionalized and spontaneous contexts, with developmental differences in the prevalence and diversity of contexts, also shows that a large amount of variability is present in environmental characteristics. In addition, even personal action seems to play a role in these developmental transitions. Since these transitions probably are experienced by a child as changes in context, it is difficult to see why this kind of research should be regarded as not taking into account environmental change.

Summarizing, this would imply that models that are entirely indifferent to environmental development do not seem to underlie developmental research, at least not in the examples mentioned by Kindermann and Skinner. This does not mean that every research of this type explicitly takes into account environmental development and that the identification of these models is useless. Instead, it shows that researchers have to be pushed to make their theoretical ideas about environmental change more explicit. Apparently, implicit notions of a developing environment are often already present in models of individual development.

The second issue in this comment refers to the fact that whereas the models described by Kindermann and Skinner may be useful in describing already existing research programs, it may be more difficult to use them in planning future research. The authors have made clear, through their extensive and illustrative use of examples, that research can be *described* in terms of different models, but should research also be *planned* based on one of these models? The question arises whether the models are mutually exclusive. Are the simple models essentially different from the more complex ones, or are they just more simple formulations of the most complex one?

The difficulty in deciding what research is planned in what kind of model incorporating environmental change, is also present in some of the examples provided by Kindermann and Skinner. The example of the birth of a sibling, given for the weather model, might also be valid for other models. Of course, a child has no direct influence on the birth of a sibling. The child has influence, however, on the reactions of the parents afterwards. Children may try to attract more attention from one parent or the other. This way the example would fit in with the developmental co-adaptation model. It might even be that the planning of the birth of a sibling and/or the parents' reactions to the first child afterwards are related to the developmental agenda the parents have for the child. More attention for the newborn child might be related to the elder child going to a day-care center or kindergarten. This way, the birth-of-a-sibling example even refers to the developmental attunement model.

Apparently, knowledge of the models is not sufficient for the production of manageable research questions. In my opinion, the placement of research in one of the models has to be driven by a strong theory, or at least a strong heuristic framework about what development is about.

This refers to a recent trend in research, also described by Kindermann and Skinner, namely a trend toward an increasing interest in explanatory (theory-based) models of environment, which includes questions on components and processes of mutual effects between persons and environment.

A theoretical or heuristic notion that may be helpful here is that of developmental tasks. The concept of developmental tasks was originally described by Havighurst (see, e.g., Havighurst, 1973) and has gained much interest in recent years, including this chapter (in addition see Kindermann & Skinner, 1988). Developmental tasks can be defined as "a series of problems and life-adjustment tasks to be achieved by the growing person in relation to his environment" (Havighurst, 1973, p. 10). The problems that form a developmental task may consist of demands and of opportunities for a person. Demands refers to the fact that adaptation to certain developmental tasks is almost inevitable. Opportunities refers to the fact that the person is not regarded as a passive recipient of developmental influences, but is expected to be able to capitalize on environmental resources. This leaves room for a recognition of the active role of persons themselves in constructing their environment and in determining environmental reactions. In addition, Baltes, Reese, and Lipsitt (1980) extended the idea of developmental tasks into a three-factor model, including not only age-related developmental influences, but also influences such as the effects of historical changes, or the effects of nonnormative life-events.

This notion of developmental tasks also fits in with Kindermann and Skinner's idea of a developmental frame, or windows of susceptibility to contextual influences. The saliency of a developmental task may change over the life span. For example, school achievements probably are important at their first occurrence, in the beginning of elementary school. After this, they may be somewhat in the background, in favor of a more socially oriented curriculum, but they may regain some importance at the end of elementary school, related to the choice of secondary education.

If we look at the three models that do incorporate environmental development and change, we see that the essence of these models can also be formulated (and demonstrated) in terms of developmental tasks. Let us look from this perspective at the weather model, the developmental co-adaptation model, and the developmental attunement model.

The weather model takes into account the unidirectional influences of environments on individuals. According to Kindermann and Skinner, these influences are not affected in any way by the individual. As examples, the birth of a sibling and the effects of parents' critical life events are described. Conceiving coping with the birth of a sibling as a developmental task for a child makes clear, as has been described before, that such an event cannot be regarded as an isolated, unidirectional effect. Children may not have an influence on the event itself, but they will certainly have an effect on what happens next: on how the child and other members of the family are going to handle this new situation.

In the developmental co-adaptation model, reciprocal individual-environment changes are described. In addition to the previous model, changes in the environment can be produced by the individual's behaviors or characteristics. Individual or environmental changes may either compensate for or magnify each other. The examples mentioned by Kindermann and Skinner are clearly related to developmental tasks: interaction in the peer group, coping with changes produced by stressful life-events, and school motivation. Again, it may be not so easy to see why these examples would not fit with a more complex model. In the example of a teacher's effect on student motivation, for example, the teacher probably will have a clear developmental agenda for the students. Also, the study of coping with stressful life events can be placed in this co-adaptation model, but might also be placed in a more complex one. For example, parental support to a child in a coping situation might be provided with a clear developmental agenda in mind.

In the developmental attunement model, the environmental changes are developmentally adjusted. As Kindermann and Skinner have already mentioned, the importance of the concept of developmental tasks is obvious here in the fact that persons in the environment have their own motives and goals and in the fact that the timing of measurement can also be assumed to be related to this agenda.

This description of the three models incorporating environmental development, along with their examples, shows that it may not be easy to decide which of the models should be used for studying an isolated psychological phenomenon. In fact, the most fruitful strategy may be to try to fit the phenomenon in the most sophisticated model, the developmental attunement model. Based on the theoretical considerations that accompany this process of fitting, decisions about what dimensions of the phenomenon to study and when to measure them can be made.

Summarizing, the chapter by Kindermann and Skinner provides a creative and extensively documented overview of different ways to look at the relation between the development of an individual and the development of the context in which that individual resides. The increasing complexity of the models they describe calls for a strong theoretical, or at least heuristic, framework of what the important issues are in development. The framework of developmental tasks served as an example in this comment.

References

Baltes, P. B., Reese, H. W., & Lipsitt, L. P. (1980). Life-span developmental psychology. *Annual Review of Psychology, 31,* 65-110.

Havighurst, R. J. (1973). History of developmental psychology: Socialization and personality development through the life span. In P. B. Baltes & K. W. Schaie (Eds.), *Life-span developmental psychology: Personality and socialization* (pp. 3-24). New York: Academic Press.

Higgins, E. T., & Parsons, J. E. (1983). Social cognition and the social life of the child: Stages as subcultures. In E. T. Higgins, D. N. Ruble, & W. W. Hartup (Eds.), *Social cognition and social behavior: Developmental issues* (pp. 15-62). New York: Cambridge University Press.

Kindermann, T. A., & Skinner, E. A. (1988). Developmental tasks as organizers of children's ecologies: Mothers' contingencies as children learn to walk, eat, and dress. In J. Valsiner (Ed.), *Child development within culturally structured environments: Vol. 2. Social co-construction and environmental guidance in development* (pp. 66-105). Norwood, NJ: Ablex.

Sroufe, L. A., & Waters, E. (1977). Attachment as an organizational construct. *Child Development, 48,* 1184-1199.

Waters, E., & Sroufe, L. A. (1983). Social competence as a developmental construct. *Developmental Review, 3,* 79-97.

COMMENTARY ON CHAPTER 6:

Modeling Environmental Development: The Necessity of Discussing Some Other Basic Assumptions

MARIA CLOTILDE ROSSETTI-FERREIRA

ZILMA MORAES RAMOS DE OLIVEIRA

Recent conceptions in the history of developmental psychology have increasingly elected, as their privileged focus of attention, the processes by which environments and individuals reciprocally influence each other. Pierre Janet is a great precursor of this tradition and has surely influenced many authors, such as Piaget, Vygotsky, Wallon, and others.

Assuming a contextual view of human development, Kindermann and Skinner's chapter explores the idea that an explanation of individual development is closely tied to an understanding of how contexts change over time. The discussion proposed by the authors about the conception of environmental development implied in models of psychological reasoning on human development is provocative when their methodological implications in producing manageable programs of research are considered.

Although they propose to look for explanations of the individual-environment interchanges across time, however, they were unable to entirely escape from a dichotomous view of those relations and from the artificial duality between stability and change.

They do call attention to more interactionist models, such as the co-adaption and attunement models, but were nevertheless influenced by the dichotomous view prevalent in the area. To overcome this duality is a difficult challenge to be faced by developmental psychology.

The basic idea usually implied in words like *environment* and *context* is the separateness between the individual and his or her surrounding conditions, both taken as already constituted elements with some kind of interdependence. In this conception, environment exists apart from the individual, it contains him or her, it influences and is influenced by him or her.

This theoretical position is rather different from a dialectical one that postulates a mutual constitution of the individual and the environment while in interaction. One is the necessary counterpart of the other.

The individual is always being constituted, evolving in a sociohistorical milieu created by human interaction with its symbolic meanings. Thus it seems too narrow to explain individual-environment relationships only as a set of reciprocal influences between already constituted elements to be investigated by interdisciplinary theories and multifactorial methods of data analysis. As stated by the authors, developmental phenomena can be better apprehended if the dynamic nature of individual-milieu relationships and their evolution are considered.

The dichotomy between stability and change raises many questions. Since human development is a continuous process occurring in the direction and rhythm valued by a concrete culture with its historical goals, to discuss stability and change in psychological development one has to investigate how individuals were and will become. It is the intrinsic movement of a tense equilibrium between intraindividual stability and change (two sides of the same coin) that one has to look for, while recognizing that this enterprise involves the cultural referents assumed by the investigator.

Nevertheless, a critical discussion about the models of environmental change proposed by Kindermann and Skinner is important not only for promoting a theoretical progress in human development research, but also for improving the efficiency of intervention-oriented research.

Some basic requirements for a model of psychological environment in the study of human development have been proposed in the chapter. Such models require the specification of the target phenomenon under study and the definition of a developmental frame according to a psychological theory in order to identify those points in time during which the target phenomenon is opened to the influence of environmental factors.

The authors arrived at a categorization of models of environmental stability and environmental development that consider diverse parameters. The most explicit parameter proposed is the stable or changeable nature of the environment. Three classes have been distinguished: (1) environmental stability, represented by what they label the "launch model," traditionally used in psychology, in which the initial forces of the contextual antecedents are the major determinants of the shape of the outcome curve. Although contextual changes are seen as a possibility, they are assumed to be irrelevant to the prediction of the target outcome; (2) age-graded environments represented by the "developmental transition model," in which the experience of environmental change for individuals represents transitions across presumably stable contexts; (3) dynamic or changeable environments that contain three models: (3.1) the "weather model," in which the sources of change range from accidental, random events to historical changes that are not initiated or steered in any way by the target individual; (3.2) the "developmental co-adaptation model," in which the changes and developments of the context are reciprocally linked to the target individual; (3.3) the "developmental attunement model," characterized by a pattern of environmental change that is calibrated according to the target individual's development and is guided by the contexts' goals to shape the individual's trajectory.

In their presentation, the authors discussed each model according to other parameters and dimensions, such as the direction of the effects, the active or passive role of the subjects, the levels of contextual influences (micro, meso, exo, macro), the presence and nature of intervening variables in the chain of effects, the timing of the contextual shift or impact, and the character (preestablished, randomic, or historical) of the changes.

This makes the models nonexclusive and introduces some difficulties in the apprehension of the differences between them. Consequently, it generates some problems for the investigator facing a concrete task of choosing the best model to fit a particular developmental study.

In our critical remarks about the models proposed, we will try to point out some of their advantages and inadequacies for the analysis of the multiple processes of environment—individual influences, and eventually for the design and evaluation of intervention programs.

Regarding the launch model, we agree with the authors that it is the most commonly used in psychological research. It has been previously called "the main effect model" by Sameroff and Chandler (1975, p. 232) in their discussion on the reproductive risk and the continuum of caretaking casualty. The direction of the effect is preestablished as it focuses on the product/outcome of a specified antecedent.

In our view, this model is suitable to analyze the influence of complex variables, such as low socio-economic status (SES), which is usually defined by the low economic, occupational, and educational position of the family in the social structure. Such complex variables involve a network of variables that may range from low and unstable income and poor sanitary conditions to family instability, low parental attention, and high restrictivity to child—as stated by Christiansen, Vuori, Mora, and Wagner (1974) when discussing social environment as it relates to malnutrition and mental development according to what they call a "social structural model." Those variables encompass, and might have differing although interrelated influences on, each of the various contextual systems proposed by Bronfenbrenner (1979). Consequently, different models might be better suited to focus the specific influence of each of those embedded variables on the individual developmental trajectory.

The stability of the environment or of the environmental influence on that trajectory does not imply a stability in the environment per se, or a stability in the influence of each of the variables included in the network. It is related, in our view, to the more general, macrostructural level of the complex category SES in which a much longer time is required for significant historical transformations to occur.

Let us try to explain this idea with the theoretical model proposed by Pollitt (1982) and modified by Rossetti-Ferreira, 1984b (Figure 1) to analyze the effects of various intervention programs in Latin America on the developmental trajectories of children born in very poor families, in which malnutrition is an endemic condition.

In the graphic presented in Figure 1, function a depicts the developmental trajectory of children from families of middle and high socioeconomic status. Function b refers to children from families who live below the poverty level, defined according to their possibility of getting the food needed to guarantee a minimum adequate diet for each member of the family. Functions b_1 and b_2 represent the developmental trajectories of children submitted to intervention programs that involved a single intervention, such as food supplementation (b_1), or a multidimensional intervention (b_2) when—besides food supplementation—the programs comprised coordinated actions in health, sanitation, and education. In his original model, Pollitt (1982) considered mental development as the basic outcome measure. In Rossetti-Ferreira's

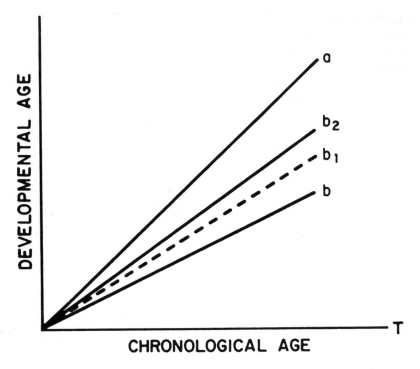

Figure 1. Developmental Trajectories of Children Born in Favorable (a) and Unfavorable (b, b_1, b_2) Conditions.

NOTE: On the abscissa, the chronological age of the children extends from birth to the end of the preschool period (T). The ordinate indicates the attained developmental age of a child. Line a describes the trajectory of development of a "normal" child with a perfect matching between developmental measures and chronological age. Line b represents the trajectory of development of a malnourished child, living in an environment of extreme poverty. Line b_1 describes the development of a child raised in similar conditions, but benefiting from a program of long-term food supplementation. In b_2, the child lives in the same unfavorable conditions as b and b_1, but has been a beneficiary of a multiple intervention program, including nutrition, health, and education.
SOURCE: Adapted from Rossetti-Ferreira, 1984b.

(1984b) modification, the *Y* variable represents any measure of individual development, ranging from quotients of mental development to measures of social and school performance.

Analyzing Figure 1, it can be seen that some improvement was observed (b_1, b_2), but the curve never reached the rate of development of middle and upper middle class children (trajectory a). Furthermore, as Bronfenbrenner (1979) pointed out, the effects tended to wash out sometime after the program was discontinued. Only with drastic changes in the environmental conditions is it possible to move a child from trajectory b to a. In individual cases this has been observed when undernourished children from very poor families were adopted by middle-class parents (Winick, Meyer, & Harris, 1975). This kind of change usually cannot be obtained by means of intervention programs unless they are accompanied by basic socioeconomic and political actions that profoundly change the macrostructures of the society (Rossetti-Ferreira, 1984a). We do not, however, deny some enduring changes occurring with specific individuals, chiefly when the family is also involved in a process of change. In this case, the effective environmental change occurs basically at the microsystem level and probably can be better explained by one of the proposed models of environmental development.

Kindermann and Skinner state that the launch model may also be a useful representation for phenomena that are open to influence from the environment at one point and subsequently become "sealed off." In this case, a kind of contextual-individual influence is defined not by the static nature of the environment, but by the individual's sensitivity or openness to influences from the environment at a certain period in life and its subsequent immunity to it. In our view, this agrees more with the notion of a critical or sensitive period—explained by the long human dependence early in life, when the human organism is more susceptible to close environmental influences, chiefly to the influence of significant others—than with a model of environmental stability. Although changes can be observed in the construct referents of "sensitive parenting" according to the developmental level of the children, as indicated by the authors, there might be stability in another, more general, macrostructural level that describes the environment in which sensitive parenting is provided for children of different ages. The launch model may be more suitable for explaining variations at this macrostructural level, while the developmental attunement would be more appropriate for analyzing how parents adjust their behavior to the developmental level of 18-month-olds and 5-year-olds. Nevertheless, later on in life, the target phenomenon individual trajectory will not be opened to that kind of influence. Thus it will not be modified by a change in parenting style.

The developmental transition model, which postulates systematic age differences in environments, is a clear-cut and useful model for examining systematic age changes that are supposed by the investigator to be connected to context transitions that are themselves organized or stratified according to age. The authors, however, have tried to make a more encompassing model that also takes into account the active role of the individuals in determining the micro-contextual influences to which they will be exposed. They have distinguished culturally designed or institutionalized environments to which individuals of specific ages are exposed, from self-selected environments in which "individuals are the creators of any age-specificity and to some extent the designers of the environment's characteristics." This enlargement of the model in our view restricts its usefulness. The active role of the individual in selecting his or her environments and in influencing their characteristics can probably be better focused through other models, such as the co-adaptation model.

The weather model of parallel play between individual and environment is defined by the fact that the environmental random or historical facts, which influence individual trajectories, are in no way initiated or steered by the target individual. The label "model of co-development" used to define it, as well as the graphic proposed to represent it, raise some doubts as they assume a continuity between the various moments of context development that does not seem to be implied in this model. A progressive chain of effects is suggested. Those effects can be filtered across different layers of meso, exo, and macro systems, with a final impact on the microecology of the target individual. The weather model emphasizes the importance of the timing of the contextual shift or impact, that is, of the changeable susceptibility of individuals and microsystems to that impact at different moments in life. The idea of developmental psychosocial crisis, proposed by Erikson (1963), seems to be quite useful for the analysis of those time "windows." On the other hand, the interchange between individual and contextual characteristics at those periods of crisis can probably be better explained by the reciprocal models of co-adaptation or of developmental attunement.

Those two reciprocal models focus on the mutual influences between the target individual and his or her social partners, which occur at a microsystem level if one uses Bronfenbrenner's taxonomy (1979). They focus on the ongoing process of interaction, assuming that in it the subject, and his partners, as well as their physical and social context are being continuously constructed and transformed. They constitute the models better suited to attend to most of the recent advances in the conception of environment-individual influences presented by the authors.

Our studies on child development involve a conception of reciprocal individual-environment change that agrees with the attunement model, when it focuses on adult-child interaction (Lyra & Rossetti-Ferreira, 1987), and with the co-adaptation model, when early peer interaction is being considered (Oliveira & Rossetti-Ferreira, 1989). In our theoretical perspective, based on Mead (1934), Wallon (1942), and Vygotsky (1962), human development occurs in and through multiple interactions with the environment, especially with privileged partners. Thus our focus is on the microsetting. We entirely agree, however, that the exo, meso, and macro levels proposed by Bronfenbrenner (1979) influence the interpersonal relationships, the routines people create, the roles they play, the objects they use, the objectives they reach for and, above all, the symbolic meanings of their actions. Those and other elements create some concrete conditions for human actions, paving the way for consciousness in Vygotsky's (1962) and Wallon's (1942) terms.

From that perspective, the social context does not comprehend only interpersonal relationships but all kinds of objects, activities, and representations created by persons and presented in the situations. It involves material artifacts and technologies, symbolic ways of behaving and dealing with information, and it is permeated and structured by language.

Discussing our perspective according to the points raised in the chapter, we can say that when the interactions are the focus of the research, their dynamic character prevails over other more stable aspects. In our studies, this standpoint has required a qualitative approach to data collection and a microgenetic level of analysis able to encompass the dialectical relations established between individuals and contexts. We presented this approach during the Bernried Conference, but it does not seem appropriate to extend it further in this volume.

In conclusion, it is a difficult challenge to find models able to encompass such a variety of levels and dimensions of the environment. The authors' contribution is very important considering the present "state of the art" in psychological developmental studies, because it calls for attention to the dynamic nature of human contexts. Their purpose of stimulating reflection and discussion among researchers was fully achieved.

References

Bronfenbrenner, U. (1979). *The ecology of human development: Experiments by nature and design*. Cambridge, MA: Harvard University Press.

Christiansen, N., Vuori, L., Mora, J. O., & Wagner, M. (1974). Social environment as it relates to malnutrition and mental development. In J. Cravioto, L. Hambraeus, & B. Vahlquist (Eds.), *Early malnutrition and mental development* (pp. 186-198). Uppsala, Sweden: Almqvist & Wiksell.

Erikson, E. H. (1963). *Childhood and society* (2nd ed.). New York: Norton.

Lyra, M. C., & Rossetti-Ferreira, M. C. (1987). *Dialogue and the construction of the mother-infant dyad*. Paper presented at the 10th Biennial Meetings of ISSBD, Tokyo, Japan.

Mead, G. H. (1934). *Mind, self and society*. Chicago: Charles W. Morris.

Oliveira, Z.M.R., & Rossetti-Ferreira, M. C. (1989). The construction of roles in early peer interaction. In B. H. Schneider, G. Attili, J. Nadel, & R. Weissberg (Eds.), *Social competence in developmental perspective* (pp. 407-408). Dordrecht, Netherlands: Kluwer.

Pollitt, E. (1982). *Desnutricion, inteligencia y politica social* [Malnutrition, intelligence, and social policy]. Lima, Peru: Studium Ediciones.

Rossetti-Ferreira, M. C. (1984a). Comments on nutrition interventions, research and social change. In J. Brozek & B. Schurch (Eds.), *Malnutrition and behavior: Critical assessment of key issues* (pp. 490-498). Lausanne, Switzerland: Nestlé Foundation.

Rossetti-Ferreira, M. C. (1984b). Limites de psicologia preventiva enquanto instrumento de mudança social. *Ciencia e Cultura, 36,* 1723-1739.

Sameroff, A. J., & Chandler, M. J. (1975). Reproductive risk and the continuum of caretaking casualty. In F. D. Horowitz (Ed.), *Review of child development research* (pp. 187-244). Chicago: University of Chicago Press.

Vygotsky, L. S. (1962). *Thought and language*. Cambridge: MIT Press.

Wallon, H. (1942). *De l'acte à la pensée: Essai de psychologie comparée* [From acting to thinking: Essay on comparative psychology]. Paris: Flammarion.

Winick, M., Meyer, K. K., & Harris, R. C. (1975). Malnutrition and environmental enrichment by early adoption. *Science, 190,* 1173-1175.

7

Description and Explanation in Developmental
Research: Separate Agendas

CYNTHIA LIGHTFOOT

TRISHA FOLDS-BENNETT

Invitations to the Bernried meetings were somewhat unusual in that
they included an assignment to design an ideal developmental study
unfettered by the practical concerns of finding money, subjects, sym-
pathetic school boards, and so forth. Although we were free to choose
a content area, we were instructed to specify the *developmental* questions we would address, to outline the *processes* on which we would
focus, and to define the *mechanisms* that might underlie temporal stability or change in processes.

As the first day of the conference drew to a close, it was clear that
participants had different and often conflicting ideas about what an
exemplary developmental study should look like. One source of controversy concerned distinctions that were presumed to exist between
processes and mechanisms. Although some thought the distinction
was more problematic than useful, others considered it vital to the design and execution of developmental research. This chapter is presented in defense of the second position.

We began by examining participants' responses to the preconference assignment and found, by and large, that the difference between

processes and mechanisms had been interpreted along the lines of the more familiar distinction between descriptive and explanatory analyses of development. Although the distinction has been recognized and respected throughout the history of developmental psychology, its impact on contemporary research design and analysis has been subtle at best. At worst, it remains one of those issues that psychologists debate eagerly, but have difficulty translating into concrete research practices. The position developed here is that the issue is central to developmental research because the study of processes and mechanisms requires distinct research strategies. In particular, we propose that intraindividual analysis is essential for answering questions about the developmental mechanisms that underlie human behavior.

Description and Explanation in Developmental Theory

RESPONSES TO THE PRECONFERENCE ASSIGNMENT

We reviewed responses to the preconference assignment because we thought they might provide insight into some of the assumptions that developmentalists maintain regarding the process-mechanism distinction. Participants were asked to respond to the questions: "What are the processes that you will focus upon in your analysis (of stability and change)?" and "What developmental mechanisms underlie this expected pattern of stability or change?" Table 7.1 indicates that most responses reflected a hierarchy of causality: Mechanisms were presumed to provide the setting conditions for the development or functioning of processes. Suggested processes, on the other hand, tended to be lower order, overt behavioral sequences or performance capabilities made possible by the operation of particular mechanisms.

Thus hierarchical organization, equilibration, internalization, and adaptation were all nominated as potential mechanisms but never as processes, while the more descriptive constructs, such as goal-setting and cooperative behavior, were nominated as processes. Even when "lower order" constructs were defined as mechanisms (e.g., perspective-taking abilities), it was in the context of explaining still lower order behaviors (e.g., helping behavior). So, regardless of what was called "process" or "mechanism," participants implied a distinction between developmental outcomes and the phenomena that produce

TABLE 7.1 Responses to Questions of Process and Mechanism

Process	Mechanism
Cooperative and helping behavior	Perspective-taking abilities
Patterns of acquiring cognitive abilities; e.g., sequential or simultaneous	Hierarchial organization, equilibrium of cognitive structures
Mental representation ability, goal setting, self-monitoring ability	Open system mechanisms; e.g., equilibration, disequilibration
Role/counter role differentiation	Fusion-differentiation, equilibration, internalization, perspective-taking
Reciprocal socialization processes	Child maturation, parent experience, support in home environment
Interaction processes	?
Processes indicated by microanalysis of behavior in test situation, stability and change over time and tests, stability and change in social ecology, e.g., relationships	? Perhaps different mechanisms for different subgroups and tasks
?	Adaptation through developmental and genetic homeostasis
Gravitation and problem generation	? Treat as complex, wholistic systems
Accentuation of individual differences	Genetic/environmental stability, person-environment transactions

them. In this respect, at least, their responses seemed derivative of the distinction between descriptive and explanatory levels of analysis. Indeed, the issue of description versus explanation recurred throughout the conference, particularly during discussions of whether one or another type of analysis—for example, statistical, mathematical, symbolic-logical—was better suited to exploring the *causes* of human development.

UBIQUITY OF INTEREST IN THE "WHAT" AND "HOW" OF DEVELOPMENT

In his preface to the volume *Mechanisms of Cognitive Development,* Sternberg (1984) argued that developmental psychologists face two fundamental questions: First, through what psychological states do individuals move in the course of development, and second, what mechanisms permit movement from one state to another? Regarding their relative importance or potential contribution to understanding development, Sternberg considered answers to the second question to be more significant. In his discussion of the volume, Flavell (1984) took a similar position when he distinguished between developmental outcomes and developmental mechanisms—the *what* and *how* of development, respectively. He suggested that each constitutes half of the "developmental story": However, because the question of *how* is a question of explanation—"the ultimate objective of any science" (p. 188)—he considered it the more important half.

Although this recent interest in explaining development may seem fresh and novel, the distinction between descriptive and explanatory levels of analysis is as old as the discipline. James Mark Baldwin (1895), the progenitor of modern developmental psychology, proposed three descriptive stages of development (reflexive, sensorimotor, symbolic) and a mechanism (circular reactions) of stage transition. He focused his subsequent work on detailing the causal-genetic laws or principles by which knowledge is generated over the course of childhood (e.g., Baldwin, 1906). Piaget's life work, as well, represented an ongoing struggle to coordinate the descriptive with the explanatory (Beilin, 1971). Similarly, Myrtle McGraw (1941) expressed the hardship involved in *failing* to distinguish between the two. In the course of formalizing an account of motor development, she found herself unable to make sense of literally thousands of recorded motor movements until she adopted an explanatory theory of neuromuscular maturation. She described her problem, and its solution in the following way:

> On examining the mass of records it appeared possible to select nine distinct phases in such a way that any child could be rated, regardless of his individual peculiarity in creeping, so as to reflect the essential advancement in his neuromuscular maturation. . . . The nine phases became apparent only after a rationale, based upon a theoretical interpretation of the maturation of the nervous system, had been realized. . . . After various efforts to organize the data into categories based upon overt descriptions of overt motor activity only, it was realized that in many instances verbal descriptions of only motor movements may read essentially the same for both voluntary and involuntary activities. . . . Moreover, it was also recognized that two babies may engage in movements which in pattern appear to be different but in fact reflect the same level of neuro-maturation. (McGraw, 1941, pp. 86-87).

McGraw solved her problem by going beyond overt motor movements to consider underlying maturational mechanisms. Her conclusion, in fact, was that these mechanisms operate such that different individuals may exhibit the same behavioral patterns for different reasons, or different behavioral patterns for the same reason. If McGraw had not structured her behavioral observations in light of an explanatory theory, she would not have been able to distinguish between descriptively similar patterns. Her experience illustrates how explanatory systems allow one to formalize a collection of observed events (as in the manner through which her nine phases of motor advancement "became apparent"), and to discern relationships between events (as in the transformation from subcortical to cortical mediation).

GENOTYPE AND PHENOTYPE

The distinction between process and mechanism, description and explanation, or the *what* and *how* of development became controversial during the heyday of normative developmental research begun in the late 1920s. At that time, the nature-nurture controversy inspired a groundswell of research designed to catalog developmental milestones that were presumably generated by the unfolding of a biogenetic blueprint. A fraction of developmentalists, however, questioned the value of such work for identifying causal-generative mechanisms. Kurt Lewin and Lev Vygotsky, in particular, took strong positions against a "psychology of numbers" that was destined to provide developmental descriptions alone.

Lewin (1933) argued vigorously that mechanisms should be at the forefront of developmental research. Adopting the language of evolutionary biology, he distinguished between *genotypic* and *phenotypic* levels of analysis. His primary goal was to discern the psychological laws that dictate the behavior of individuals within environments. His concern with dynamic relations—the psychological structures that unite child and situation—made him critical of statistical methods that characterized the "average" individual rather than the psychological structures underlying an individual's behavior. He argued that such quantitative methodologies brought individuals together at a phenotypic, descriptive level, and masked potential genotypic (psychological) dissimilarities:

For, in the investigation of the fundamental dynamic relations between the individual and the environment, it is essential to keep constantly in mind the actual total situation in its concrete individuality. The statistical method is usually compelled to define its groups on the basis not of purely psychological characteristics but of more or less extrinsic ones (such as number of siblings), so that particular cases having quite different or even opposed *psychological* structure may be included in the same group. (Lewin, 1933, p. 591)

According to Lewin, insight into child-environment dynamics and their development could only be achieved by means of genotypic analysis, and this involved investigating individual children acting within particular environments. Inferences from the statistically derived average child to a particular child were impossible by his reckoning:

The concepts of the average child and of the average situation are abstractions that have no utility whatever for the investigation of dynamics. . . . For the discovery of dynamic laws . . . it does not suffice to segregate a single property or a phenotypically defined event, without regard to the total situation. . . . The laws of falling bodies in physics cannot be discovered by taking the average of actual falling movements, say of leaves, stones and other objects, but only by proceeding from so-called "pure" cases. Likewise, in psychology the forces of the environment and the laws of their operation on child behavior can be discovered only by proceeding from certain total situations that are "simple," but well defined in their concrete individuality. (Lewin, 1933, p. 591)

Vygotsky was impressed by Lewin's phenotype-genotype distinction (Valsiner, 1988), and argued that in the absence of genetic analysis, the psychology of human development resembled a pre-Darwinian taxonomy in which whales were classified as fish on the basis of outward or morphological similarities (Vygotsky, 1934/1986, p. 122). Confusing morphological appearances with causal-developmental phenomena constitutes a theoretical error from the outset; but the *degree* of error, practically speaking, corresponds to the complexity of the "genotype":

When the morphological analysis of psychological structures lacks its genetic counterpart, it becomes inadequate. With the growth of the complexity of psychological processes, the importance of the preceding developmental stages also grows. The greater organization and differentiation of psychological structures, the more inadequate a pure morphological analysis becomes. Without genetic analysis and synthesis, without a study of early developmental stages, we would never be able to recognize those elementary forms that become bearers of the essential relations. (Vygotsky, 1934/1986, p. 125)

Both Lewin and Vygotsky believed that genotypic analysis was the most direct route to understanding development. Indeed, they considered it the *only* route to discovering fundamental developmental laws and principles. Most would agree that identifying general laws and principles is fundamental to the developmental sciences. Recall that Flavell (1984) considered explanation the ultimate objective of *any* science. Lewin and Vygotsky distinguish themselves from the mainstream, however, on the issue of the source of lawful behavior and the methods by which it could be discerned. Conventional methodologies emphasize large numbers of representative individuals, mathematical averages, and sample generalizability as mainstays of a "scientific" method; "lawfulness" is equated with generalizability. Thus the source of lawfulness is located in group performance, and the group becomes the prototype for the individual. In contrast, Lewin and Vygotsky held that development proceeds according to the reciprocal and systemic relationships that exist between individuals and the environments in which they function. This assumption requires different analytic methods—notably those that focus on how particular children psychologically structure their behaviors within particular contexts.

The theoretical posture adopted by Lewin and by Vygotsky on the issue of quantitative versus developmental methodologies dovetails neatly with modern criticisms of the "scientism" that pervades psychological research (Koch, 1981; Shames, 1990). Valsiner (1989) has spoken against psychology's dependence on the "law of large numbers" and the presumed equivalence of statistical methodology and the scientific method. Harré and Madden (1975) and Secord (1986), among others (e.g., Bhaskar, 1975; Margolis, 1984), have cast reasonable doubt on the ability of traditional "science" to illuminate human action. In particular, they take issue with conceptions of behavioral science as the pursuit of universal laws inferred from regularities across a set of specifiable variables. The alternative proposed is to start from the premise that mechanisms, explanations, and lawfulness reside within natural behavioral and social structures that enable and constrain action possibilities. The goal of behavioral science, then, is neither to discern regularities nor predict outcomes from a given set of variables, both of which are inherent in traditional developmental research. Instead, the aim is to specify the psychological structures

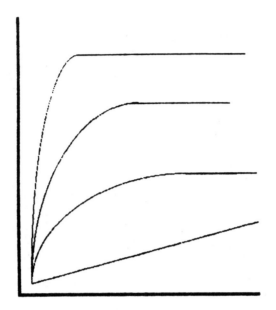

Figure 7.1. Sample Set of Individual Curves—Continuous Function
SOURCE: Adapted from Sidman, 1952.

with which particular individuals construct and adapt to particular realities. The distinction between these two conceptual systems has dramatic implications for research on human development.

Issues of Method

AGGREGATED DATA AND FALSE INFERENCES

Typically, as in most areas of psychology, analyses of developmental data employ ANOVA statistical models in which data are summarized in the form of group means. However, as the reader has no
doubt anticipated, ANOVA models are of limited utility in understanding the development of individuals. In fact, as Lewin argued,
group and individual performances may have little in common. His
caveat against averaging across individuals is given force by
Sidman's (1952) demonstration of differences between functions for

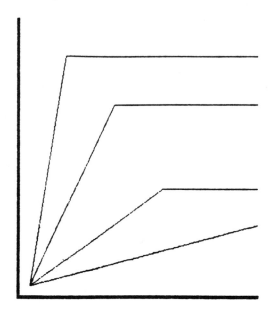

Figure 7.2. Sample Set of Individual Curves—Discontinuous Function
SOURCE: Adapted from Sidman, 1952.

individuals and for groups. Sidman mathematically generated a set of individual curves similar to those shown in Figure 7.1.

Here, interorganism variability is shown in both the asymptotes approached by the curves, and the rates of approach to the asymptotes. Sidman went on to show that the mean curve derived bore no relation to the form of the individual curves, and furthermore, that similar mean curves could be generated by individual curves of vastly different forms. For example, the individual curves shown in Figure 7.2, if averaged, will provide an equally good approximation to the original mean curve generated by the curves shown in Figure 7.1.

Although Sidman presented only these two cases in detail, he argued that his analysis applied equally to any functional relation. That is, for many functions, the means curve will not be of the same form as the individual curves. It follows that any particular mean curve does not uniquely specify the form of individual curves, and does not provide information necessary to make inferences about individuals.

TABLE 7.2   Typical Rehearsal Protocols

Word Presented	Rehearsal Sets Eighth-Grade Subject	Third-Grade Subject
1. yard	yard, yard, yard	yard, yard, yard, yard, yard
2. cat	cat, yard, yard, cat	cat, cat, cat, cat, yard
3. man	man, cat, yard, man, yard, cat	man, man, man, man, man
4. desk	desk, man, yard, cat, man, desk, cat, yard	desk, desk, desk, desk

SOURCE: From "Rehearsal and Organization Processes in Children's Memory" by P. Ornstein, J. Naus, and C. Liberty, 1975, *Child Development, 26*, p. 822. © The Society for Research in Child Development, Inc. Reprinted by permission.

More recently, Ornstein, Naus, and Liberty (1975) encountered a similar problem in using mean performance to study children's memory strategies. They had third graders attempt to remember a set of words. The children were taught to use an "active" rehearsal strategy in which they rehearsed each item aloud in combination with other to-be-remembered items. Third graders were able to perform this strategy, but when their recall was compared to a group of eighth graders, it was discovered that they were still unable to recall as many items as these older children. Ornstein and his colleagues were perplexed about the lack of correlation between strategy use and recall until they examined how individual children executed the active rehearsal strategy. They found that although third graders were responding to the training instructions to rehearse words in combination, their rehearsal had a "rote-like" quality to it (see Table 7.2).

Third graders, they discovered, tended to take the first presented word and combine it with each subsequently presented item, whereas eighth graders rehearsed several combinations of items. Therefore, third graders rehearsed the first couple of items disproportionately more than the later items. In this example, the mean indicated that the two *groups* did not differ with regard to average performance on a measure of strategy use; however, examination of individuals indicated differences in the sophistication and effectiveness of strategy use.

These results indicate the value of looking beyond group performances in order to understand the behavior of individuals. ANOVA models intentionally obscure the individual; individual variation is considered a nuisance variable to be controlled (Appelbaum &

McCall, 1983). Nonetheless, they are often used as a basis for interpreting individuals' behaviors. Moving from the level of the group to that of the individual, however, also involves moving beyond results that are generated by the models. As stated by Rogoff and Gauvain (1986), "interpretation of the theoretical meaning of statistical results generally draws on a deeper understanding of the data base than is captured in the summary of the results"; it is of utmost importance, therefore, that the statistical representation of the results reliably capture the "realities of specific cases" (pp. 266-267). On the basis of Sidman's demonstration, however, we would argue that the realities of specific cases may be beyond the scope of current statistical methods.

To their credit, psychologists are becoming increasingly convinced that change with age inferred from group data may not correspond to change within any one individual (e.g., Wohlwill, 1973). The examples presented above illustrate how developmental phenomena may be lost or obscured by aggregating data across individuals, and that group data may lead to false inferences regarding the performance of individuals. The obvious solution is to adopt methods that preserve changes in *individuals'* behaviors over time. In keeping with this suggestion, a distinction must be made between interindividual and intraindividual methods of analysis. Lewin and Vygotsky both favored the latter, and studies have shown the importance of using them. But most contemporary methods that are intended to study the development of individuals are of the interindividual ilk, and we will argue that they undermine the goals of genetic—as opposed to phenotypic—analysis.

CHANGES ACROSS INDIVIDUALS: INTERINDIVIDUAL ANALYSIS

The study of developing organisms is known to present special difficulties from the standpoint of statistical methodology (Appelbaum & McCall, 1983). Most statistical methods have the effect of eliminating variance and individual differences, and yield descriptions of static outcomes rather than explanations of dynamic processes. Consistent with the argument presented above, Green (1990) has stated that "analysis of individual differences in behavior over time is one avenue that can lead toward a better understanding of the *mechanisms* of development" (p. 1, emphasis added). Individual difference methodologies are gaining favor among developmentalists; in fact, most of the conference participants expressed a preference for examining individual as opposed to group differences. Generally, one of two conceptual models is used to analyze individual differences in development—one involves the assessment of developmental functions and the other assesses individual difference stability (Appelbaum & McCall, 1983; Green, 1990). Both employ longitudinal designs and are essentially interindividual in that they permit comparisons between individuals and groups of individuals. Each is associated with a different class of statistical techniques, however—developmental functions with profile analysis and individual difference stability with correlational analysis.

Profile analysis techniques are meant to provide answers to questions concerning *developmental functions*. The goal is to determine common developmental profiles displayed by individuals (Appelbaum & McCall, 1983). Data are generally organized in the form of growth curves, or plots of the relation between an individual's age and the characteristic of interest (e.g., IQ score, see McCall, Appelbaum, & Hogarty, 1973). The individual's pattern of changes over time (i.e., the "profile") is determined and correlated for the purpose of determining heterogeneity and homogeneity of classes of individuals.

The second class of procedures is essentially correlational and meant to investigate *individual difference stability*. That is, it examines the relative standing of individuals on a particular developmental characteristic at different points in time. Structural equation modeling, path analysis, and regression procedures are some of the methods used to determine individual difference stability. Basically, these procedures involve apportioning variance among a constellation of correlated variables. If the relative standing of individuals remains stable over time, inferences are made regarding the trait-like nature of the characteristic of interest. However, if instability occurs, it is taken as evidence for the transient nature of a particular characteristic.

Both classes of procedures provide comprehensive information about changes across individuals over time, yet neither can address questions regarding underlying mechanisms. Profile analysis provides purely descriptive information about individual differences (Green, 1990). Although useful for identifying individuals who have similar and different patterns of development, it cannot speak to the issue of *how* certain individuals came to show some patterns as opposed to others, or whether or not individuals may show the same pattern for different reasons, or different patterns for the same reason. Correlational analyses of individual difference stability, which necessarily aggregate across individuals and are thus subject to Sidman's criticisms, are further limited to analyzing linear models. Models that posit reciprocal relationships among variables are beyond the scope of current correlational procedures (Green, 1990).

Although it is generally acknowledged that the classes of procedures described above cannot provide answers to causal-genetic questions, an exception has been made in the case of structural equation modeling because it permits the testing of competing theoretical models. In this case, "cause" translates to "which explanatory model, A or B, accounts for most of the variance?" The cause, then, is the model that has been defined a priori. Obviously, unstated causes (i.e., untested models) are also possible. So, as Green warns us, these procedures do not permit causal inferences in the true sense of the word. They can only provide, in the spirit of Popper, evidence of a disconfirmatory nature; that is, evidence that one model should be rejected because another does a better job of accounting for correlational relationships among variables. More importantly, perhaps, is the fact that the explanatory models are being evaluated with respect to how well they characterize patterns of aggregated data. As we argued previously, a model reputed to explain a particular constellation of correlations is addressing a different form of causality than that which is relevant to intraindividual development.

Thus far we have provided a number of reasons and examples supporting the need for genetic analysis. On the other hand, little has been said about what such an analysis might entail. Strong statements made by Lewin and Vygotsky on this subject would suggest that they were prepared with intraindividually based alternatives to standard methods of quantification and measurement. And indeed, they were.

DEVELOPMENT WITHIN INDIVIDUALS: INTRAINDIVIDUAL ANALYSIS

> Kramer found in 100 percent of his cases that bestial children lost their bestial behavior so completely when brought into an appropriate environment that they might better be characterized as dainty. (Lewin, 1933, p. 393)

Lewin cited Kramer's finding to illustrate the hazards of inferring trait-like tendencies or dispositions (e.g., bestiality) without taking into account the particular environments in which individuals behave. His premise that psychological systems are distinct from behavioral and situational events formed the backbone of his theory. Psychological systems were considered dynamic in that they unite the child with its environment. They define the "real environments" of the child, as opposed to, say, the "objective" physical or social environments as seen through the eyes of others. Within this constructivist perspective, Lewin's genetic analysis took the form of characterizing changes to a psychological system; changes, that is, in the "life-space" of the individual. These ideas formed the basis of Lewin's field theory in which development was described in terms of specific changes in the psychological force, direction, and distribution of environmental objects or events (i.e., the life space). Lewin wrote:

> Objects are not neutral to the child, but have an immediate psychological effect on its behavior: many things *attract* the child to eating, others to climbing, to grasping, to manipulation, to sucking, to raging at them, etc. These imperative environmental facts—we shall call them valences *(Aufforderungscharakter)*—determine the *direction* of the behavior. . . . The valence of an object usually derives from the fact that the object is a means to the satisfaction of a need. . . . The objects bearing valences are different for the baby, the toddler, the kindergartner, and the pubescent. (Lewin, 1933, pp. 596-597)

Lewin's "detour problem" provides a simple and elegant demonstration of genetic analysis within the field theory paradigm (see Figure 7.3). Here we have a situation in which a child (C) must navigate around two different types of barriers (B) in order to reach a piece of chocolate (Ch). The vector (V) indicates the direction of the field force associated with the positive valence. Young children solve the first problem more easily than the second because it does not require movement in a direction opposed to the direction of the valence. Solution to the second problem, in contrast, reflects a psychological restructuring of the field such that the initial movement, although "objectively" a movement *away* from the valence, becomes the first of several steps *toward* the chocolate; a child who can understand this has begun to perceive the "whole situation."

In addition to its direction, the strength of a valence also influences problem solutions. When the strength is especially strong, it is more difficult to move away from the valence initially:

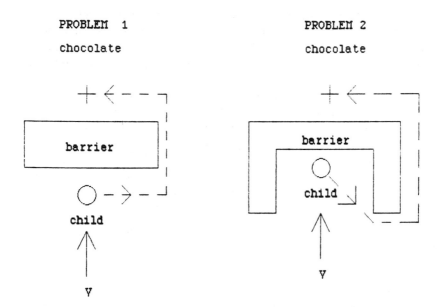

Figure 7.3. Lewin's Barrier Problems

SOURCE: From *Handbook of Child Psychology,* (p. 600) Murchison (Ed.), 1933. Reprinted by permission.

Instead, the child will execute, with all its energy, affective meaningless actions in the direction of the valence. Above all, that relative detachment and inward "retirement" from the valence which is so favorable to perception of the whole situation and hence to the transformation of the total field, which occurs in the act of insight, is made much more difficult. (Lewin, 1933, p. 601)

In understanding Lewin's methodology, it is critical to remember that his use of the terms *direction* and *strength* is meant in the psychological, not the physical sense. Young children's difficulty with the second barrier, and with problems that involve stronger valences, is a consequence of psychologically structuring the field at a perceptual level. Therefore, a young child may negotiate the first boundary easily because its solution does not require extreme violation of physical direction toward the goal. The second boundary, however, requires the individual to transcend perceptual limitations to achieve the goal.

Lewin's insight into the development of children's construction of the life space was achieved in the context of careful experimentation and manipulation. If one were to study goal activation using the first barrier problem alone, one might conclude that there are no developmental differences; both younger and older children make easy progress and reach the chocolate. Likewise, if the second barrier problem were used alone the investigator would be led to conclude that older, but not younger children are able to establish and work toward goals. It is only in the context of studying individuals' action patterns in both settings that the understanding of developmental change emerges.

The way the child structures and transforms the task and, consequently, its possible solutions, was also at the heart of Vygotsky's version of genetic analysis. His "method of double stimulation" was influenced strongly by Piaget's clinical method and Kohler's method for studying problem solving in apes (see Valsiner, 1988, for a more thorough historical analysis). At the time of his work, Vygotsky believed psychology to be in a state of crisis that was primarily methodological in nature, and symptomatic of its transformation into a "true science" (Vygotsky, 1934/1987, p. 54). The crisis was marked, most notably, by the lack of a unitary perspective within the discipline. Each new set of empirical findings, Vygotsky complained, required the construction of a new theory. Piaget's method overcame this to a certain extent because it could be applied to a diversity of developmental domains, and generated a wholistic account of developing thought:

> Piaget owes this gold mine of empirical data to his *clinical method,* a method whose power and unique character has advanced him to the front ranks of contributors to the development of research methods in psychology. Piaget's clinical method is a necessary tool for studying the complex, unified formations of the child's thought in transition and development. It provides a unity to his varied studies, bringing them together into a connected and vital clinical picture of the child's thinking. (Vygotsky, 1934/1987, p. 55)

So Vygotsky considered Piaget's new method a means of uniting the science, and also the various developments of the child. An example of such theoretical integration born of the clinical method is the developing relationship between thought and language. Although Piaget and Vygotsky reached different conclusions about the relationship—its manifestation in egocentric speech, for example—it was only by virtue of their methods that they were able to attempt synthetic solutions to the problem of the development of thought and language.

As an example, consider Vygotsky's studies of concept formation for which he employed the method of double stimulation. At the time of his writing, evidence was accruing as to the equivalence of concepts formed by adults and children. His studies were designed to show that although phenotypically similar, the concepts formed by adults and children were genetically different. That is, concept *formation,* or the *underlying processes* by which concepts were attained, differed for children compared to adults in spite of seemingly similar outcomes. The primary focus of all of Vygotsky's work concerned the genesis of higher mental functions. Higher mental functions, in contrast to lower mental functions, are reflected in the ways that individuals mediate their behavior on the basis of cultural signs and symbols—language, in particular. His argument regarding concept formation was that children's concepts were formed according to lower mental functions, whereas adults' concepts were formed according to higher mental functions. Basically, the method of double stimulation involved presenting the subject with two sets of stimuli: One provided content for the operation of lower mental functions, whereas the other required higher mental functions (Vygotsky, 1934/1986, p. 103). Specifically, children were given a number of wooden blocks of various colors, shapes, heights, and sizes. The underside of each block, not seen by the children, contained one of four nonsense words. One nonsense word (e.g., *lag*) was written on all tall and large blocks, another word was written on all flat and large blocks, and so forth. The experiment began when the investigator turned over one block, showed the word to the child, and asked the child to select all blocks that might be of the same kind. After the child completed this task, the investigator turned over one of the wrongly chosen blocks, indicated that it had a different word on it, and asked the child to continue sorting. The experiment continued in this way—child sorted, investigator corrected, child re-sorted—until the child, if able, successfully sorted the blocks as indicated by the nonsense words. Success, for Vygotsky, meant that the child's activity had become sign-mediated; that is, cultural mental functions had superseded natural mental functions in determining behavior such that the nonsense words took precedence over the perceptual features of the objects. Only adolescents and adults succeeded on this task:

> Learning to direct one's own mental processes with the aid of words or sign is an integral part of the process of concept formation. The ability to

regulate one's actions by using auxiliary means reaches its full development only in adolescence. . . . The new significative use of the word, its
use *as a means of concept formation,* is the immediate psychological
cause of the radical change in the intellectual process that occurs on the
threshold of adolescence. No new *elementary* function, essentially different from those already present, appears at this age, but all existing functions are incorporated into a new structure, form a new synthesis,
become parts of a new complex whole (Vygotsky, 1934/1986, p. 108,
original emphasis).

For Vygotsky, the new complex whole assembled during adolescence forms the basis of all higher mental functions; activity becomes
sign-mediated as cultural mental functions supersede natural mental
functions in determining behavior. His conclusion was based on the
microgenetic study of individuals within constrained problem solving
contexts. His enthusiasm for systematic experimentation was shared
by Lewin who claimed that the manipulation of controlled environments was essential for understanding children's actions within natural settings. Although his distinction between "experimental" and
"natural" environments appears to us artificial, we would agree that
Lewin's and Vygotsky's insights into the psychological development
of children were facilitated by their ability to specify the constructive
opportunities afforded by the different environments. Lewin and
Vygotsky constrained such opportunities experimentally. In nonexperi-
mental settings, however, children's constructions are also constrained;
we would argue, in fact, that they are *always* constrained—by a variety of social-historical forces—and that a primary goal of intraindividual analysis is to specify how the child organizes and
transforms constraints across the life course. This idea, in fact, constituted a basic premise for Lewin's and Vygotsky's experimental work:
The relationship between the child and its environment is essentially
one of interdependence, and development, most broadly conceived,
may be defined in terms of relational transformations.

Final Comments on the Issue of Causality
and the Lawfulness of Human Development

For the past 50 years or so, developmentalists have relied mostly
on data aggregated across individuals for the purpose of making inferences about developmental changes observed between groups.

ANOVA models have contributed to vast stores of information about age differences in average or typical skills, competencies, and behavior. On the other hand, these methods have reduced or eliminated entirely the very phenomenon that the discipline presumes to address: psychological development. Perhaps this state of affairs is the legacy of normative research begun in the 1930s, as suggested by Dixon and Lerner (1988). Or perhaps it is due more generally to psychology's adoption of a mechanistic rather than an organic metaphor, which emphasizes systemic stasis rather than transformation (Feldman, 1986). Regardless, it is becoming acknowledged increasingly that the focus on descriptive outcomes and averages must shift to explanatory mechanisms and individuals (e.g., Riegel, 1976; Bidell, 1988).

Recent advances in the study of individual differences, although moving in the right direction, have been disappointing in their interindividual focus. Profile analytic techniques are meant to correlate individuals' patterns of change rather than explain them; and methods of analyzing individual difference stability lose the individual within patterns of correlated variables ("models") that can only be derived from aggregated data. The claim is often made (and particularly strongly by those exploring individual difference stability methods) that quantitative methods are simply "tools" that may be used for the purpose of informing developmental theory. We would argue, however, that statistical "tool use" is not theory-neutral, but sets significant limits on the types of theoretical inferences that can legitimately be made. To the extent that statistical tools are used to organize and interpret scientific activities, they are constitutive of particular conceptual systems that psychologists use to ask and answer questions about development.

At this point it may be useful to highlight two significant differences implied by phenotypic versus causal-genetic methodologies as described here. The first concerns the difference between generality and lawfulness, which have tended to be falsely equated in developmental psychology. A common argument in favor of large-*N* designs and quantification is that they reveal levels of generality that intraindividual methods cannot approach. A criticism of intraindividual methods, from this perspective, is that results cannot be applied for the purpose of understanding the development of other individuals. However, knowledge that many or most members of a population exhibit similar behaviors or follow similar developmental trajectories is distinct from knowledge about developmental laws or principles that generate behavioral similarities. We would argue for a distinction, then, between *patterns* that might hold for groups of individuals, and *laws* that characterize the operation of psychological systems. As we have emphasized throughout this chapter, determinations of patterns and laws require distinct methodologies (quantitative and intra-individual, respectively) and permit different theoretical inferences (regarding normative outcomes versus developmental mechanisms). Again, *lawfulness*, as applied to developing psychological systems, is not meant to invoke conceptions of universality, generalizability, or predictability—all sacred cows of a conventional view of "science." Instead, it is understood to characterize psychological and social structural conditions that enable, facilitate, and constrain action possibilities (Harré & Madden, 1975; Lewin, 1933; Secord, 1986). In a similar vein, we would also argue the importance of distinguishing between *interdependence* and *correlation*. Early champions of the causal-genetic method (e.g., Lewin and Vygotsky) assumed an inter-dependence between developing individuals and their environments. The microanalytic approach that typified their work followed quite naturally. Recognition of child-environment interdependence is now in vogue, and efforts are being made to capture the multidetermined nature of children's development. Interdependence has lost its meaning, however, in large factorial designs and path analyses that confuse the correlations of multiple child and environment variables with the psychological systems by which children construct and adapt to reality.

Our point, finally, is that we are dealing with two distinct conceptual systems that require distinct research methodologies. Unfortunately, one conceptual system, the one that is least suited to exploring psychological development, has become the yardstick by which we measure the scientific merit of research. As Vygotsky forecast more than 50 years ago, the transformation of psychology into a "true science" has everything to gain by developing methodological tools appropriate to the phenomena it seeks to explain.

References

Appelbaum, M., & McCall, R. (1983). Design and analysis in developmental psychology. In W. Kessen (Ed.), *Handbook of child development* (Vol. 1, pp. 415-476). New York: Academic Press.

Baldwin, J. M. (1895). *Mental development in the child and the race.* New York: Macmillan.

Baldwin, J. M. (1906). *Thought and things: A study of the development and meaning of thought or genetic logic: Vol. I. Functional logic, or genetic theory of knowledge.* New York: Macmillan.

Bhaskar, R. (1975). *A realist theory of science.* Leeds, UK: Leeds Books.

Beilin, J. (1971). Developmental stages and developmental processes. In D. Green, M. Ford, & G. Flamer (Eds.), *Measurement and Piaget* (pp. 172-189). New York: McGraw-Hill.

Bidell, T. (1988). Vygotsky, Piaget and the dialectic of human development. *Human Development, 31,* 329-345.

Dixon, R., & Lerner, R. M. (1988). A history of systems in developmental psychology. In M. Bornstein & M. Lamb (Eds.), *Developmental psychology: An advanced textbook* (pp. 3-50). Hillsdale, NJ: Lawrence Erlbaum.

Feldman, H. (1986). How development works. In I. Levin (Ed.), *Stage and structure: Reopening the debate* (pp. 284-306). Norwood, NJ: Ablex.

Flavell, J. (1984). Discussion. In R. J. Sternberg (Ed.), *Mechanisms of cognitive development* (pp. 187-209). New York: Freeman.

Green, J. (1990). Analyzing individual differences in development: Correlations and cluster analysis. In J. Colombo & J. Fagan (Eds.), *Individual differences in infancy,* Hillsdale, NJ: Lawrence Erlbaum.

Harré, R., & Madden, E. (1975). *Causal powers.* Totowa, NJ: Littlefield, Adams.

Koch, S. (1981). The nature and limits of psychological knowledge: Lessons of a century qua "science." *American Psychologist, 36,* 257-269.

Lewin, K. (1933). Environmental forces. In C. Murchison (Ed.), *Handbook of child psychology* (pp. 590-625). Worcester, MA: Clark University Press.

Margolis, J. (1984). *Philosophy of psychology.* Englewood Cliffs, NJ: Prentice-Hall.

McCall, R., Appelbaum, M., & Hogarty, P. (1973). Developmental changes in mental performance. *Monographs of the Society for Research in Child Development, 38* (Serial No. 150).

McGraw, M. (1941). Development of neuro-muscular mechanisms as reflected in the crawling and creeping behavior of the human infant. *Journal of Genetic Psychology, 58,* 83-111.

Ornstein, P., Naus, J., & Liberty, C. (1975). Rehearsal and organization processes in children's memory. *Child Development, 26,* 818-830.

Riegel, K. (1976, October). The dialectics of human development. *American Psychologist,* 689-699.

Rogoff, B., & Gauvain, M. (1986). A method for the analysis of patterns, illustrated with data on mother-child instructional interaction. In J. Valsiner (Ed.), *The individual subject and scientific psychology* (pp. 261-290). New York: Plenum.

Secord, P. (1986). Explanations in the social sciences and in life situations. In D. Fiske & R. Shweder (Eds.), *Metatheory in social science: Pluralisms and subjectivities.* Chicago: University of Chicago Press.

Sidman, M. (1952). A note on functional relations obtained from group data. *Psychological Bulletin, 49,* 263-269.

Shames, M. (1990). On data, methods, and theory: An epistemological evaluation of psychology. *Canadian Psychology, 31,* 229-238.

Sternberg, R. (Ed.). (1984). *Mechanisms of cognitive development.* New York: Freeman.

Valsiner, J. (Ed.). (1988). *Developmental psychology in the Soviet Union.* Brighton, Sussex, UK: Harvester Press.

Valsiner, J. (1989). From group comparisons to knowledge: A lesson from cross-cultural psychology. In J. P. Forgas & J. M. Innes (Eds.), *Recent advances in social psychology: An international perspective.* North Holland: Elsevier Science Publishers B. V.

Vygotsky, L. (1986). *Thought and language.* Cambridge: MIT Press. (Original work published 1934)

Vygotsky, L. (1987). Thinking and speech. In R. Rieber & A. Carton (Eds.), *The collected works of L. S. Vygotsky* (Vol. 1, pp. 39-285). New York: Plenum. (Original work published 1934)

Wohlwill, J. F. (1973). *The study of behavioral development.* New York: Academic Press.

The "What" and "How" of Development: Really Two Separate Research Agendas?

WOLFGANG SCHNEIDER

As already pointed out by Lightfoot and Folds-Bennett (this volume), the participants in the Bernried meetings had different and often conflicting opinions about many issues concerning human development. Among these issues, the distinction between developmental processes and developmental mechanisms and its implications for developmental research attracted special interest, leading to both stimulating and controversial discussions. If my recollections of those debates are correct, the majority of participants took the position that the distinction between process and mechanism has important implications, a view elaborated by Lightfoot and Folds-Bennett (Chapter 7). A stable minority, however, including myself, saw the distinction as presenting a conceptually complicated and confusing problem. In particular, these participants felt uncomfortable with the term *mechanism,* a word that is derived from the notion of mechanics and that suggests a decontextualized model of the human mind analogous to a machine with moving elements (see also Sigel, 1986). These participants argued that comparably neutral terms like *developmental transitions* or *sources of developmental changes* seem better suited to address the issue of explanation.

Admittedly, the controversy concerning terminology—although interesting from a theoretical point of view—addresses only a minor

AUTHOR'S NOTE: I wish to thank Merry Bullock for her thoughtful and critical comments on this chapter.

problem when compared to the issue of judging the importance of the distinction between (descriptive) processes and (explanatory) mechanisms for developmental research and theory. This is the topic Lightfoot and Folds-Bennett have chosen for their interesting and provoking essay. When reading through the chapter, I was immediately reminded of the discussions in Bernried: Similar to the debates at the monastery, the ideas expressed in the chapter very much stimulated my thinking about issues of cognitive development. However, they also generated some confusion on my part. Given the amount of stimulation/provocation provided by this chapter, I thought it helpful to comment on its major points.

Before discussing the issues in detail, I will first outline what I see as the most important assumptions treated in Chapter 7. These can be summarized as follows: (1) Like many leading developmental theorists, the authors assume that the question of explanation is more important than the question of description. Accordingly, future research should give more emphasis to the issue of developmental mechanisms. (2) Traditional developmental methodology based on ANOVA models cannot achieve this goal: Because the available methods focus on the analysis of group means, they may lead to incorrect inferences concerning developmental changes in individuals. Instead of using "interindividual" methods, future research should focus on methods of "intraindividual" or "genetic" analysis. (3) Today's research can profit from looking at the past: For example, Lewin's experiments based on his field-theoretical approach and Vygotsky's studies on concept formation (strongly influenced by Piaget's "clinical method") seem well-suited to give deep insights into the "lawfulness" of children's development. (4) *Conclusion:* Issues of developmental processes and developmental mechanisms require different methodologies; they should be kept distinct.

In the remainder of this chapter, I will elaborate on these four major points.

Should Our Research Focus More on the "Mechanisms" Issue?

At first glance, the answer to this question seems clear. There is little doubt that explaining development is more important than simply describing it. Like Lightfoot and Folds-Bennett, I fully agree with Flavell's (1984) contention that the question of explanation should be "the ultimate objective of any science" (p. 188). Unlike Lightfoot and Folds-Bennett, however, I am not convinced that the state-of-the-art of developmental theory requires a particular emphasis on mechanisms, at least not of the sort described in recent models of cognitive development.

Why this negative attitude? In my view, a careful reading of the volume edited by Sternberg (1984), devoted to the exploration of mechanisms of cognitive development, elicits some skepticism concerning the fruitfulness of this enterprise. First of all, it is surprising to see that there is little overlap among the six models of cognitive development presented in this volume (cf. Sigel, 1986). As Flavell (1984) put it: "Whenever one sees six different theories supposedly trying to explain the same thing, one should suspect that Truth is not yet at hand!" (p. 190).

A second problem is that most theoretical approaches operate at a high level of abstraction, making a large number of "bold and imaginative claims" (Flavell, 1984) about various aspects of cognitive development. In principle, there is nothing wrong with trying to capture the "big picture" of human development, a goal that most of these theories try to reach. Given the high level of abstraction, however, it is difficult to see how the theories could be falsified by experimental test.

Third, and most important in the present context, the basic concept of developmental mechanism is never directly addressed in the various theoretical approaches (cf. Sigel, 1986). The large collecion of "mechanisms" includes transformation rules, differentiation, coordination, hierarchical integration, discrimination, encoding processes, equilibration, and adaptation. Do these terms indeed denote explanatory concepts? Let us take Piaget's concept of equilibration as an example. Aebli, one of Piaget's most prominent European students, has serious doubts in this regard (see Aebli, 1984). In his view, Piaget's (unproven) core assumption is that children typically strive for consistency in their thinking. Whenever children experience a state of imbalance, they try to overcome it, a process called "equilibration." According to Aebli, the term *equilibration* does not provide an explanation for developmental change. While it indicates *that* consistency was reestablished, it does not tell us *how* this might happen.

Unfortunately, this is true for most concepts considered as mechanisms in developmental theory. As emphasized by Sigel (1986), the mechanisms do not inform us about what governs developmental change. For example, to what extent is change controlled by

children's social interactions? Or what is the impact of biologi-
cal/maturational components? We need to know much more about the
various sources of developmental change and their interrelations at
different age levels.

Does this mean that we should intensify our search for more salient
developmental mechanisms, as Lightfoot and Folds-Bennett suggest?
Although this must be an important goal in the long run, I do not
think that current research should focus solely on issues of explanation. In my view, problems of generalizability inherent in many contemporary models of cognitive development stem from the fact that
the available data base is still weak. Despite the large number of empirical studies on numerous issues in cognitive development, the
number of robust, cross-validated findings is comparably restricted
(see van der Veer, van IJzendoorn, & Valsiner, in press, for a discussion of the problem of replicability). Thus more emphasis should be
given to a careful *description* of developmental changes over the life
span. I do hope that an emphasis on systematic data collection will
eventually enable us to come up with low-level inferences about
mechanisms of developmental changes that are better founded than
many of the high-level "explanations" offered in contemporary developmental theory. But do we really need a different methodology to accomplish this goal? This is what I want to discuss in the next section.

How Bad Is Our Developmental Methodology?

As briefly mentioned above, Lightfoot and Folds-Bennett believe
that current problems of the state-of-the-art of developmental theory
are closely linked to the use of ANOVA models in data analysis. Because ANOVA models focus on group means, they are of limited utility in understanding the development of individuals.

I agree with the authors that a focus on ANOVA models restricts
our knowledge about individual differences and their changes over
time. Along with Lightfoot and Folds-Bennett, I also believe that
ANOVA models still dominate developmental research. In my view,
however, a more serious shortcoming of traditional developmental
methodology is that it has been dominated by cross-sectional analyses, comparing different age groups at one point in time. While many
have voted for longitudinal designs, only a few have actually used

them. When Lightfoot and Folds-Bennett raised the issue that we need "intraindividual methods," I first thought they were referring to longitudinal methodology. A more careful reading of the chapter, however, revealed that I was wrong in this regard. The authors distinguish between two conceptual models of developmental analysis—the analysis of developmental functions and the analysis of individual differences—claiming that both approaches employ longitudinal designs that are essentially *interindividual.*

Frankly, I have problems with this claim. I still believe that one of the major advantages of longitudinal methods over cross-sectional designs is that they allow for *intraindividual* analyses in addition to interindividual comparisons. In particular, recent developments in growth curve modeling such as the Hierarchical Linear Modeling (HLM) procedure developed by Bryk and Raudenbush (1987; see also Chapter 4) represent a nice example for the progress we have made in this regard: HLM not only gives an estimate of (intraindividual) growth curve parameters but also provides a statistical procedure that tries to "explain" the variation found among intraindividual growth curves. Despite the various conceptual and methodological problems of longitudinal studies (for overviews see Rogosa, 1988; Schneider, 1989), there is no doubt that we have made considerable progress regarding the design and analysis of developmental studies over the last few years. As a matter of fact, we have overcome many of the disadvantages linked to the (cross-sectional) ANOVA methodologies alluded to by Lightfoot and Folds-Bennett.

What Can We Really Learn From the Past?

As you may well imagine, I was curious to learn more about the type of "intraindividual analysis" that Lightfoot and Folds-Bennett conceive of as "the king's road" for the explanation of developmental change. In order to clarify their position, the authors refer to the theoretical framework elaborated by Lewin and by Vygotsky, focusing on an experimental method called "genetic analysis." Because this term has several connotations in the literature, I discuss the major characteristics of the experimental approaches used by Lewin and Vygotsky before judging their importance for the explanation of developmental changes.

LEWIN'S VERSION OF "GENETIC ANALYSIS"

Lewin's "detour problem" is presented as an illustrative example for genetic analysis within the field theory paradigm. In this task, a child must navigate around two different types of barriers in order to reach a piece of chocolate (see Figure 7.2). As Lightfoot and Folds-Bennett point out, young children typically have more problems with the type of barrier that requires initial movement in a direction opposed to the location of the chocolate. In Lewin's terminology, this means a movement away from the "positive valence" associated with the piece of chocolate: Solution to this problem requires a "psychological restructuring" of the problem situation in that the first movement, although away from the "valence," becomes the first of several steps toward the chocolate. According to Lewin, successful performance in this task depends on the child's age (older children perform better than younger ones), on the strength of a valence (the stronger the valence, the more difficult the task), and on the ability to restructure the task as a set of related movements rather than a series of separate movements.

Undoubtedly, this is an interesting experimental task. It is difficult, however, to see how this "genetic analysis" differs from more modern approaches used in experimental methodology. One possible difference may be that Lewin operated with theoretical concepts like *field force, valence,* or *psychological restructuring* that he took for granted, whereas modern experimenters probably would like to make these concepts more accessible and testable in their experimental designs.

For example, Lewin's claim that performance in the detour problem task varies as a function of the strength of valence could be easily tested by varying the degree of attractiveness of the target. Lewin's theory would be confirmed if even older children fail to solve the more difficult barrier problem when the target is very attractive to them. It would be falsified, however, if we found a positive correlation between degree of target attractiveness and successful task solutions, regardless of age (i.e., the more attractive the target, the higher the percentage of successful solutions).

In my view, Lewin's experimental procedure cannot be conceived of as qualitatively different from modern experimental methodologies. The major difference concerns terminology: Modern problem solving theories would probably avoid Lewin's rather abstract explanations of successful task performance like "an understanding of the difference between physical and psychological realities" or "a successful construction of the life space" in favor of more concrete, observable behaviors. Thus it is really difficult for me to see how Lewin's approach of genetic analysis can lead to the detection of general "developmental mechanisms." The explanatory value of a term such as *psychological restructuring* seems similarly restricted as the Piagetian concept of *equilibration*.

VYGOTSKY'S VERSION OF "GENETIC ANALYSIS"

Lightfoot and Folds-Bennett use Vygotsky's studies of concept formation based on his "method of double stimulation" as an example for his version of genetic analysis. This method involved presenting subjects (i.e., children, adolescents, and adults) with two sets of stimuli. For example, children were given a number of wooden blocks that could be sorted according to features such as color, shape, height, and size. The underside of each block, not seen by the subjects, contained one of four nonsense words. Children were asked to select all blocks that might be of the same kind. Whenever a block was "wrongly chosen," the experimenter turned over the block, indicated that it had a different word on it, and asked the child to continue sorting. The experiment consisted of a sequence of child sorts and experimenter corrections, until the child correctly sorted the blocks as indicated by the nonsense words. As a main result, Vygotsky found that the ability to regulate one's action by auxiliary means (i.e., the use of nonsense words) was not fully developed before adolescence where "all existing functions are incorporated into a new structure. . . , become parts of a new complex whole." (Vygotsky, 1934/1986, p. 108).

What is the essentially new information about developmental changes in children's concept formation that we can derive from Vygotsky's approach? According to Lightfoot and Folds-Bennett, the core message is that "the new complex whole assembled during adolescence forms the basis of all higher mental functions; activity becomes sign-mediated as cultural mental functions supersede natural mental functions in the determination of behavior." In my view, however, we do not learn much about "natural mental functions" in Vygotsky's experiment, mainly because the method of double stimulation forces children to adopt rules provided by the experimenter. It is difficult to see how this methodological approach fits with the basic theoretical assumption of interdependence between developing individuals and their environments, a claim inherent in both Lewin's and Vygotsky's theories.

As emphasized by Lightfoot and Folds-Bennett, Vygotsky's approach was strongly influenced by Piaget's "clinical method," a procedure highly regarded even in contemporary textbooks of developmental psychology. This method, which involves first confronting children with a problem solving task, then urging them to come up with a solution (judgment), and finally asking them to justify their judgment, has been assumed to be an elegant procedure to explore the way children make use of their existing "cognitive structures." However, critics like Aebli are not convinced that the clinical method tells us much about children's problem solving in everyday situations. At about the time when Piaget's theory was introduced into American psychology, Aebli (1963) published his critical analysis of the Piagetian procedure. In his view, the clinical method leads to instable, ad hoc productions that are of no relevance for children's decision making in everyday problem solving situations. In subsequent experiments conducted by Aebli and his coworkers (cf. Aebli, 1984; Riesen, 1988), it indeed could be shown that children's performance in Piagetian conservation tasks does not predict their behavior in similar everyday problem solving situations. For example, when confronted with the problem that there was not enough tea available in a glass that should be given to a sick child, all of the children who did not master Piaget's conservation task (i.e., who believed that transferring liquid from a broad, low glass into a thin, high glass will produce more liquid) recommended adding new tea in order to help the sick child; none of the children spontaneously suggested that the experimenter should pour the tea from the glass into a (thinner and higher) tea bottle in order to produce more tea for the sick child. Of course, most of these "nonconservers" found the experimenter's idea of pouring the tea from the glass into the tea bottle helpful in order to improve the sick child's situation. However, when asked to decide between the options of either transferring the tea from the glass to the bottle or to add a small amount of tea to the liquid already in the bottle, almost all of the children preferred the latter possibility.

If Aebli is right—and there is reason to agree with his position—using the clinical method does not give us much insight into the relationship between the child and its environment. It is difficult to imagine that Piaget, Lewin, or Vygotsky were able to create experimental test situations that suitably mirrored the "constructive opportunities" afforded by children's everyday-life, natural environments. This is not to say that these great researchers were unable to stimulate our thinking about human development. Undoubtedly, the opposite is the case. What I doubt is that their experimental methodology gets us to the ambitious goals Lightfoot and Folds-Bennett have in mind.

Thus I do not see any new feature in this type of intraindividual analysis that overcomes the basic shortcomings of traditional experimental research. Like most contemporary experimental paradigms, the "genetic method" does not attend to the child's perspective regarding the task. Rather, the child is viewed as a passive respondent faced with tasks of relevance to the experimenter (cf. Sigel, 1986). In order to better understand the outcomes of experimental tests, it seems important to know more about children's constructions of the situation and their interpretation of this experience.

Do We Really Need Different Agendas for Studying "Descriptive" Processes and "Explanatory" Mechanisms?

As the reader may have inferred from the previous section, I am not convinced that searching for "general laws of development" or general "explanatory mechanisms" will benefit much from the "genetic method" described above. Actually, I do not believe that searching for rather global developmental mechanisms constitutes a promising research strategy for the future. The research findings presented in recent books and journal articles on issues of cognitive development suggest that there is much more variety, domain-specificity, and complexity in cognitive development than indicated by the six theories presented in Sternberg's book. As noted by Flavell (1984), there is more variety in *what* gets developed and also more variety in *how* developmental changes get accomplished. Accordingly, we may be obliged to devise specific theories for specific transitions.

How do we get to such theories? In my view, approaches such as the hierarchical linear modeling procedure devised by Bryk and Raudenbush (1987), based on the analysis of individual growth curve parameters does have the potential to promote our understanding of interindividual differences in intraindividual developmental changes for a wide range of domains. Another promising methodological approach—although probably not similarly suited for complex statistical analysis—is what Siegler and Jenkins (1989) have labeled the "microgenetic method." The two key properties of microgenetic methods are that (1) the same subjects are observed over an extended period of time, and (2) their learning is subjected to intensive trial-by-trial analysis, with a goal of inferring the underlying processes that gave rise to both qualitative and quantitative aspects of learning (cf. Siegler & Jenkins, 1989, p. 9). One of the major advantages of this approach over traditional longitudinal methods is that the time intervals between measurement points are very small, thus allowing for the assessment of transitional periods (e.g., the identification of the exact point at which a new behavior was first shown). Siegler and Jenkins demonstrated the utility of this approach for studying strategy construction in young children, showing that careful observation and description of the children's problem solving activities over many trials led to the identification of a set of transitional processes preceding the discovery of a counting strategy.

In my view, this approach combines intra- and interindividual analysis in that it is based on a collection of single-case studies, enabling the researcher to compare individual developmental paths in order to detect commonalities that can be conceived of as more general transition rules. Although the microgenetic method entails certain disadvantages because it is expensive and based on small sample sizes, it not only provides us with a detailed picture of the idiosyncracies of individual performance, but may also allow low-level inferences about "developmental mechanisms" better suited for "explaining" behavioral changes than the global conceptualizations predominant in current developmental theories.

As I have emphasized before, I was very impressed by the way Lightfoot and Folds-Bennett handled the very complicated issue of processes and mechanisms of cognitive development. Their chapter helped in stimulating my thinking about this issue in several ways. It is mainly due to space restrictions that I have focused on those points where we have different opinions. Obviously, the main difference between our positions is that Lightfoot and Folds-Bennett ask for different research agendas in order to explore descriptive processes versus explanatory mechanisms, whereas I believe that careful and sophisticated experimental (longitudinal) research can help in reaching both goals. Thus my conviction is that we do not need different methodologies but more fine-grained, domain-specific analyses than before in order to move from descriptions of development to the detection of transitional mechanisms. As several longitudinal studies on cognitive development are currently conducted, we soon may be in a position to evaluate this claim.

References

Aebli, H. (1963). *Über die geistige Entwicklung des Kindes* [Cognitive development in children]. Stuttgart: Klett-Verlag.

Aebli, H. (1984). Kognitive Entwicklung: Was entwickelt sich, und bei welchen Anlässen? [Cognitive development: What develops, and under which circumstances?]. *Zeitschrift für Entwicklungspsychologie und Pädagogische Psychologie, 16*, 102-118.

Bryk, A. S., & Raudenbush, S. W. (1987). Applications of hierarchical linear models to assessing change. *Psychological Bulletin, 101*, 147-158.

Flavell, J. H. (1984). Discussion. In R. J. Sternberg (Ed.), *Mechanisms of cognitive development* (pp. 187-209). New York: Freeman.

Riesen, M. (1988). *Zur Entwicklung von Invarianzbegriffen beim Kinde* [The development of conservation in children]. Unpublished master's thesis, University of Bern, Switzerland.

Rogosa, D. (1988). Myths about longitudinal research. In K. W. Schaie, R. T. Campbell, W. Meredith, & S. C. Rawlings (Eds.), *Methodological issues in aging research* (pp. 171-209). New York: Springer.

Schneider, W. (1989). Problems of longitudinal studies with children: Practical, conceptual, and methodological issues. In M. Brambring, F. Lösel, & H. Skowronek (Eds.), *Children at risk: Assessment, longitudinal research, and intervention* (pp. 313-335). Berlin: deGruyter.

Siegler, R. S., & Jenkins, E. (1989). *How children discover strategies*. Hillsdale, NJ: Lawrence Erlbaum.

Sigel, I. E. (1986). Mechanism: A metaphor for cognitive development? A review of Sternberg's "Mechanisms of cognitive development." *Merrill-Palmer Quarterly, 32*, 93-101.

Sternberg, R. J. (1984) (Ed.). *Mechanisms of cognitive development*. New York: Freeman.

Van der Veer, R., van IJzendoorn, M. H., & Valsiner, J. (Eds.) (in press). *Reconstructing the mind: Replicability in research on human development*. Norwood, NJ: Ablex.

Vygotsky, L. (1986). *Thought and language*. Cambridge, MIT Press. (Original work published 1934)

COMMENTARY ON CHAPTER 7:

What If the How Is a Why?

JEANETTE A. LAWRENCE

Lightfoot and Folds-Bennett's chapter is a celebration of the difference between explanation and description, with a plea for fresh attention to the issues involved in explaining developmental change and stability. The chapter makes three major points about the description/explanation distinction. First, Lightfoot and Folds-Bennett argue that there is a hierarchical distinction between processes and mechanisms, with mechanisms underlying any processes of development that are described empirically. The process/mechanism distinction reduces to the differentiation of description from explanation. Explanations of developmental change and stability, and by association mechanisms of development, are the major pursuit of the developmentalist. Descriptive techniques, such as profile analyses, allow us to observe only what has happened, but not how it came about. I will argue that this reduction is costly if it leads us to miss the significance of processes (in the sense of temporal sequences of actions), and if it masks the ways and means leading to developmental outcomes, involving interacting circumstances and activities.

The second major point is that only some methods yield explanations, by revealing the general mechanisms that propel change. Therefore, developmentalists should give more attention to those methods that allow them to make causal inferences about the forces energizing development. This position leads to discounting the usefulness of linear correlational methods and causal methods, such as structural equation techniques, that are confined to dealing with aggregate data.

The third point identifies the type of method that will best reveal mechanisms. The most complete and useful explanations of developmental change involve those that focus on individuals rather than groups, and specifically explain the changes that take place in individuals in and through dynamic interactions with the environment. Such dynamic and microgenetic methods "specify how the child organizes and transforms constraints across the life course." Interactive methods that allow the researcher to understand how certain individuals initiate and react to others are most likely to reveal the transformations that occur in developing individuals' behaviors as they occur in contexts of relationships and transactions between themselves and other people.

The reduction of the process/mechanism distinction to description/explanation begins with Lightfoot and Folds-Bennett's analysis of the Bernried preconference assignments. They discovered an order of abstraction in more than 20 contributors' efforts to specify the processes and mechanisms of change. Of course, the assignment may have suggested a hierarchy by referring to mechanisms that might underlie the processes' temporal stability or change. As Table 7.1 shows, processes such as helping behaviors and goal-setting are identified as phenomena that are propelled by mechanisms such as perspective-taking, equilibration, and internalization. So, processes constitute the *whats* of change and stability, and therefore in Lightfoot and Folds-Bennett's terms, descriptions. Mechanisms constitute the *hows,* and therefore explanations.

A refinement of the use of what/how interrogatives may resolve one potential confusion in the argument, and allow us to get the idea of "process" and description back into the type of analysis of developmental change that Lightfoot and Folds-Bennett are advocating. The whats of development undoubtedly cover emerging behavioral patterns and newly acquired abilities and skills. There is, however, potential for confusion if how is reserved for causal mechanisms. In that type of scheme we are left with no label for intermediate sequences and routes. In order to develop authentically interactive accounts of development, we need to describe in detail what happens at the level of the changing interactions between persons, and then to build causal models about those dynamic, moving features of the events being described. So, it may be productive to identify two levels of how, or more constructively, to reserve why for that most abstract and paradigmatic level of explanation, and to keep how for the activities and circumstances observable within the phenomena under investigation.

The case for interactive, microanalytic methods is strengthened when the researcher can identify the constraining and enabling forces at work, and chart the routes of change that move back and forward between environmental forces and internally generated responses and initiatives. Lightfoot and Folds-Bennett present an example in Vygotsky's experiment of a child's interactions with an adult when learning a new concept. The child acquired the concept by internalizing a word sign during interactions that the adult structured, and then by using the word to sort blocks into categories. Lightfoot and Folds-Bennett argue that this and other examples illustrate how Vygotsky and also Lewin were able to explain developmental change, because they specified the opportunities that particular environments gave children to generate more adequate ways of interpreting phenomena. Yet, even in this type of interactive situation, there seem to be levels of explanation. Two things are happening. Qualitative analyses are made of the transactions that occur between two parties within a situation, for example, when an adult presents a child with counterexamples of how to use a concept and gives the child opportunities to correct the error. General laws or replicable patterns are used to interpret why/how those transactions are effective, for example, applying the dialectical principle as a theoretical framework for interpreting the situation as the child's creation of a synthesis out of the antithetical, negative instance taken with the original positive instances.

At the level of immediate phenomena, the significance of the transaction and its unfolding is unproblematic. However, while one researcher (using the method of double stimulation) claims that the dialectics of the reciprocal interaction caused the developmental change, another may question why a dialectical explanation is most appropriate. Advocates of both environmentalist and genetic naturist theories may be uncomfortable with the emergent aspects of the dialectical model. For instance, Kindermann and Valsiner (1989) demonstrate how the same parent/child interactions involved in learning to dress oneself may be explained differently by learning theorists and dialecticians.

No data set yields interpretable concepts exclusive to a single theory (Feyerabend, 1987). Focus of attention and weight of interpretation are fine-tuned according to prior commitments to particular theoretical concepts (e.g., socialization, internalization). Terwee's (1990) argument for the influence of the individual researcher's interpretation supports this point, by showing how different philosophers and social scientists propose contradictory explanations of the same contextual description. Interpretations range from narrative through motivational to teleological, depending on the interpreter's basic philosophical position.

Explanation lies at the heart of each researcher's theory of development. The hermeneutic principles that sit comfortably with a particular view of developmental change come from the larger scheme in which the theory's assumptions and concepts are connected in causal networks. This idea of the deeply theoretical nature of explanatory devices is supported in Flavell's (1984) critique of the six theories of the mechanisms of cognitive development in the Sternberg (1984) volume. Not surprisingly, as many different mechanisms as theories appear in the chapters, for each theorist puts forward a causal explanation that is fundamentally tied to his or her own account of the child's growing understanding and interpretation of the world, and there is little ground for drawing general principles from the six accounts, as Flavell so cogently observes.

A classic example of two researchers laying different interpretive frames around a data set comes from Allport's (1937) reinterpretation of Hartshorne and May's (1930) finding of low correlations among different measures of children's morality across different situations. Allport disagreed with the original interpretation that there was no generality in children's morality, and argued instead for underlying general traits and consistent patterns of socialization to conformity. The data were not in dispute, nor were the trends observed. Two distinct theories of personality and two distinct analytic approaches provoked dispute over the explanation of the data.

Even if researchers were to agree about the forces operating in a particular situation, they might still propose causal connections that transcend the patterns found in the actual interactions between individuals. With their example of attitude change, Harré and Secord (1973) argue that when a detailed description of what is actually happening yields any two-variable PQ pattern, the nature of that pattern must be explained. P may cause Q, or there simply may be a high degree of regularity that does not of itself suggest causality. "But what is wanted beyond critical description is the *explanation* of why the pattern (PQ) occurs, that is why and by what mechanism in those circumstances (P) produces (Q). . . . More generally what is required is some understanding of the mode of *connection* between (*P*) and (*Q*)" (Harré & Secord, 1973, p. 130).

When it is possible to infer patterns in connections between variables, the researcher's task is to describe as accurately as possible the antecedents (*P*s) of outcomes (*Q*s). But such *PQ* linking statements will need to have a deductive system of theoretical concepts behind them to establish that the *PQ* links are produced by causal mechanisms of the order of self-regulation or dialectical adjustments.

Nevertheless, loose associations in one developmental episode may become the causal factors in another, since interactions naturally allow significant things to emerge that were not important before. Development of X at Time 1 allows the development of Y at Time 2, because the changing person now has a greater repertoire of actions at his or her disposal. For example, perspective taking and a chain of triggered events can act as the antecedents of cooperative behavior in one situation, but the very ability to take the perspective of the other person may have been the outcome of one or more prior encounters with the needs of another person. If we are to understand developmental change in general, we need to propose reasons why any interactions between individuals and any internal constructions of those events propel change. We must ask if there are any classes of activities that occur within and between individuals that are consistently likely to push one or another individual to change. The most obvious examples are Piagetian self-regulating equilibration cycles, and the contradictory forces of dialectics. In each, a person makes adjustments to new states and the operations involved in adjusting bring about changes in the person. The why question (or a deeper level of how) is fundamental to the notion of explanation (Kim, 1967).

In an interpretation of developmental change and stability employing the three interrogatives, the how process is used for the finer descriptions that allow researchers to include more information, in terms of temporal events and multiagent interactions in the phenomena that are interpreted. Or, if we want to think about conditions and consequential chains causally, then processes would be the phenomenal sequences and connections that are revealed in the data. They do not yield a full blown account of the developmental change, anymore than a time-sequenced observation of the life of a butterfly explains why this creature goes through that particular life cycle. Neither general laws nor hermeneutic principles immediately fall out of the data (Terwee, 1990).

What would a three-way division gain? It should allow us to go behind developmental outcomes to identify some of their antecedent phenomena operating in linking networks without necessarily invoking one particular mechanism as that which effects the change. Examining the processes behind the new state or skill adds precision to the developmental descriptions that Flavell (1968) argues precede causal-analytic, antecedent-consequent explanations.

Let us take a hypothetical case of development as a way of reexamining Lightfoot and Folds-Bennett's distinction of outcome and process in terms of "whats" and "hows" of developmental change, reserving "why" for explanatory mechanisms. Jill is a college sophomore who has an automobile accident, and becomes a paraplegic. Once she is out of the hospital, Jill decides to return to college and build a career. Obviously, her world has changed. She has adjustments to make (both physical and psychological) that are specific to her circumstances and condition, and tasks to accomplish that she shares with other students of her age (e.g., knowledge to acquire, social bondings to make, career trajectories to choose). So there are specialized adaptations required of Jill as a young adult who has experienced a catastrophe, as well as normative developmental tasks. As Valsiner (1987) and Karmiloff-Smith (1984) point out in different domains, there will be a number of significant bifurcations where the choices that she makes will become antecedent conditions of other immediate and long-term changes in Jill's personal development. These choices may be developmental outcomes of particular experiences, and then in turn lead to further choice points that canalize her subsequent choices along particular routes.

The adjustments that Jill makes to constraints and opportunities, and her decision processes are likely to be covert. Whatever the mechanisms of change may be, we will not immediately be able to inspect them. Nor will we be able to interpret the transformations in her thoughts and feelings that occur along the way, if we only examine her developmental achievements. The end products of adaptation are the aspects of change most visible and amenable to quantitative analysis, but neither the routes to those outcomes, nor their causes, will be revealed by gross or aggregate measures. For comparative purposes, it will be possible to measure Jill's newly acquired skills and self-concept with coarse, group-oriented instruments. But these data will not reveal the factors operating during the period while these skills and reactions were being acquired, and they will not reveal what causes their acquisition. Yet, while the pathways to such attainments vary across persons and situations and are not immediately accessible to the observer, they constitute important information for interpreting observable differences as developmental change, rather than as inter-individual differences at a single point in time. Then, the plausibility of explanations and predictions will be grounded in the comprehensiveness and appropriateness of the descriptions for the type of phenomena that constitute developmental change or constancy.

For instance, take Jill's choice to use a motorized vehicle that allows her to drive herself to and around campus, or her choice to depend on a family member to drive her to college and manipulate her wheelchair. Consequences for her independence arise from the alternative decisions. Family and friends can actively assist her growing confidence and independence, or their concern can set up conditions either for her dependency choices or for her contrary choices leading to independence. We would want to incorporate the event sequences that issue in either dependency or independency outcomes. Although making choices for greater independence are among the developmental tasks of all adolescents (Erikson, 1963), they have enormous personal consequences for Jill.

We see Jill arriving in her totally independent motorized vehicle, negotiating halls and pathways with what appears to be confidence after a period of isolation and withdrawal. The change in Jill can be described with observational statements about Jill's activities, or with inferences about her emotional state. Both types of descriptions are part of the whats of Jill's development. But it would be inappropriate to think of these as the processes of change, for they are outcomes of a series of episodes that have been taking place within and around Jill, even if some outcomes are interim to other different choices and achievements.

According to Lightfoot and Folds-Bennett, the most useful accounts of what has occurred will cover the complexities of the interacting personal and environmental factors that led to the behavioral and emotional changes in Jill. If we had observed daily episodes in which Jill and a parent worked on her mastery of the controls of the vehicle, we would be able to generate a description of the physical and social actions that led to a whole, multifaceted aspect of Jill's development and learning. Learning to simultaneously manage the vehicle and her physical limitations is likely to take Jill and her parent some time, and to involve choices and adjustments that have other ramifications for Jill's developing self, for example, handing over control and changes in the relationship. The genuinely interactive nature of their activities with the vehicle means that we cannot know what aspects of Jill's development will emerge as critical in successive episodes. New personal and ego structures will be constructed in the interactions.

Methodologies need to capture the activities involved in the interactions that occur in sequences of episodes where Jill and her parent interact while managing Jill's handling of the vehicle, and these activities are not very different in nature from the structuring, handing over, and taking up activities that occur in the progressive episodes leading to a child's acquisition of dressing skills (Kindermann & Valsiner, 1989). I believe that the fine-grained descriptions of how Jill arrives at her new independent actions and feelings are the type of microgenetic analyses Lightfoot and Folds-Bennett want us to generate in order to understand developmental changes in children. These analyses are not explanations in the sense of being able to say why the interactions between persons help to bring about change. They will not reveal why Jill seeks independence and develops personally over a series of episodes involving a new task, or why another individual may make different choices and become totally dependent on outside assistance. Nor can they tell why one young child rather than another becomes proficient at tying shoelaces or managing a fork. What fine descriptions do reveal are the elements of new types of interactions and new achievements that emerge over time.

Although it may be easier to identify questions about development in the study of children than in the special case of Jill, as Lightfoot and Folds-Bennett demonstrate, they are not easily resolved. At Time 1, Child A has begun to perform X (a performance culturally expected of children of A's age). A is successful in meeting cultural expectations and displaying the developmentally appropriate achievement, for example, taking the perspective of another child needing help, or reading a story. But Child B, of whom the same type of performance is anticipated, does not perform X. What does one pose as an explanation of the A,B difference, and at what level is the explanation pitched? Differentiation of the different performances by Child A over time (prior to and at Time 1), and between A and B at a given single point in time (Time 1) need to be interpreted in developmental terms. To mount those explanations, we will need to invoke abstract theoretical mechanisms such as dialectics. Nevertheless, the sequences of interactive transactions can reveal in fine detail the routes by which the invoked causal forces lead to new states and functions. The "hows" serve the "whys."

Lightfoot and Folds-Bennett's position echoes Harré and Secord's (1973) argument for the observation of human behavior in its complete episodes, and their claim that it is not possible to understand a single element of a social episode without examining it in its naturally occurring sequences and interactions. My case is that an understanding of developmental change is acquired at the level of empirically inspectable phenomena, and most appropriately involves documenting the temporal sequences, interacting circumstances, and activities that issue in new states or structures. Then, to explain why such forces are effective and how different aspects of the phenomena work together to produce change in humans, it is necessary to call on theoretically derived mechanisms of development. Whether we think of these mechanisms as the hows or whys of change, they need to be grounded in sequenced and interactive process descriptions. Therefore, while description and explanation are different and it is useful to preserve the distinction, their agenda are intertwined. The refinement of description with contextualized process analyses is a prelude to explanation.

References

Allport, G. (1937). *Personality: A psychological interpretation.* London: Constable.

Erikson, E. H. (1963). *Childhood and society* (2nd ed.). New York: Norton.

Feyerabend, P. (1987). *Farewell to reason.* London: Verso.

Flavell, J. H. (1968). *The development of role-taking and communication skills in children.* Huntington, NY: Krieger.

Flavell, J. H. (1984). Discussion. In R. J. Sternberg (Ed.), *Mechanisms of cognitive development* (pp. 187-209). New York: Freeman.

Hartshorne, H., & May, M. A. (1930). *Studies in organization of character.* New York: Macmillan.

Harré, R., & Secord, P. F. (1973). *The explanation of social behavior.* Totowa, NJ: Littlefield, Adams.

Karmiloff-Smith, A. (1984). Children's problem solving. In M. Lamb, A. L. Brown, & B. Rogoff (Eds.), *Advances in developmental psychology* (pp. 39-90). Hillsdale, NJ: Lawrence Erlbaum.

Kim, J. (1967). Explanation. In P. Edwards (Ed.), *Encyclopedia of Philosophy, Vol. III* (pp. 159-163). New York: Macmillan.

Kindermann, T. A., & Valsiner, J. (1989). Research strategies in culture-inclusive developmental psychology. In J. Valsiner (Ed.), *Child development in cultural context* (pp. 13-50). Toronto: Hogrefe & Huber.

Sternberg, R. J. (1984). *Mechanisms of cognitive development.* New York: Freeman.

Terwee, S.J.S. (1990). *Hermeneutics in psychology and psychoanalysis.* Berlin: Springer-Verlag.

Valsiner, J. (1987). *Culture and the development of children's actions.* New York: John Wiley.

Editors' Integration: Six Biases in Contemporary Developmental Psychology

JENS B. ASENDORPF

JAAN VALSINER

The chapters and commentaries of this volume have provided an empirical data base for a methodological evaluation of present developmental psychology. This data base is far from being representative, but it entails sufficient heterogeneity for such a methodological endeavor. As we have pointed out in the introduction, by "methodological" we mean the Continental-European concept of examining the tacit assumptions underlying general approaches as well as particular methods of science. In this concluding chapter we review the various contributions to this volume from such a methodological point of view.

This methodological evaluation is organized around six polarities that provide some structure to the heterogeneity of developmental approaches, and that are closely related to the three dimensions of developmental perspectives that we have discussed in the introduction. Contrary to the introductory chapter, however, we do not consider these polarities value-free dimensions. Instead, we regard them as biases of present developmental psychology that may limit its further progress. Hence these biases need to be transcended in the future (by some other, it is hoped, more productive ones). Spelling out a bias is the first step of overcoming it, and so our hope is that this concluding chapter may stimulate some readers to reevaluate these and other biases in their own developmental research.

Domain-Specific Preferences for the
General Versus the Differential

The first bias is related to the polarity between the general and the differential perspectives on development. The present volume has a clear bias toward the differential view because the Bernried workshop was designed around the question of *differential* stability and change in development. In this focus, the present volume differs from contemporary developmental psychology that, taken as a whole, appears to be fairly balanced in respect to the duality general-differential. When it comes to particular domains of development, however, strong biases become evident. A clear majority of research on cognitive development is devoted to universal-developmental as opposed to differential-developmental questions, whereas the opposite is true for social-emotional development (see also Maccoby, 1984).

It does not seem to be accidental that the only chapter in this volume that deals exclusively with general development (Chapter 1) uses an example from the cognitive domain for illustration (conservation of quantities), whereas Chapter 2, which is devoted to differential questions, uses examples predominantly from the social-emotional domain (criminal behavior, interpersonal conflicts, marital happiness, parental control of children's behavior). The discussions in Bernried also showed a strong association between cognitive and general development, and social-emotional and differential development.

There are a number of reasons why this bias can be detected in contemporary psychology (e.g., lack of appropriate theoretical models, or the prevalence of research traditions that do not recognize the bias). We would prefer not to address this issue here, but rather make evident that the need to overcome that bias is quite serious. Fortunately, there exist some efforts in different research domains that are oriented toward this objective.

To give an example for cognitive development, research on memory development has typically focused on the description of universal developmental trends. Only recently, differential-developmental questions such as the development of individual differences in memory strategies, of memory performance in experts versus novices in a particular domain of knowledge, or of individual differences in the memory performance of the elderly have become the focus of empirical research (see Weinert, Schneider, & Knopf, 1988). Or, to give an example for social development, the overwhelming majority of developmental studies on social interaction are concerned with the prediction and explanation of interindividual differences in social behavior—such as aggressiveness, shyness, or prosocial behavior—whereas universal developmental trends in social interaction have been nearly always restricted to early childhood (e.g., the early development of social coordination among peers; see Eckerman, Davis, & Didow, 1989).

Emphasis on Outcomes Versus Mechanisms

The second bias in present developmental psychology is the strong tendency to study intermediate developmental outcomes as opposed to developmental mechanisms. It is quite remarkable that contemporary research on human development is struggling with the issues of which earlier developmental psychology was acutely aware (e.g., Vygotsky, 1929; Werner, 1937). It may be the case that the eternal problem of lack of direct access to the "internal" psychological world of our subjects (particularly of children) is the reason for the overemphasis on the externally manifest facets of psychological development. Those facets themselves, however, are intermediate outcomes of some underlying mechanisms that may guide development over some longer time frame.

We follow here the usage of the term *mechanism* as it was introduced in Chapter 7, despite some reservations about this term because it can be easily associated with a mechanistic world view. Neither we nor the authors and commentators of Chapter 7 would subscribe to this very specific interpretation of the concept of developmental mechanisms.

Our observations of intermediate developmental outcomes are only a selective sample of actually relevant aspects of the underlying developmental mechanisms. Therefore it is very difficult to recreate a model of those mechanisms on the basis of these intermediate outcomes. It is here that the coordination of the deductive and inductive lines of scientific inquiry is most necessary—and most difficult.

In order to study the underlying psychological mechanisms on the basis of the post factum account of their intermediate outcomes, we need to make some educated guesses about what these mechanisms might be like. Of course, these guesses are informed by previous evidence we have at our disposal. In order for that evidence to be productive (rather than misleading), the methodological underpinnings of it need to be analyzed. Still, even then, we are faced with a formidable difficulty in conceptualizing the mechanisms involved.

This becomes evident from Chapter 7 and its commentaries. Making sense of the underlying mechanisms of development led our contributors to have another look at the methodological traditions of Kurt Lewin and Lev Vygotsky. Of course, ready answers could not be found to be waiting for us under the dust that these old contributions have gathered in the libraries of our contemporary academic institutions. Without an explicit methodological stance in the sense of our Introduction, this issue cannot be solved. On the other hand, no progress in methodology will be made unless the idea that development is not directly explainable on just the basis of careful registration of its intermediate outcomes becomes accepted in all of its disturbing complexity.

Focus on Individuals Versus Environments

The four remaining biases that we spell out here refer to the polarity *individual-environment*. The third bias is the strong tendency of today's developmentalists to focus on individuals as opposed to environments or person-environment relationships. It is quite surprising that the tendency to separate the person and the environment from each other (and to view them as opposite competing entities) perseveres so strongly in psychology—despite all the efforts in the history of the discipline to overcome it (e.g., the research traditions of Kurt Lewin, Egon Brunswick, Urie Bronfenbrenner, Robert Cairns, and others). This perseverance must have its own metatheoretical reasons (rather than be a mere historical coincidence). It could be that our conceptualization of the idea of relationship between person and environment is poorly differentiated.

It is therefore of central importance that this shortcoming was a main target of discussion in this volume (see Chapter 6 by Kindermann & Skinner, and the commentaries by Rossetti-Ferreira & Oliveira, and by van Aken). The introduction of the assumption that persons and environmental contexts are co-developing (rather than persons being "molded" or "shaped" by "contexts") can be considered to be of fundamental relevance for contemporary developmental psychology.

Of course, reflecting upon the co-developmental nature of person and environment constitutes no automatic solution to our conceptual and methodological problems. Instead (and as the contributions to this volume indicate) we need to construct explicit models of how that co-development is organized in its microgenetic and ontogenetic time frame. For example, psychologists use terms such as *influence* (e.g., "environment influences person" or "person influences environment"), but elaborations of what that influence actually means are largely absent. In fact, any notion ranging from "influence" = "strict determination" to "weak probabilistic or episodic effect" can be meant (and then the notion of *effect* is similarly ill-defined!). It would be very helpful if developmentalists made it more clear in what sense the terms denoting relationships between person and environment (e.g., *effect* and *influence*; also *interaction* and *transaction*) are used in their discourse.

These difficulties are complicated even further if developmental psychologists try to look at the dynamics of the co-developmental relationship. It is here that our theoretical and methodological assumptions can easily lead our empirical research astray. For some unspecifiable reasons many developmental psychologists tend to assume that if a person-environment relationship at some stage of their co-development takes a certain form, that form might be retained at other stages too, or that the form of a person-environment relationship within a certain stage of development is the same for all individuals in the population.

We therefore call for efforts to enrich our repertoire of concepts that allow us to make sense of the person-environment co-development. For instance, it seems feasible that during ontogenesis there can be convergencies and divergencies of person-environment relationships. At one stage, the co-development may show the same form for all person-environment relationships, whereas at a later stage there may suddenly exist two or more ways in which different individuals relate with their different environments. If our methodological schemes at that stage are set up to look for only one form of relationship, we are rather likely to overlook the others.

Variable-Orientation Versus Person-Orientation

If the focus is on individuals, a fourth bias is evident: The unit of analysis is most often one variable as opposed to the developing person as an organized *system* of variables. If we follow Allport's (1937) definition of personality as the "individual organization of behavior," this latter person-oriented approach to development combines the personality and the developmental perspective, and only this combination of perspectives can seriously answer questions about *personality* development. One method of studying personality development is to describe individuals by patterns or profiles of variables, either directly with the Q-sort method (see Chapter 5), or indirectly by individual configurations or qualitative or quantitative variables (see Chapter 2 and Bergman's commentary on Chapter 5).

Profile approaches to individual development cannot be replaced by many single-variable studies because a profile is more than the sum of its constituents. For example, a profile approach allows the study of compensatory effects between developmental changes in different variables on a subject-by-subject basis. Therefore, profile approaches to development appear to be a useful (and still largely unexplored) area of developmental research. Their practical implementation in empirical studies has to overcome two obstacles, however. Many variables have to be assessed repeatedly over time in the same individuals, and the reliability of a profile is usually lower than the mean reliability of its constituents; therefore, care must often be taken to improve the reliability of the profiles by aggregating them over many observations (time points, judges, or situations). Hence studies of profiles are much more costly than studies of single variables.

A profile approach is not the ultima ratio of a person-oriented view of development, however. Allport (1961, p. 16) already noted that "a profile brings us near, but not very near, to our goal of individuality" because "a profile tells us nothing about the *organization* of the qualities in question." Therefore Allport regarded a profile approach to personality only as a "halfway approach to individuality." Future studies may use more sophisticated methods of studying the individual organization of behavior and its change during development.

Focus on the Aggregate Level
Versus the Individual Level

If present developmental psychologists study the change in single variables, they very often investigate this change at the sample level (aggregate level) as opposed to the individual level; this we consider the fifth bias. For example, most empirical studies of general development make claims about the universal development in a particular population but support these claims with data about the mean developmental change in a sample. What is ignored here is the problem that change at the level of aggregates of persons cannot always be generalized to all or even a majority of these persons; sometimes a small minority of "strong changers" produce significant change at the aggregate level whereas the majority do not change, or even change in the opposite direction. That universal change cannot be inferred from aggregate change has been repeatedly pointed out in this volume. As alternative procedures, analyses of individual developmental functions were proposed in Chapters 1 and 4, and tests of individual ordinal predictions in Chapter 3.

The same problem arises in differential-developmental studies when the stability of traits is analyzed by correlations. Medium-sized correlations are very often misinterpreted as moderate stability at the individual level. In Chapter 5 it was demonstrated that this can be a false inference because of the interindividual variance of the individual stabilities, and a method of analyzing individual stability scores was described that safeguards against this misinterpretation.

It should be noted that a related problem can arise in log-linear analyses of the differential change of groups (see Chapter 2). In these analyses, the members of a group are considered to be homogeneous, and probabilities of change patterns that are estimated for a group are often interpreted in terms of the individual likelihood of the change pattern for all members of the group. This would again be a false inference; a more correct interpretation would be that a particular change pattern is more often found in one group as compared to another group.

Culture-Neutral Versus Culture-Bound
Views of the Environment

The sixth bias of present developmental psychology refers to the tendency to treat environmental influences in isolation as opposed to culturally structured systems. In a way, this bias is a special version of the third bias described above. It is relevant, however, to differentiate it from the former because it may have been the main theoretical constraint on our discussions in Bernried and contributions to this volume. We have scarcely touched upon the possibility (see Chapter 6 for exceptions) that all or at least most aspects of the human environment are culturally organized.

This cultural organization can be seen as a mediator between the developing persons and their developing environments (Valsiner, 1989). Thus culture is the result of the previous co-adaptation of persons and their environment as well as an important constraint for their possible future. In this respect some intermediate outcomes of development—cultural "mediating devices"—reenter the processes of further development in a productive way.

The methodological problem that comes with any recognition of this kind of culture-as-instrument view on development can be seen in the inevitable open-endedness of development (new psychological forms can emerge in the history of person-environment co-development), as well as the difficulty with assuming the presence of merely one way in which a psychologist might build a developmental picture of some phenomenon.

For example, in our occidental child psychology we are habitually tempted to view the birth of a child as a necessarily positive event (and treat counterexamples to that, which do occur in our society, as in some sense abnormal). That perspective will bring our psychologists to a large mismatch with culturally constructed symbol systems in those societies that view the birth of twins as a cultural sign of "bad luck," and demand the use of infanticide to remedy the culturally created state of "danger" to the whole of the community. Unless we consider the whole community in this case to be in some sense "abnormal" (in the requirement of infanticide), we will need to adjust our assumptions of the environment to include the culturally constructed meaning systems (see also Valsiner & Benigni, 1986).

We do not want to suggest that these six biases of today's developmental psychology are the most important ones. The most critical biases of a particular historical period in the development of a scientific discipline become visible only after the fact, because they are shared by almost *all* scientists of that historical period. For example, correlations between parenting styles and childhood personality have been nearly always interpreted in terms of parental influences on children's personality before it was realized that the same correlational results are also consistent with the opposite view—child effects on their parents, or reciprocal influences between both sides (Bell, 1977). But we would insist that the six biases that we have identified here shape present developmental research to a significant degree, and put some unhealthy constraints on its future development.

Of course, there are other possible ways of distinguishing between different approaches to developmental questions. Distinctions such as formalists versus naturalists (a difference that was so nicely spelled out in Chapter 3) or mechanistic versus organismic models of development (Reese & Overton, 1970), refer to dualities that are quite appealing to everybody who has attended large conferences of developmental psychologists. With all dualities at a high level of abstraction these distinctions share the danger that too many attributes are clustered together. We have chosen for our methodological analysis an intermediate level of abstraction that provides more degrees of freedom for "interapproach differences" at the cost of being perhaps less intuitively appealing.

Last but not least we hasten to add that both the selection and the discussion of the biases of present developmental psychology are revealing of our own personal biases. These were similar enough to ensure cooperation, and hopefully they were different enough to prevent an all-too-strong metabias in our methodological reasoning. At this metalevel of abstraction the air is rather thin and dry, and so we conclude with a happy regression to our memories of the pleasant Benedictine Convent at Bernried with the wonderful Andechs beer where all this began.

References

Allport, G. (1937). *Personality: A psychological interpretation.* New York: Holt & Co.

Allport, G. (1961). *Pattern and growth in personality.* New York: Holt, Rinehart & Winston.

Bell, R. Q. (1977). Socialization findings re-examined. In R. Q. Bell & R. V. Harper (Eds.), *Child effects on adults* (pp. 53-84). Hillsdale, NJ: Lawrence Erlbaum.

Eckerman, C. O., Davis, C. C., & Didow, S. M. (1989). Toddlers' emerging ways of achieving social coordinations with a peer. *Child Development, 60,* 440-453.

Maccoby, E. E. (1984). Socialization and developmental change. *Child Development, 55,* 317-328.

Reese, W. H., & Overton, W. F. (1970). Models of development and theories of development. In L. R. Goulet & P. B. Baltes (Eds.), *Life-span developmental psychology: Research and theory* (pp. 116-149). New York: Academic Press.

Valsiner, J. (1989). *Human development and culture.* Lexington, MA: Lexington.

Valsiner, J., & Benigni, L. (1986). Naturalistic research and ecological thinking in the study of child development. *Developmental Review, 6,* 203-223.

Vygotsky, L. S. (1929). The problem of the cultural development of the child. *Pedagogical Seminary and Journal of Genetic Psychology, 36,* 415-434.

Weinert, F. E., Schneider, W., & Knopf, M. (1988). Individual differences in memory development across the life span. In P. B. Baltes (Eds.), *Life-span development and behavior* (Vol. 9, pp. 39-85). Hillsdale, NJ: Lawrence Erlbaum.

Werner, H. (1937). Process and achievement: A basic problem of education and developmental psychology. *Harvard Educational Review, 7,* 353-368.

About the Contributors

Françoise D. Alsaker is an Associate Professor in the Division of Personality and Developmental Psychology at the University of Bergen, Norway. She is in charge of the curriculum in developmental psychology at the University of Bergen, where she also received her doctorate. Her major research interest has been on the study of the development of self-evaluation in early adolescence and its relation to factors such as achievement, school context, and pubertal development. She is currently involved in research on psychosocial health in early adolescence, including self-evaluation, depression, social anxiety, peer relations, and parental relations. She has recently initiated a project on self-perception and peer relations in the transition from kindergarten to elementary school.

Jens B. Asendorpf is a Senior Researcher at the Max-Planck-Institut für Psychologische Forschung in Munich, Germany, and a lecturer for personality development at the University of Munich. He completed full studies in mathematics/computer science and psychology, and spent a year at Yale University preparing his Ph.D. thesis on affect repression. For the past eight years he has studied social competence in both adults and children, with a special focus on the development of social anxiety and aggressiveness. He has authored three monographs

259

and numerous journal articles in the areas of psychology of emotion, personality, methodology, and social development.

Lars R. Bergman is a professor in the Department of Psychology, Stockholm University. He also holds a position at Statistics Sweden as an expert in measurement techniques. Since receiving his Ph.D. in psychology from Stockholm University in 1972, he has been pursuing research in differential psychology and developmental psychology. Being also trained as a statistician, he has made contributions in the field of research methodology, especially methods for analyzing longitudinal data. Within these areas he has published extensively in scientific journals and books. His current research interests are the study of the growth of patterns of adjustment problems and methods for studying development from a person perspective where the gestalt or profile of an individual's information is at focus. He also pursues applied research in the field of measurement techniques, especially questionnaire construction and testing.

Agnes E. Dodds is a lecturer in the Centre for the Study of Higher Education at the University of Melbourne. She is involved in faculty staff development with a focus on innovative teaching. Her research interests are professional problem solving and professional ethics. Current projects include social and ethical problem solving of nurses and the professional education of engineers in developing countries.

Trisha Folds-Bennett is a Visiting Assistant Professor at the College of Charleston in Charleston, South Carolina. In addition to her teaching responsibilities at the College of Charleston, she is completing doctoral work at the University of North Carolina at Chapel Hill. Her dissertation is focused on the context specificity of motivation in elementary school-aged children. She has also done research on the context specificity of memory strategies in young children. She is interested in bringing her work in motivation and memory development together by focusing on the development of cognitive skills in the context of the family.

Thomas A. Kindermann is an Assistant Professor of Psychology at Portland State University in Portland, Oregon. He received his Ph.D. in developmental psychology from the Free University Berlin. His research interests focus on human development within a life span perspective, specifically on the study of plasticity and change within developmentally relevant contexts. Special interests include observational methodologies in the study of natural interactions between related partners, the formation of peer groups in school, and social interactions in old age.

Kurt Kreppner is a Senior Research Scientist at the Max Planck Institute for Human Development and Education in Berlin, Germany. He received his Ph.D. in 1969 from the Technical University of Darmstadt. He has pursued research in the area of family socialization with emphases on early childhood and adolescence. Research questions concern changes in family structure caused by the integration of a new child and, in adolescence, by the beginning separation of adolescents from their families. His research is observational and takes place in natural settings. He has authored a monograph on measurement, coedited a volume on family systems development from a lifespan perspective, and published numerous scholarly articles.

Jeanette A. Lawrence is a senior lecturer in the Department of Psychology, University of Melbourne. She received her Ph.D. in educational and developmental psychology at the University of Minnesota. She has been active in research on problem solving and decision making in professional life, especially magistrates' courtroom judgments and sentencing and nurses' and anaesthetists' problem solving. Her research on ethical and moral development involves the analysis of the processes of judgment making.

Cynthia Lightfoot is an Assistant Professor of Psychology at the State University of New York, Plattsburgh. She received a master's degree in psychology from the University of British Columbia, Vancouver, and a Ph.D. in psychology from the University of North Carolina, Chapel Hill. Her work is informed by the theoretical traditions of Lev Vygotsky and James Mark Baldwin, and explores the social and cultural contexts of human development. She is currently researching the role of shared adventures in creating adolescent peer culture and social definitions of self.

Zilma Moraes Ramos de Oliveira is an Assistant Professor of Developmental Psychology at the Faculty of Philosophy, Sciences, and Arts of Ribeirão Preto, University of São Paulo, in Ribeirão Preto,

Brazil. She completed her doctoral degree in experimental psychology at the Institute of Psychology at the University of São Paulo. She has been involved as a teacher, consultant, and researcher in early child development and education. Her research interests include analysis of adult-child dialogs in day care instructional situations and curriculum for day-care centers.

Maria Clotilde Rossetti-Ferreira is a Full Professor of Developmental Psychology and Head of the Department of Psychology and Education at the Faculty of Philosophy, Sciences, and Arts of Ribeirão Preto, University of São Paulo. She had her training as Clinical Psychologist and obtained her Ph.D. in developmental psychology at the University of London. She has lectured for a number of years on life span developmental psychology for medical and psychology students and is involved as a consultant and researcher on early child development and education. Her research interests include social interaction in early childhood, the process of construction and the role of the physical and social contexts, and mother-infant attachment and the child's and the family's adaptation to the day care center.

Wolfgang Schneider is a Professor of Psychology at the University of Würzburg. He completed his Ph.D. in educational psychology at the University of Heidelberg and worked as a Senior Researcher at the Max Planck Institute for Psychological Research for almost 10 years. His research interests include cognitive development, prediction of academic outcomes, and methodological problems of longitudinal studies. He has published widely on topics in developmental psychology, educational psychology, and methodology.

Eberhard Schröder works as a research scientist at the Max Planck Institute for Human Development and Education in Berlin, Germany. He is member of an interdisciplinary team conducting a longitudinal project focused on the interface between social structure and child development. Since obtaining his doctoral degree in psychology from the Technical University in Berlin in 1988, he has been involved in research on the developmental and contextual constraints on cognitive processes, in particular focusing on intra- and interindividual differences in intraindividual change. His research interests include methodological questions in longitudinal research, theories of evolutionary and developmental processes, genetic epistemology, and cognitive science.

Ellen A. Skinner is an Associate Professor with a joint appointment at the Graduate School of Education and Human Development and the Department of Psychology at the University of Rochester, New York. She is also an Adjunct Research Scientist at the Max Planck Institute for Human Development and Education in Berlin, Germany. She received her Ph.D. in developmental psychology from Pennsylvania State University. Her research interests focus on the study of human development from early childhood to adolescence within a life span perspective. Content areas include motivation, perceived control, and coping processes; a special interest of hers is in how close relationships encourage or undermine individuals' perceived control and coping.

Warren Thorngate is a Professor of Psychology at Carleton University, Ottawa, Ontario, Canada. Since obtaining his Ph.D. at the University of British Columbia in 1971, he has pursued research on social aspects of human judgment and decision making. He is currently involved in studies of adjudicated contests, attentional economics, and computer communication in developing countries, and is writing *Conceptual Research Methods for Psychologists*.

Jaan Valsiner is an Associate Professor of Psychology at the Developmental Psychology Program of the University of North Carolina at Chapel Hill, and a member of the Carolina Consortium on Human Development. A native of Estonia, he started his academic career as a member of the Faculty of Psychology at Tartu University. After leaving the Soviet Union in 1980, he saw his work become known worldwide. He has been a Visiting Professor at Justus-Liebig-Universität Giessen, at the University of Melbourne, and at the Universidade Federal de Brasilia, as well as a Visiting Research Scientist at Max-Planck-Institut für Psychologische Forschung, Istituto di Psicologia del C.N.R., and Leiden University. His research interests are in the domain of cultural organization of human affective and mental processes. His recent books include *Culture and the Development of Children's Action* (Chichester, UK: John Wiley, 1987), *Developmental Psychology in the Soviet Union* (Brighton, Sussex, UK: Harvester Press, 1988), *Human Development and Culture* (Lexington: D. C. Heath, 1989), and *A Quest for Synthesis: The Life and Work of Lev Vygotsky* (with René van der Veer; Oxford, UK: Basil Blackwell, 1991). He has also been the editor (and coeditor) of eight scholarly volumes.

Marcel A. G. van Aken is a postdoctoral fellow at the Max Planck Institute for Psychological Research in Munich, Germany. He completed his Ph.D. in developmental psychology at the University of Nijmegen, The Netherlands. The subject of his dissertation was a longitudinal study of the development of children's competence in a transactional relationship with social support provided by parents, teachers, and peers. His current research interests concern the development of social competence, the development of the self-concept, and the role of environmental demands and social support (both related to developmental tasks) in this development.

Alexander von Eye is a Professor of Human Development and Psychology at The Pennsylvania State University in State College, Pennsylvania since 1986. He has held Assistant Professorships at the Universities of Trier and Erlangen-Nuremberg, Germany, and was Senior Research Scientist at the Max Planck Institute for Human Development and Education in Berlin, Germany. He has published more than 100 articles in the areas of cognitive development and methodology, specifically categorical data analysis. He has both authored and edited a number of books chiefly in the area of social science methodology and statistics.

Holger Wessels is an Assistant Professor of Early Childhood Socialization and Sociology at the Free University of Berlin, Germany. He received his Ph.D. from the Technical University of Berlin. His research focuses on the effects of day care on early child development and methodology and statistics. His substantive interests include the prediction of patterns of early childhood development from characteristics of day care institutions and teachers. His interests in statistics involve log-linear modeling of developmental and change processes. He developed a novel method for interpreting residuals in lag-analyses. Presently he is writing a textbook on introduction into log-linear modeling.